WITHDRAWN
No longer the property of the
Boston Public Library.
Sale of this material benefits the Library.

CAMBRIDGE

INSTANT IELTS

READY-TO-USE TASKS AND ACTIVITIES

GUY BROOK-HART

Cambridge Books for Cambridge Exams ...

WITHDRAWN

No longer the property of the
Boston Public Library.
Sale of this material benefits the Library.

CAMBRIDGE
UNIVERSITY PRESS

PUBLISHED BY THE PRESS SYNDICATE OF THE UNIVERSITY OF CAMBRIDGE
The Pitt Building, Trumpington Street, Cambridge, United Kingdom

CAMBRIDGE UNIVERSITY PRESS
the Edinburgh Building, Cambridge CB2 2RU, UK
40 West 20th Street, New York, NY 10011-4211, USA
477 Williamstown Road, Port Melbourne, VIC 3207, Australia
Ruiz de Alarcón 13, 28014 Madrid, Spain
Dock House, The Waterfront, Cape Town 8001, South Africa

http://www.cambridge.org

© Cambridge University Press 2004

This book is in copyright. Subject to statutory exception
and to the provisions of relevant collective licensing agreements,
no reproduction of any part may take place without
the written permission of Cambridge University Press.

First published 2004
Third printing 2005

Printed in the United Kingdom at the University Press, Cambridge

Typeface Syntax 10/13pt. *System* QuarkXpress® [GD]

A catalogue record for this book is available from the British Library

Library of Congress Cataloguing in Publication data

ISBN 0 521 75533 6 paperback

Contents

Introduction   4

Listening Section 1   A House to Rent   5
                             At the Doctor's   8

Listening Section 2   Coping with Stress   11
                             Mentoring   14

Listening Section 3   Bridging the Digital Divide   17
                             Changes in Intelligence   20

Listening Section 4   Emblematic Buildings   23
                             Changes at Work   26

Academic Reading Passage 1   GM Food   29
                             Light Pollution   33

Academic Reading Passage 2   Television Addiction   37
                             Increased Life Expectancy   41

Academic Reading Passage 3   The History of Migration   45
                             Homegrown Maps   49

General Training Reading Passage 1   Traveller's Tips   53
                                     London's Markets   57

General Training Reading Passage 2   Distance Learning   60
                                     Revision for Exams   64

General Training Reading Passage 3   Australia Fights Back   68
                                     Canals on Mars   72

Academic Writing Task 1   Student Finances   76
                             Activities by Gender   79
                             Cinema Trends   82
                             Describing a Process   85

Academic Writing Task 2   Children and Lifestyles   88
                             Multinational Companies   91
                             Too Many Rules?   94

General Training Writing Task 1   Letter to a Magazine   97
                                  Job Application   100
                                  Letter Giving Advice   103
                                  Letter of Request   106

General Training Writing Task 2   Neighbours   109
                                  Working from Home   112
                                  Studying Abroad   115

Speaking Module Part 1   118

Speaking Module Parts 1, 2 and 3   119

Recording Scripts   123

WITHDRAWN
No longer the property of the
Boston Public Library.
Sale of this material benefits the Library.

Introduction

About this book

This book contains realistic tasks covering all parts of the IELTS test on photocopiable pages. The tasks are preceded by a 'warm-up activity' called **Introduction** and followed by one or more **follow-up activities** to provide you with a complete lesson which your students should find enjoyable, interesting and, above all, useful preparation for the IELTS test.

Timing

The lessons take from 45 minutes to about 1 hour 30 minutes. Detailed guidance on timing is given in the teacher's notes. If the lessons are too long for the period of your class, the teacher's notes contain suggestions for giving activities for homework or for doing them in a following lesson.

Levels

The IELTS test is designed to give each candidate doing the test a result in a Band from Band 1 (Non-user) to Band 9 (Expert User). The tasks in this book are at the same level of difficulty as the tasks in the IELTS test. The activities and the teacher's notes are designed to give practice and preparation for both **Intermediate** and **Advanced** students taking the test in order to optimise their performance.

  For the purposes of this book:
  Intermediate students would be expected to achieve Band 4, 5 or 6 in the test.
  Advanced students would be expected to achieve Band 6, 7 or 8.

Teacher's notes

The teacher's notes give detailed advice on how to prepare your students for each part of the IELTS test and each question-type. There is separate advice for **Intermediate** and **Advanced** classes. You should choose the advice which best suits your students' level, but you can always use advice from the **Advanced** boxes with **Intermediate** classes and vice versa, if you think it is useful. You may wish to supplement these lessons with extra grammar practice. Our recommended grammar books are *Advanced Grammar in Use – a reference and practice book for advanced learners of English*, (*with answers*), ISBN: 0 521 498686 and *English Grammar in Use – reference and practice for intermediate students*, (*with answers*), ISBN: 0 521 43680X.

Answer keys

These contain the complete range of possible answers. Answers must coincide exactly with the key (including correct spelling) for them to be correct.

Reading passages

These are designed to be done in class, though they are also suitable as homework tasks. The teacher's notes give detailed advice on teaching different reading techniques, ways of dealing with different IELTS question-types and ways of dealing with reading passages in class.

Many passages have a **vocabulary follow-up.** These are placed after the passage to give students experience in dealing with reading passages *in spite of* difficult vocabulary. These activities can be done first, if you think this will help your students deal with the reading more confidently.

Listening sections

In the IELTS test, candidates hear each section *once only*. However, in classroom practice it may often be beneficial, especially for **Intermediate** students, to play these twice. As in the IELTS test, each listening activity comes in two parts, with a pause in the middle for students to read the next set of questions.

Speaking follow-ups and role plays

These follow most reading passages and listening sections, and are designed to give students an opportunity to express their opinions and ideas on the topic of the lesson. The teacher's notes give detailed advice on how to handle these in class. However, please note that in the IELTS test the topics of the speaking module are *not* related to the topics dealt with in other parts of the test.

Writing tasks

Each of these contains an introduction to the topic and practice in planning answers to writing tasks. They also contain **sample answers** to the task with exercises based on them. When the exercises have been completed correctly, the answers should serve as models for your students when they do their own writing tasks. The sample answers are followed by work on useful structures or vocabulary. The final activity is a similar writing task for students to do themselves. This can be given for homework or, if you think it is more suitable, as class work.

Speaking

These activities are designed to give practice in the three parts of the speaking module of the IELTS test. In the test, the speaking module takes 11–14 minutes, so it is probably not a good idea to do all these activities at the same time. Photocopy and cut up a few activities to fill ten- or fifteen-minute gaps in your lessons on different days. Read the teacher's notes for advice on how to manage these activities in class.

1 Introduction

Read about Lucy and then, in groups of three, discuss

- what things will probably worry Lucy about going to study in Canada.
- which type of accommodation would be most suitable for her and which least suitable. Put them in order from **1–6**.

☐ a hall of residence or dormitory
☐ a shared flat or apartment with other students
☐ a bedsitter or studio
☐ a room in a family house
☐ a basement flat or basement suite
☐ a terraced house or row house

Lucy is a 24-year-old graduate student at the University of Natal, in Durban, South Africa. She has just won a scholarship to study for part of her doctorate at the University of British Columbia in Vancouver, Canada. She is single and this will be her first time abroad.

2 ⊙ Listening

You will hear a man in Vancouver, Canada, phoning a real-estate agent in order to rent out rooms in his house.

Work in pairs and look at Questions 1–7.

- Before you listen predict the type of information you will need for the answer to each question.

  Example: *in Question **7** you will need a telephone number.*

- Then listen and answer the questions.

Questions 1–7

Complete the form below.
Use **NO MORE THAN THREE WORDS OR A NUMBER.**

BELLINGHAM REAL-ESTATE AGENTS

Property to rent

Type of property: (**1**) ....

Architectural type: **2 storey**

Address: 3281 (**2**) ....

  Richmond, British Columbia.

Monthly rent: $700 (**3**) ....

plus $30 for (**4**) ....

View of: (**5**) ....

Seller information

Name: (**6**) ....

Address: **as above**

Telephone: (**7**) ....

Cell phone: **903 2773987**

a terraced house or row house

a basement flat or basement suite

Now you will listen to the second part of the conversation.

Before you listen, work in pairs and:
- read the questions and check you understand the vocabulary.
- suggest other ways of expressing the options (**A, B, C, D** or **E**) in the questions.

Example:	Answer:
8C dryer	machine for drying clothes

Then listen to the second part and answer Questions 8–10.

Questions 8–10

Circle two letters A–E.

8 Which of the following does the kitchen contain?
   A dishwasher
   B washing machine
   C dryer
   D gas stove
   E microwave

9 Which of the following does the house have?
   A a swimming pool
   B air conditioning
   C central heating
   D a games room
   E a fireplace

10 Which amenities are nearby?
   A the university
   B a shopping mall
   C a park
   D a sports centre
   E a movie theatre

3 Follow-up

Role play

Read the advertisement below and then work in pairs to prepare either Role A or Role B. When you have prepared, change partners and do the role play.

Family House for Rent		
$700 per room	**2 bedrooms**	**Richmond**

Two big bedrooms in large 2-storey Richmond home with view over ocean and 2-minute walk from beach and park. Shopping mall 1 block away. Fully-equipped kitchen including microwave and dishwasher. Washing machine and dryer in basement. Games room with ping pong and pool. Central heating. Would suit single students.

Role A: Real-Estate Agent You put the advertisement at the bottom of the page on your website. You should deal with enquiries about it. You are keen to rent out this property as you have not had many enquiries about it – it's rather far from the city centre and the university. Before you start, think of extra details about the property and questions you would ask people enquiring about the room.

Role B: Lucy You have seen the advertisement at the bottom of the page on the Internet. Phone the estate agent to find out more details about the house. You are worried that the house is a little far from the university – you don't have a car at the moment and would have to rely on public transport, at least until you can find a part-time job and earn some extra money. Before you start, think of questions you want to ask the real-estate agent.

Vocabulary

When you travel to English-speaking countries, you may hear either British English vocabulary or American English vocabulary, or something different depending on where you go. Here are some words which are different in British English and American English. (Canadian English is likely to be similar to American English.)

Match the words in British English on the left with their American English equivalents on the right.

British	American
1 cinema*	a yard
2 cooker	b stove*
3 distance between two parallel streets	c sidewalk
4 flat*	d movie theatre
5 garden*	e mall*
6 lift*	f line
7 motorway*	g gas* or gasoline
8 pavement*	h garbage*
9 petrol*	i freeway*
10 queue*	j faucet
11 rubbish*	k elevator
12 shopping centre*	l downtown
13 tap*	m block*
14 the town centre	n apartment*
15 sea	o ocean

*These are the words most often used in Australia.

From *Instant IELTS* by Guy Brook-Hart © Cambridge University Press 2004 **PHOTOCOPIABLE**

Estimated class time: 1 hour

1 Introduction *(10 minutes)*

You can personalise the activity by asking your students to tell their partners what type of accommodation would suit them if they were moving to study in a foreign country.

2 🔘 Listening

For the complete recording script, please see page 123.

Questions 1–7 *(15 minutes)*

Before listening

- Tell your students that although they won't be able to predict the *actual* answers in the test, trying to predict *the type of information needed* is the most effective way of approaching the task.
- Although in the test they will have less time to do this than in class, they should try to predict *how* the answer will be said.

Intermediate

Ask your students to say for which questions they may be asked to write down a word which is spelt out (Answer: Questions **2** and **6**).

Elicit the problems which they may have in this type of exercise *e.g. one of the speakers repeats the spelling wrongly.*

Ask them to look at Questions **1–5** in pairs and suggest 2 or 3 possible answers for each, so they think about the *type* of information they should be listening for.

Advanced

You may wish to turn this into a vocabulary revision exercise by brainstorming different types of property *town house, apartment etc.*, different types of road to live in *street, avenue, square etc.* and talk about vocabulary differences between British and American English.

ANSWER KEY
1 (modern) (family) house
2 Number One / No 1 / Road
3 per room
4 (the) cleaner / cleaning
5 (over) (the) ocean
6 Peter Truboise
7 60474106

Questions 8–10 *(15 minutes)*

Point out that with multiple selection questions, the speakers will probably use different words from the ones that appear in the questions.

- Point out the example and elicit some suggestions for other options *e.g. washer, cooker.*

Play the second part of the listening task.

- Ask your students to check their answers in pairs before checking with the whole class.
- Play the second part again and compare the words the speakers used with the words in the questions.

ANSWER KEY
  8 A E
  9 C D
10 B C

3 Follow-up *(20 minutes)*

Role play

Before doing the role play:
- Ask your students to prepare the same roles in pairs.
- The real-estate agents should think up extra details for the property and questions they should ask Lucy – *e.g. How long do you want to rent for? What's your job or occupation?*
- For the Lucy role, they should think of possible questions. *E.g. How much is the rent? Do I have to pay a deposit?*

Remix the pairs to do the role play.

Vocabulary

ANSWER KEY
1d 2b 3m 4n 5a 6k 7i 8c 9g 10f 11h 12e 13j
14l 15o

1 Introduction

Work in pairs and discuss
- which of these symptoms you would go to the doctor for and which you would treat yourself.
- what illnesses they might be symptoms of. (Choose from the box below.)

Symptoms
a cough
sneezing
a rash
spots
a runny nose
a headache
a back ache
a sore throat
diarrhoea
dizziness
nausea and vomiting
a temperature

Illnesses
the flu
a cold
an allergy
food poisoning
chicken pox
over-tiredness
bronchitis

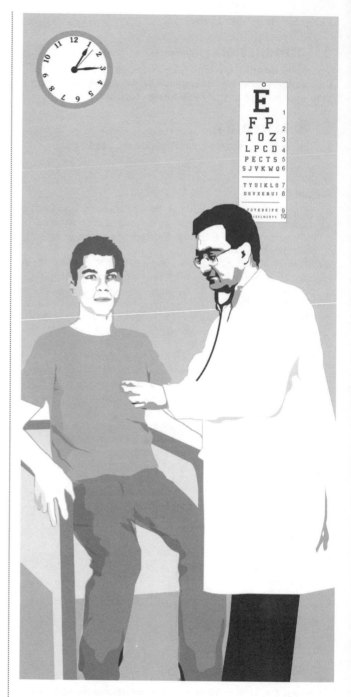

2 ⊕ Listening

Martin is visiting a doctor at a student health centre. You will hear a conversation between Martin and the doctor.

Before you listen, look at Questions 1–6 and predict what type of information you should listen for in each question. (In the example you have to listen for the patient's name and also listen to how it is spelt.)

Questions 1–3

Complete the form below.
Write NO MORE THAN ONE WORD OR A NUMBER for each answer.

STUDENT HEALTH CENTRE
MEDICAL RECORD

Example	Answer
Patient's name:	Martin Hansen

Faculty of (**1**) ....

Address: 13 (**2**) .... Street, Perth.

Telephone: (**3**) ....

Date of Birth: 15th June, 1986.

Questions 4–6

Complete the notes below.
Write NO MORE THAN THREE WORDS for each answer.

Serious illnesses / accidents: (**4**) ....

Operations: (**5**) ....

Allergies: (**6**) ....

From *Instant IELTS* by Guy Brook-Hart © Cambridge University Press 2004 **PHOTOCOPIABLE**

Now you will listen to the second part of the conversation.
- Before you listen, look at Questions 7–10.
- Work in pairs and suggest other ways of expressing the alternatives in the questions.

Example:	Answer:
7C He has an infection	I might have got a germ / I probably picked up the flu from someone

- When you have done this, listen and answer the questions.

Questions 7–9

Circle the correct letters A–C.

7 Why is Martin visiting the doctor?
  A He suffers from headaches.
  B He suffers from nausea.
  C He has an infection.

8 How many hours does Martin usually sleep each night?
  A Less than eight.
  B Between eight and nine.
  C More than nine.

9 Which of these describes Martin's problem?
  A It's continuous and constant.
  B It's worse during the daytime.
  C It's worse in the evening and at night.

Question 10

Circle two letters A–E.

10 Which of these things does the doctor suggest Martin should do?
  A change his diet
  B have his eyes tested
  C sleep more
  D take more exercise
  E take some medicine

3 Follow-up

Speaking Module Part 3

In Part 3 of the speaking module the interviewer asks you some questions and discusses them with you.
Work in pairs. Ask each other these questions and discuss your answers together.

a Why is it important to stay healthy?
b Which do you think is more important: health or money?
c What things should people do to protect their health?
d What are the main health problems in your country?

Estimated class time: 50 minutes–1 hour

1 Introduction (10 minutes)

Ask your students to discuss these things fairly briefly.

> **ANSWER KEY**
>
> **1** This is a question of personal inclination – some people are readier to visit the doctor than others for a number of reasons. Also, it will depend on how long the symptoms persist and how serious they are.
>
> **2** (Possible answers):
>
> **the flu:** sneezing, a headache, a back ache, a sore throat, nausea and vomiting, a temperature
>
> **a cold:** a cough, sneezing, a runny nose, a headache, a sore throat, a temperature
>
> **an allergy:** a cough, sneezing, a rash, spots, a runny nose, nausea and vomiting
>
> **food poisoning:** a headache, diarrhoea, dizziness, nausea and vomiting, a temperature
>
> **chicken pox:** a rash, spots, a headache, a temperature
>
> **over-tiredness:** a headache, dizziness
>
> **bronchitis:** a cough, a sore throat, a temperature.

2 🔊 Listening

For the complete recording script, please see page 123.

Optional pre-listening activity (10 minutes)

Ask your students to look at the questions (1–10) and the photo.

- Ask them to work in pairs and predict what questions the doctor will ask the patient – they needn't write these down.
- Discuss their suggestions and correct their English where necessary.

Questions 1–6 (15 minutes)

Before you play the listening, ask your students to look at the form (Questions 1–3) and predict possible problems when listening for information of this type. These will include:

- Spelling of names – which letters do they find confusing? *E.g. G and J, C and S, A and H*
- Telephone numbers e.g. *double 3, Oh and zero in British and American English etc.*
- Other things which confuse students e.g. *mistakes made by one of the speakers, numbers – 15 and 50, A and 8 with American speakers etc.*

> **Intermediate**
>
> **If necessary, give your students some practice with the problems they mention. You can:**
> - Ask them to spell a few names.
> - Do a minimal pairs exercise on the board i.e. write:
>
>   **A** **B**
>   13   30
>   14   40
>   15   50 etc.
> - Read the numbers at random and ask students to say whether each number is from '**A**' or '**B**'. They then work in pairs and test each other by reading the numbers in the same way.
> - In groups get them to dictate their telephone numbers.

> **Advanced**
>
> *Extra activity*
> - Ask students to work in pairs and invent their own dialogue for this part of the listening in which they include some of the problems you have elicited.

- Put pairs together in groups of 4 or 6 to read their scripts to each other – the others note down the answers.
- Get a pair whose dialogue you think is particularly good to read it to the whole class.
- Ask students to comment on which dialogues gave them the most problems and why.

Ask your students to look at Questions 4–6 and brainstorm possible answers from the whole class.

- Tell them that although they won't be able to predict the *actual* answers in the test, trying to predict *possible* answers in this way is the most effective way of approaching the task.
- Remind them that to get the marks they must spell their answers correctly.
- Play the first part of the listening (**Questions 1–6**), then ask students to check their answers first in pairs, then with the whole class.

> **ANSWER KEY**
> 1 Medicine
> 2 Chatham
> 3 01734 24655
> 4 (a) broken leg / broke leg
> 5 none / no (operations)
> 6 dust (and) cats

Questions 7–10 (15 minutes)

Point out to your students that with multiple choice (Questions 7–9) and multiple selection (Question 10), the speakers rarely use the same words as appear in the questions.

- Elicit ways of rewording some of the alternatives in the questions, *e.g. 7B: he feels sick, or C he's caught a virus.*
- Ask students to work in pairs and think of other alternatives.

Play the second part of the listening.

- Ask your students to check their answers in pairs, then with the whole class.
- Play the second part again to hear what words the speakers used to produce the correct answers for Questions **7–10**.

> **ANSWER KEY**
> 7 A
> 8 B
> 9 C
> 10 B and E

3 Follow-up (10 minutes)

Speaking Module Part 3

When candidates answer these questions in the test, it's important that they give fairly long answers – not just a few words. To do this, encourage them to

- give reasons for their answers.
- give examples to support their ideas.

> **Intermediate**
>
> **You can work with the whole class first and**
> - brainstorm ideas, reasons and examples for each question.
> - brainstorm vocabulary they will need to answer the questions well e.g. *check-up, balanced diet and disease.*
> **Then put them in pairs to do the task.**

> **Advanced**
>
> **You can put them in small groups to brainstorm useful vocabulary before they start.**

1 Introduction

Discussion

Work in pairs and answer these questions.
a   What does each of the pictures show?
b   Why could each of them be a source of stress at work?
c   What other sources of stress at work can you think of?
d   How can you cope with stress at work?

Vocabulary

Check you know the meanings of these words and phrases which you will hear in the listening. Then complete the sentences below using each word or phrase once.

workplace   personal goals   overwork   trivialities   set money aside

1   I put your headaches down to .... You need to take some time off and have a holiday.
2   It's a good idea to .... so that you don't have financial problems if you become unemployed.
3   It's important in your job to meet your own .... as well as fulfilling your company's objectives.
4   She has difficulty dealing with really important issues in the office because she gets too involved in ....
5   We've carried out a 5-year study into stress in the .... – particularly in factories and offices.

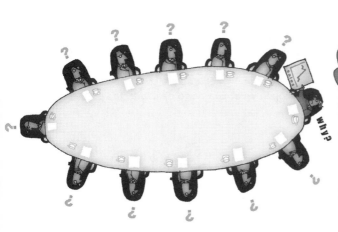

2 🎧 Listening

You will hear part of a radio programme in which a researcher talks about stress at work.
- Before you listen, look at Questions **1–4** below.
- Study the list of possible causes of stress and explain why each of them can cause stress.

Questions 1–4

Complete the list of reasons why these people suffer from stress. Choose from the list of possible causes in the box.

What did each person say was the **principal** cause of stress for them?

| *Example* | *Answer* |
| Ramon | Team work |

Kikuko	(1) ....
Boris	(2) ....
Etienne	(3) ....
Nagwa	(4) ....

> **Possible causes of stress**
> **A** bad management
> **B** dual-career family
> **C** fear of unemployment
> **D** new technologies
> **E** physical surroundings
> **F** powerlessness
> **G** too much work

Now listen to the second part of the listening, and answer Questions 5–10 below.

Questions 5–7

List THREE parts of one's daily routine that can help reduce stress.
Write NO MORE THAN THREE WORDS for each answer.

5 ....
....
6 ....
....
7 ....
....

Questions 8–10

Complete the table below.
Write NO MORE THAN THREE WORDS in each space.

| Strategies for reducing stress from specific causes | |
Cause of stress	Strategy for reducing stress
Overwork	(8) ....
Fear of job loss	(9) ....
New technologies	(10) ....

3 Follow-up

Speaking Module Part 2

In Part 2 of the speaking module you are given a prompt card and you have to speak for one or two minutes about the subject on the card.
Look at this prompt card and prepare to give a short talk.
Do the following steps:

- Work in pairs. Brainstorm ideas for the talk and make notes.
- Change partners and take it in turns to give your talks.

> Describe some things which cause you stress.
> You should say:
>   when you get stressed
>   why certain things cause you stress
>   how you feel when you are stressed
> and explain what you do to deal with the problem.

From *Instant IELTS* by Guy Brook-Hart © Cambridge University Press 2004 **PHOTOCOPIABLE**

Estimated class time: 1 hour

1 Introduction *(10 minutes)*

Discussion *(5 minutes)*

The sources of stress arising from the pictures include:

- conflict with colleagues, bosses or customers
- work-related travel
- overwork
- coping with new technologies
- poor physical working conditions.

Vocabulary *(5 minutes)*

Ask your students to work in pairs. Encourage them to use their dictionaries where necessary.

> **ANSWER KEY**
>
> **1** overwork   **2** set money aside   **3** personal goals   **4** trivialities
> **5** workplace

2 🕮 Listening

For the complete recording script, please see page 124.

Questions 1–4 *(20 minutes)*

Before listening

Ask your students to explain how each of the items in the box 'Possible causes of stress' can cause stress. Then follow the advice for Intermediate or Advanced students.

Intermediate

- Remind them that when they listen, they won't hear these exact words or phrases.
- Ask them to suggest how they might be phrased in the listening *e.g. for dual-career family: 'both husband and wife have jobs'.*
- If you wish, play the listening down to *acute source of stress* as an example.

Advanced

- Play the example i.e. what is said about Ramon down to *an acute source of stress.*
- To show students how the speakers will not use the same vocabulary as appears in the questions, elicit how the idea of teamwork as a cause of stress is expressed in the listening activity i.e. *work in teams, conflict between personal goals and the need to cooperate with one's colleagues.*
- Ask students to work in pairs and each pair write a part of the script for one of the causes in the box. Encourage them to paraphrase the cause, not repeat the same words.
- They then read their extract to the rest of the class who have to say which cause it is.
- When doing this, you should encourage them to use different words as merely repeating *bad management* (for example) makes the answer obvious.

Play the first part of the listening and ask your students to check their answers first in pairs and then with the rest of the class.

> **ANSWER KEY**
> **1** C   **2** G   **3** D   **4** E

Intermediate

- If necessary, play the listening activity again for them to improve on their answers (though they won't have this opportunity in the IELTS test).
- Elicit what things confused them while they were listening and, where necessary, play extracts to show why each answer is correct – in this way they become familiar with the ways unwary candidates are distracted from getting the correct answer.

Advanced

- Play the recording again and ask your students to compare the differences between the words in the list of possible causes and the words Dr Greenhill used in the listening task.

Questions 5–10 *(15 minutes)*

Questions 5–7 and 8–10 are basically the same type: students may use no more than 3 words.

Intermediate

- To prepare for this, go back to their list of ways of coping with stress at work from the Introduction, and ask them to rephrase them so that they express them in no more than 3 words.
- Then play the second part of the listening task and ask them to check their answers in pairs.

Advanced

- Before listening, ask them to predict what they think the answers will be – they may use ideas already expressed in the Introduction.
- Get feedback from the whole class, but discount any answers which are more than 3 words.
- Play the listening activity and check the answers in pairs and then with the whole class.

> **ANSWER KEY**
> **5** a balanced diet / vary your diet
> **6** drink less coffee
> **7** take regular exercise
> **8** manage time better / manage your time
> **9** make plans / (set money aside / update your c.v.)
> **10** do training courses

3 Follow-up

Speaking Module Part 2 *(15 minutes)*

- Don't allow students to write out what they are going to say in full – just brief notes.
- Tell the listening student in each pair to give their partner feedback when they have finished.
- Students may then repeat their 'improved' talk to someone else.

1 Introduction

Work in pairs or small groups.

● Match the first half of the phrases below with the second half to make a list of typical things that worry students when they are starting university.

● Discuss which would be serious problems for you and which would be less serious.

1	Finding	a	around a strange city.
2	Living	b	away from home for the first time.
3	Missing	c	enough money.
4	Not being able to keep up with	d	friends and family.
5	Not being able to understand	e	members of the opposite sex for the first time.
6	Not finding	f	somewhere pleasant to live.
7	Not finding one's way	g	the food.
8	Not having	h	the weather unpleasant.
9	Not liking	i	the work.
10	Studying with	j	what's being said in class.

2 ◉ Listening

You will hear part of a talk to new students at a university.
Before you listen, look at Questions 1–3.

● Work in pairs and quickly suggest alternative ways of stating the three options for each question.

> *Example:*   *Answer*
> 1A New students   Students just beginning at university.

● Then listen to the talk.

Questions 1–3

Circle the correct letters A–C.

1 Who are mentors?
   A new students
   B second or third-year students
   C university teachers

2 How often should mentor groups meet?
   A once a week
   B once a fortnight
   C once a month

3 What is it essential to do at the first meeting?
   A explain your problems
   B make new friends
   C agree when to meet again

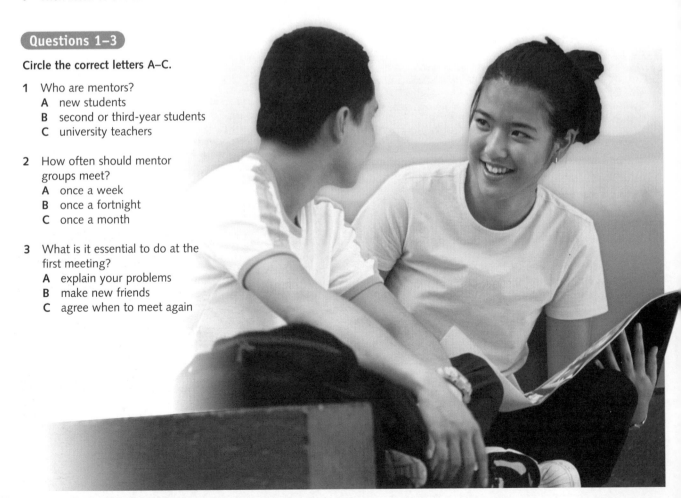

From *Instant IELTS* by Guy Brook-Hart © Cambridge University Press 2004 **PHOTOCOPIABLE**

You will now hear the second part of the talk.

Before you listen, work in pairs and

- look at Questions **4–7** and say four things you would hope to receive information about if you were a new student.
- look at Questions **8–10** and try to predict possible answers (you can make several suggestions for each question).
- then listen to the second part of the talk and answer Questions **4–10**.

Questions 4–7

List FOUR things which students may be given information about.
Write NO MORE THAN THREE WORDS for each answer.

4 ....

5 ....

6 ....

7 ....

Questions 8–10

Complete the sentences below.
Write NO MORE THAN THREE WORDS for each answer.

8 Your mentor will show you how to obtain a free

....

9 Mentoring is useful for people who are

.... for the first time.

10 Your mentor may give you advice on how to

....

3 Follow-up

Discussion

Discuss these questions in small groups.
a Have you come across a mentoring system like this?
b What was it like?
c How well did it work?
d If there wasn't a system of this kind, what methods were used to help new students settle in? Would you have liked a mentoring system like the one described?
e Do you think a system like this would be good for people starting new jobs in a company?

Role play

Do the following role play in groups of three. One person should take Role A and two people should share Role B.

Role A: You are a second-year university student, and you have volunteered to be a mentor to new students because you like meeting new people, enjoy being helpful and feel enthusiastic about university life in general. You met your 'mentees' (the new students) briefly on the first day of term, but this is your first proper meeting with them. To help bring out problems and worries they may have, ask them questions like: *How do you expect university life to be different to life as a school student?* or *What are your concerns about being at university?* Before you start, think of a few more questions like these.

Role B: You are a new university student, and you have asked to join a mentor group. You met your mentor briefly on the first day of term but this is your first proper session with him / her. You have just left school and this is your first experience of higher education, so you are full of questions such as: *How many hours a day should I spend studying?* or *What are my tutors looking for in my written assignments?* Before you start, think of a few more questions like these to ask your mentor, and also questions about social or sports facilities.

Estimated class time: 1 hour

1 Introduction *(10 minutes)*

Before handing out the photocopiable page:
- Elicit the things that would worry / worried your students on their first day at university or college.
- If they are hoping to study abroad, ask them what worries they have about this.
- List their concerns and then ask them in groups of 3 or 4 to discuss how reasonable the worry is and how the problem can be dealt with.

Ask them to do the exercise in pairs or small groups.

ANSWER KEY

1h   2b   3d   4i   5j   6f   7a   8c   9g   10e

---

2 🕪 Listening

For the complete recording script, please see page 124.

Questions 1–3 *(15 minutes)*

Before listening, your students should briefly suggest alternative ways of expressing the options.
- Give them a few minutes and then get feedback / suggestions from the whole class.
- Play the first part of the listening activity and check the answers.
- If you wish, play the extract again, and ask your students to note down what was actually said. Compare it with the wording of the correct options.

ANSWER KEY

1   B
2   B
3   C

Questions 4–10 *(15 minutes)*

For Questions 4–7, your students should quickly brainstorm possibilities.
For Questions 8–10, they should predict possible answers.
- Tell them to pay particular attention to correct spelling because if they spell words wrongly in the test, they may not get the mark.

Intermediate

- To help them, tell them that the answers contain these words. *academic, account, facilities, techniques*.
- After playing the recording, ask them to work in pairs and complete their answers.
- With a weak class, play the listening a second time (though they will not have this opportunity in the test).
- Check the answers with the class – if necessary, play extracts to show where the answers are.

Advanced

- When they brainstorm possible answers, you can:
- Ask them to work in pairs and express as many as possible in not more than 3 words.

ANSWER KEY

4   academic systems
5   study techniques / techniques for studying   } in any order
6   university facilities
7   social activities
8   e-mail account
9   away from home
10 pass (your) exams

---

3 Follow-up *(20 minutes)*

Discussion

Students discuss their experiences and opinions in groups of 3 or 4.

Role play

Although there are two roles, students should do this role play in groups of 3, with 1 person taking Role A and 2 people Role B.

Before starting

- Put students with the same role in pairs to prepare their questions and ideas. Give them 3 or 4 minutes to do this.
- Discourage them from writing their questions down as this makes the role play unnatural.
- When everyone has finished, get feedback from the whole class by asking what things they discussed.

1 Introduction

Work in small groups. Look at the photographs and answer the questions below.

1 What are the main differences in the way the people in the photos work?
2 What is the digital divide?
3 How can digital / Internet technology help people in the developing world?

2 🎧 Listening

You will hear Sanjay, a student on a social studies course, talking in a tutorial about a project which aims to reduce the digital divide. He is talking about how the Internet is being used to help the people in Veerampattinam, a village on the east coast of India near Pondicherry.

Before you listen, look at the diagram and Questions 1–4 on the next page.

● Work in pairs and discuss what the diagram shows, and what words you might put in each space.
● Then listen and answer Questions **1–4**.

Questions 1–4

The diagram below shows how Veerampattinam gets information.
- Label the numbered parts in the diagram.
- Write TWO OR THREE WORDS in each space.

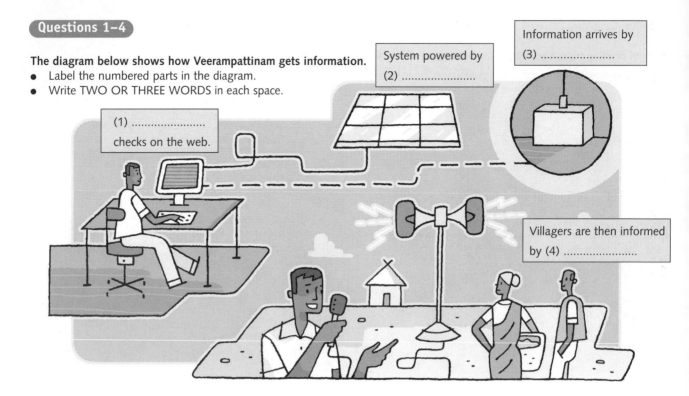

System powered by (2) ....

Information arrives by (3) ....

(1) .... checks on the web.

Villagers are then informed by (4) ....

Now study Questions 5–10. Then listen and answer the questions.

Questions 5–7

Which THREE types of information do villagers obtain from this service?

Circle THREE letters A–F.

A   agricultural prices
B   educational information
C   employment information
D   farming advice
E   government regulations
F   weather forecasts

Questions 8–10

Circle the correct letters A–C.

8   The project was designed by a well-known
   A   businessman.
   B   geneticist.
   C   politician.

9   It is important that the system is managed by
   A   government officials.
   B   external experts.
   C   the villagers themselves.

10   The project means that villagers are better able to deal with
   A   middlemen.
   B   employers.
   C   landlords.

3 Follow-up

Speaking Module Part 3

Discuss these questions in pairs or small groups.
- Do you think the world is becoming a safer place as a result of technology?
- How has the Internet changed people's lives?
- Which do you think is a more important priority: Internet access or fixed telephones and electricity?
- Do you agree that it is important that the government is not involved in a project like this, or do you think this is a service which the government should provide?
- What other examples have you heard about of information technology changing people's lives in poor regions?

Estimated class time: 55 minutes

1 Introduction *(15 minutes)*

- Ask your students to work in small groups and to compare the ways people in the different photographs work (e.g. in 3: hard physical work, poorly paid, dangerous etc., in 2: 'knowledge workers', clean, safe etc., in the middle photo: using digital technology in a 'traditional' setting).
- Get feedback from the different groups for the whole class.
- Elicit what is meant by 'the digital divide' and why it is an important issue.
- Ask students to concentrate on the middle photo and say what applications of digital / Internet technology may be used for in this setting *e.g. to check prices, to e-mail customers and suppliers, for online banking.*
- Ask them to say how it could be applied to improve the lives of people in the 3 photos which show hard physical work. *Examples:*
  - Cell phones and the Internet in villages in Bangladesh (people in remote areas have access to weather forecasts so they know if it's safe to go fishing, they can phone towns to find out if work is available or money has arrived in the bank from relatives working abroad).
  - Virtual classrooms in Laos give children in remote areas access to modern education.
- You could also ask if digital technology has had any adverse effects on the quality of life in developed countries.

2 🔊 Listening

For the complete recording script, please see page 125.

Questions 1–4 *(10 minutes)*

Before listening, ask if anyone has heard or read about this project – if so, ask them to say what they know about it.

Intermediate

- Give them a couple of minutes to discuss what the diagram shows.
- Ask them to think of vocabulary connected with the diagram.

Advanced

Ask them to work together and describe:
- what they suppose is happening (especially what sort of information interests the villagers).
- how the system works.

- When they have listened, check the answers with the whole class, and particularly spelling. Remind them that they must spell their answers correctly in the test.
  Ask if any of them successfully managed to predict the answers to the questions before they listened.
  In the test they are unlikely to be able to predict the information but this technique will help them to focus on the questions and the *type* of information required.

> **ANSWER KEY**
> 1 (a) (local) volunteer
> 2 solar panel(s)
> 3 wireless (transmission) (system)
> 4 public address system

Questions 5–10 *(20 minutes)*

Intermediate

Before listening

- Tell your students to work in pairs and decide which answers they *think* will be correct. (They should omit Question **8** as this is impossible to predict.)
- Encourage them to think of reasons for their answers.
- Discuss their ideas with the whole class.
- Check they know the meanings of *middlemen* and *landlords* in Question **10**.
- Play the second part of the listening and ask them to check their answers in pairs, and then with the whole class.
- Ask them which words gave the correct answer.
- If necessary, play the listening again, stopping to show them where the answers are given.

Advanced

Before listening

- Ask your students to look at Questions **5–7** and say why each of these types of information might be useful to the villagers.
- Tell them to look at Questions **8–10**, and imagine how the information may be presented in the listening activity as they are unlikely to hear exactly the same words.
- Play the second part of the listening. Students can check their answers with their partners, and then with the whole class.

> **ANSWER KEY**
> 5 A
> 6 C   5, 6 and 7 in any order
> 7 F
> 8 B
> 9 C
> 10 A

3 Follow-up

Speaking Module Part 3 *(10 minutes)*

If your students have difficulty dealing with these questions, suggest they compare the usefulness of the Internet versus fixed telephones and electricity for:
- people living in a remote village in a poor African country.
- people living on a small island.

Students should come up with the idea that the Internet is useful for getting practical information if they know where to look, and they speak the language. Telephones put them immediately in contact with people in the city etc. Electricity is required for basic equipment such as refrigerators and electric light. The photo shows a man cleaning solar panels.

1 Introduction

Work in small groups. Discuss whether the following statements are true or false.

a   People nowadays are on average more intelligent than their parents or grandparents were.

b   Intelligence is something which we are born with and cannot change.

c   Our intelligence is our ability to learn.

d   Intelligence is measured by our ability to solve problems.

e   People with an IQ of 130 are in the top five per cent of the population for intelligence.

f   Our intelligence is affected by our diet.

g   We're not getting more intelligent: we're just getting better at doing IQ tests.

2 🔊 Listening

You will hear three psychology students, Martin, Maria and Farouk, discussing some project work which Martin and Maria have been doing for a seminar on intelligence. Listen and answer Questions 1–7.

Questions 1–7

Who gave these explanations for rises in intelligence?

Write A   **if it was James Flynn.**
Write B   **if it was John Rust.**
Write C   **if it was Robert Howard.**

1   television and computers   ………

2   better nutrition   ………

3   smaller families   ………

4   car-driving   ………

5   more complex societies   ………

6   wider access to education   ………

7   more sophisticated concepts   ………

ANSWER KEY

a   This is the question which the listening passage deals with.

b   Apparently not. Our intelligence develops throughout our childhood and youth. Studies of identical twins brought up separately have demonstrated that environmental factors including upbringing and education can also affect intelligence.

c   According to the *Encyclopaedia Britannica*, intelligence is the 'ability to adapt effectively to the environment, either by making a change in oneself or by changing the environment or by finding a new one'.

d   Again, according to the *Encyclopaedia Britannica*, intelligence tests include tasks 'requiring recognition of analogies, classification of similar terms, extrapolation of number series, … and the like'.

e   Only one score in 20 differs by more than 30 points from the average of 100, so that five per cent of the population will score either less than 70 or more than 130.

f   Malnutrition in childhood will almost certainly affect the development of a child's intelligence.

g   This is a point of view.

Now look at Questions 8–10 and study the alternatives carefully.
Listen to the second part of the listening, and answer the questions.

Questions 8–10

Circle the correct letters A–C.

8 Which graph best illustrates changes in intelligence in Western industrialised countries over the last 40 years?

A B C

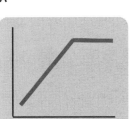  

9 Which graph best illustrates changes in intelligence in some East Asian countries over the last 40 years?

A B C

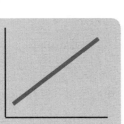  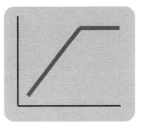

10 What explanation is given for improvements in British exam results?
   A better teaching
   B higher intelligence
   C lower standards

3 Follow-up

Speaking Module Part 3

Discuss these questions in small groups.
1 What different types of intelligence do you know of?
2 Do you agree that levels of intelligence are rising / have risen?
3 Does increased intelligence mean we make fewer mistakes, or that the world is a better place to live in?
4 In what ways does increased intelligence permit us to have a better quality of life?
5 What can we do to maximise the intelligence of our children?

Estimated class time: 1 hour

1 Introduction *(15 minutes)*

Ask your students to discuss these statements in groups of 3 or 4.

- Several students may have some knowledge of the subject. If so, use them as a resource and ask them to say what they know.
- When they have finished, one person in each group refers to the answers below and reports the 'true' answers to the rest of the group.

2 🔊 Listening *(20 minutes)*

For the complete recording script, please see page 125.

Questions 1–7

Intermediate

- Remind your students that they are unlikely to hear exactly the same words on the recording as occur in the questions.
- Ask them to work in pairs and suggest how the ideas might be expressed in the listening activity *e.g. instead of 'wider access to education' they may hear 'more children have the chance to go to school'.*
- Tell them they will have to listen carefully as neither the names nor the list occur in the same order as they are mentioned by the speakers.
- They listen and then check their answers in pairs.
- If necessary, check what was actually said on the recording.

Advanced

- Familiarise your students with the questions by asking them to work in pairs and suggest a reason why each explanation may have led to higher intelligence.
- Get feedback on this from the whole class.
- You can develop this into a discussion (some students, for example, may believe that television numbs the intelligence, or that large families stimulate the intelligence more).
- Do the listening exercise and check their answers.

ANSWER KEY
1 A
2 C
3 C
4 A
5 B
6 C
7 B

Questions 8 and 9 *(10 minutes)*

Intermediate

Before they listen, write these sentences and ask your students to match them with the graphs:
- After a dramatic rise, they levelled off a few years ago. (*8A and 9C*)
- After peaking a few years ago, levels have begun to dip slightly. (*8C*)
- Intelligence levels started to rise later and they still haven't reached their peak. (*9B*)
- Levels of intelligence are still rising dramatically. (*8B and 9A*)

ANSWER KEY 8A 9B

Advanced

Before they listen:
- Ask your students to look at the alternatives and describe the differences between them.
- Then write the sentences from the Intermediate box above on the board and discuss the differences between their descriptions and the sentences you have written.

ANSWER KEY
8 A
9 B

Question 10 *(5 minutes)*

- Ask your students to predict what the best answer for this will be before they listen.
- If necessary, play this part of the listening task again for them to check their answers.

ANSWER KEY
10 C

3 Follow-up

Speaking Module Part 3 *(10 minutes)*

- Put students in small groups to discuss these questions.
- When they have talked for about 5 minutes, remix the groups and ask students to report what they thought about each question.
- Encourage them to discuss the questions further.

1 Introduction

Work in pairs. Match the picture with the name of the building and the city where it is located. See how many you can do in two minutes.

Name
a City of Arts and Sciences
b Guggenheim Museum
c Louvre
d Opera House
e Parthenon
f Petronas Towers
g World Financial Centre

City
i Athens, Greece
ii Bilbao, Spain
iii Paris, France
iv Sydney, Australia
v Valencia, Spain
vi Shanghai, China
vii Kuala Lumpur, Malaysia

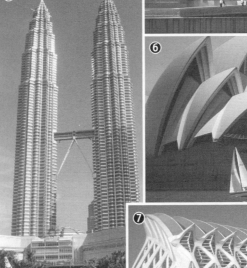

2 🔊 Listening

You will hear a university teacher giving a lecture to students on an urban planning course. He talks about emblematic buildings and their benefits.

Before you listen, look at the table below and Questions **1–4**.
• Work in pairs and try to predict what information will be needed to complete the table.
• Then listen and answer Questions **1–4**.

Questions 1–4

Complete the table below.
Write NO MORE THAN THREE WORDS OR A NUMBER for each answer.

City	Building(s)	Special feature	Number of visitors per year
Bilbao	Guggenheim	modern art collection	(1) ....
Paris	Louvre	(2)	5 million
Valencia	City of Arts and Sciences	(3)	4 million in the first year
Alexandria	(4)	—	—

Questions 5–7

Complete the notes below.
Write NO MORE THAN THREE WORDS for each answer.

Four benefits to the city of Valencia from building the City of Arts and
Sciences are that it has ...

- *boosted tourism.*
- *regenerated a (5) .... of the city.*
- *improved the city's (6) ....*
- *attracted (7) ....*

Questions 8–10

Complete the plan of the City of Arts and Sciences.
Write NO MORE THAN THREE WORDS for each answer.

Car Park and (8)...

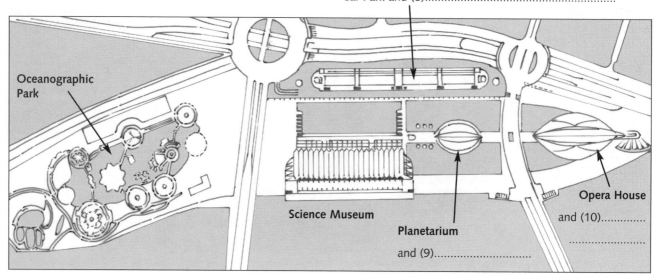

Oceanographic
Park

Science Museum

Planetarium
and (9)...............................

Opera House
and (10)..............
....

3 Follow-up

Speaking Module Part 2

Work in pairs to practise Part 2 of the speaking module.
- Choose one of the prompt cards and decide together what you can say (you
  can still do this even if you come from different countries, but your answers will
  be different). Make a few notes to help you.
- Speak for one or two minutes about the subject to a student from another pair,
  and also listen to what he / she says.
- Discuss what you find difficult about doing this speaking task, and what you
  could do to improve your performances.

Describe an important building in your country.
You should say:
where it is
what it is used for
when it was built
and explain why the building is important.

Describe a place you have visited that really impressed you.
You should say:
where it is
what it is used for
when it was built
and explain why it impressed you so much.

   From *Instant IELTS* by Guy Brook-Hart © Cambridge University Press 2004   **PHOTOCOPIABLE**

Estimated class time: 55 minutes (Intermediate)
1 hour 5 minutes (Advanced)

1 Introduction *(15 minutes)*

Ask your students to match the picture with the name of the building and its location.

ANSWER KEY

1e	i	Parthenon, Athens
2f	vii	Petronas Towers, Kuala Lumpur
3c	iii	Louvre, Paris
4b	ii	Guggenheim Museum, Bilbao
5g	vi	World Financial Centre, Shanghai
6d	iv	Opera House, Sydney
7a	v	City of Arts and Sciences, Valencia

- Ask if they have visited any of these buildings and if so what they were like.
- Put your students in small groups to brainstorm reasons:
  - why cities build emblematic buildings like these.
  - what benefits buildings like these bring to the cities where they are located.
- Get feedback from the whole class.

2 🔊 Listening

For the complete recording script, please see page 126.

Questions 1–4 *(10 minutes)*

By trying to predict the answers they are concentrating on the *type* of information they should be listening for. When they do the test, this will help them to focus their attention.

- Play the first part of the listening task. Students listen and check their answers in pairs.
- If necessary, play the relevant parts of the recording again.

Advanced *(15 minutes)*

As an alternative way of approaching these questions
Tell your students that these questions could have been written as multiple choice.
Ask them to write 3 credible alternatives for each answer (1 they believe is true and 2 good distractors). This will help to sensitise them to how multiple-choice questions work.
Tell them that to do this, they should use their general knowledge as far as possible. For example they might write:
Modern Alexandria is famous for
A *its pyramid*
B *its lighthouse*
C *its library*
Check and discuss ideas with the whole class.
Play the first part of the listening task. Your students should do the exercise they have written and the printed exercise.
Check the answers with the whole class – see if any of the alternatives they wrote appeared as correct answers!

ANSWER KEY

1. 1 million / one million / 1,000,000
2. glass pyramid
3. (futuristic) science museum
4. (new) library

Questions 5–10 *(15 minutes)*

- Before listening ask your students to work in pairs and suggest possible answers.
- After listening, ask them to discuss their answers in pairs, and then with the whole class.
- Check that answers were spelt correctly. Remind them how important this is in the test.

ANSWER KEY

5. depressed industrial area
6. image
7. (plenty of) (new) investment (from outside)
8. garden (with sculptures / on roof / with trees)
9. (large screen) film theater / film theater (with large screen)
10. theatre / theater (complex)

Advanced *(20 minutes)*

As an alternative way of approaching questions 5–7:
Tell your students that Questions **5–7** could have been written as a multiple-choice question where they would have to choose 4 correct answers out of 8 possibilities.
Ask them to write the 8 alternatives (*boosted tourism* is the example which they can include in their 8). Doing this should stimulate them to imagine all the benefits of having emblematic buildings in a city and ways of expressing the benefits.
Get feedback from the whole class and discuss together which are the most viable alternatives for this question.
Play the listening and ask them to answer the questions on the printed page *as well as* the questions they have written.
Check the answers with the whole class, paying attention to whether they predicted any of the answers when writing their multiple-choice exercise.

3 Follow-up

Speaking Module Part 2 *(15 minutes)*

- Put students in pairs to brainstorm some of the things they can mention – encourage them to cover all the points in the instructions.
- Then give them 2 or 3 minutes to work alone and prepare some **brief** notes.
- Remix the class into new pairs for them to give their talks.
- Tell the partners not giving talks to listen without interrupting and when the student has finished speaking to give him or her feedback on what they did well, what they could improve and give suggestions for improvements.

1 Introduction

Here is some vocabulary which you will hear when you listen to the lecture.
Before you listen, match the phrases in column A with their explanation in column B.

A		B	
1	beeper	a	a rise to a more senior position in the company
2	career	b	employ a person or organisation outside the company to do a job for the company
3	commute	c	finding new employees
4	contract out	d	objective
5	education	e	pager (an electronic device for contacting someone)
6	goal	f	permanent employment
7	part-time worker	g	someone who works for fewer hours than a complete working week
8	promotion	h	training
9	recruitment	i	travel to and from work
10	staff	j	work from home
11	telecommute	k	workforce
12	tenure	l	working life

From *Instant IELTS* by Guy Brook-Hart © Cambridge University Press 2004 **PHOTOCOPIABLE**

2 ⓢ Listening

You will hear a lecturer, Dr Pendleton, giving a lecture to students on a Business Administration course. He talks about changes in the way people work in recent years.

- Before you listen, look at Questions **1–6** and check that you understand the vocabulary.
- Then listen and answer Questions **1–6**.

Questions 1–6

What is Dr Pendleton's opinion of the following developments? Write

A if he thinks they have been generally beneficial for workers.
B if he thinks they have been generally harmful for workers.
C if he has no strong opinion either way.

Example:	Answer:
The shift from manufacturing to services	C

1 goal-oriented careers
2 flatter management structures
3 contracting out specialist activities
4 Internet recruitment
5 mobile phones and beepers
6 continual re-education

Now look at Questions 7–10.
- Before you listen, say what type of word / words (noun, adjective, verb etc.) are needed for each space.
- Then listen and answer Questions **7–10**.

Questions 7–10

Complete the notes below.
Write NO MORE THAN THREE WORDS for each answer.

Generally in industry the (7)..............................
of products is becoming shorter — so companies
require (8)........................... from the
workforce.
This means that there are fewer
(9)........................... jobs.
Another major change is that new technologies have
enabled people to (10)........................... .

3 Follow-up

Work in pairs and choose one of the following topics.
- Spend a few minutes preparing what you are going to say, then give a short talk (one or two minutes) to your partner.
- After your partner has spoken, give feedback on what he / she did well and what he / she could improve.

Describe a job you have done in the past which you particularly enjoyed.
You should say:
 what the job consisted of
 who you worked for
 what parts of the job were particularly difficult or challenging
and explain why you found this job so enjoyable.

Describe a job which you would particularly like to do in the future.
You should say:
 what the job consists of
 where you would like to do it
 what qualifications or experience are needed in order to get this job
and explain what attracts you to the job and what you will do in the future in order to get it.

Estimated class time: *1 hour 10 minutes (Intermediate)*
1 hour 15 minutes (Advanced)

1 Introduction *(15 minutes)*

Before you hand out the photocopiable page:

- Tell students that they are going to listen to a talk about the nature of work, and how it has changed in recent years.
- Ask them to work in small groups and brainstorm together how the way people work has changed.
- You may wish to suggest an example: *Nowadays business people don't have to travel to meetings so often; they can use video-conferencing instead.*
- Get feedback for the whole class from the different groups.
- Ask them to discuss which changes they think are a good thing for workers and which ones are not so positive.

Intermediate students may find this exercise difficult, so you may need to give some extra explanations to help them.

> **ANSWER KEY**
> 1e 2l 3i 4b 5h 6d 7g 8a 9c 10k 11j 12f

2 🔊 Listening

For the complete recording script, please see page 126.

Questions 1–6 *(20 minutes)*

Intermediate

Ask your students to read Questions 1–6.

- To make sure they know what the various items mean, ask them to work in pairs and discuss *their* opinions of whether these things have been harmful or beneficial for workers.
- Briefly get feedback from the class.
- Remind them that they probably won't hear exactly the same words / phrases used by the speaker.
- Reassure them that the answers in the listening are in the same order as the questions.
- Use the example to show how the questions work. Play the recording down to the words ... *just as badly paid.* Ask students why the answer was **C.** (Answer: he says *equally boring and just as badly paid.*)
- Play the first part of the listening task and ask students to check their answers in pairs.
- Then check with the whole class.

Advanced

To prepare your students for Questions 1–6, you may play a game:

- Put them in pairs and ask them to choose one of the items from the questions *e.g. The shift from manufacturing to services.*
- They have to write something about it which either shows that it has been beneficial, harmful or neither, but without mentioning exactly what they are talking about or saying what their opinion is *e.g. Since fewer people work in factories, work is neither so dirty nor so dangerous as it was in the past.*
- Each pair then reads out their sentence to the rest of the class, who have to say which of the items they are talking about and what their attitude to it is.
- Then play the first part of the listening task and ask students to work in pairs and answer the questions.
- Check the answers with the whole class by asking for the gist of what Dr Pendleton said about each item.

> **ANSWER KEY**
> 1 A
> 2 B
> 3 A
> 4 A
> 5 B
> 6 C

Questions 7–10 *(15 minutes)*

- Ask your students to look at the gaps and say what type of words they will need (adjectives, nouns, verbs etc.).
- Ask your students to predict what the answers will be.
- Tell them they will hear the actual words they need, but the other words on the recording will not be the same as the words in the summary.
- Play the listening task, and ask them to check their answers in pairs.

> **ANSWER KEY**
> 7 life cycle / lifecycle
> 8 (much / far) greater / more / increased flexibility
> 9 permanent (or) tenured
> 10 work from home / telecommute

Advanced *(20 minutes)*

Alternative method

- Challenge your students to complete the notes without listening (*maximum 3 words*).
- Give them 5 minutes to discuss this in small groups.
- Then get feedback on the various alternatives from the whole class.
- Play the listening to check how close their ideas were to what was actually said.

3 Follow-up

Speaking Module Part 2 *(20 minutes)*

Ask your students to choose which talk they are going to give, and then:

- Put students with the same talk in pairs to brainstorm some of the things they can mention.
- Give them 2 or 3 minutes to work alone and prepare some **brief** notes.
- Remix the class into new pairs, where possible with someone who has prepared the other talk and ask them to give their talks to each other.
- Tell the listening partners not to interrupt and to give feedback at the end on what they did well, what they could improve and suggestions for improvements.
- If they wish, they may then repeat their 'improved' talk.
- Alternatively, you may choose 1 or 2 students to give their talk to the whole class and then invite feedback from the whole class.

1 Introduction

Discuss these questions in small groups.

1 What do you know about Genetically Modified (GM) food?
2 What are the purposes of GM food?
3 Do you think there are any potential dangers of GM food? What are they?
4 What examples of GM food have you heard of?
5 Can you think of any genetic modifications to food which would make life easier?

"Nothing's labeled. How are we supposed to know which fruit has been genetically engineered?"

Look at the statements below. Which are in favour of GM foods and which are against them?

It's tampering with Mother Nature.

Most of us don't know we're eating it.

If they hadn't, we'd probably still be eating grass instead of wheat.

Scientists said that nuclear power and other things were completely harmless.

It will solve the world's hunger problems.

It could create super-weeds and super-insects.

2 Reading

You are going to read an article about GM food from a magazine called *Canada and the World Backgrounder*.

- Before dealing with the questions, 'skim' the article. This means you should read it to get a *general* impression of what it is saying, but you should not try to understand everything (after all, there may not be a question about it).
- When you have finished reading, decide whether you have the impression that it is in favour of GM foods or against them.
- Do this in a maximum of three minutes.

A **A lot of people think we could be headed for trouble by tampering with Mother Nature and producing genetically altered food.** But those who promote genetically modified foods say it's no more 5 unnatural than traditional selective breeding, to say nothing about synthetic fertilizers and chemical pesticides.

B Most Canadians regularly eat bio–engineered food. Anyone who consumes cheese, 10 potatoes, tomatoes, soybeans, corn, wheat, and salmon is taking in genetically modified (GM) food. In addition, 75% of processed foods contain GM ingredients. In fact, around 65% of the food we get from the shops has some genetically modified 15 component. GM food does not have to be labelled as such in Canada, so most of us don't know we're eating it. Some of the items that have a high likelihood of containing GM material might surprise you. They include chocolate bars, baby 20 food, margarine, canned soup, ice cream, salad dressing, yoghurt, cereals, cookies, and frozen French fries. And, there's nothing new about this.

C Farmers and plant breeders have used genetically modified foods for centuries; if they 25 hadn't, we'd probably still be eating grass instead of wheat. They've refined the foods we eat through selective crossbreeding, combining different types of wheat, for example, and eliminating weaker varieties. Today, however, genetic engineering is 30 changing the nature of plant breeding even more: it's no longer just a case of mixing different varieties of the same species. Now, genes from completely different life forms are being combined – fish genes into tomatoes to make the latter more frost resistant, 35 for example.

D Such "tampering with Nature" makes a lot of people anxious. They wonder if the foods that come out of genetic modification are safe for human consumption. Scientists say they are completely 40 safe; GM is just a way of adding genes to plants to make it possible for them to survive without the use of pesticides and to increase yields. But, the non-believers point out that scientists said that nuclear power, the toxic insecticide DDT, and a host of 45 other things, were also completely harmless.

E Fans of agricultural biotechnology think producing GM food is a move in the right direction, that it will ultimately improve health, the environment, and the economy. They're convinced 50 it will solve the world's hunger problems by boosting the nutritional content of foods, lead to a drop in pesticide and herbicide use, and result in more efficient and profitable farming. Critics say it could also create superweeds and insects, disrupt global 55 food systems, destroy ecological diversity, put small farms out of business, and cause long-term environmental problems. All that aside, they think consumers have a right to know what is in their food. 60

F After all, GM products do pose some problems. In 1998, a researcher at the Rowett Institute for Agriculture in Aberdeen announced to the world that genetically engineered potatoes did some nasty things to the rats they were tested on. 65 The potatoes were engineered to produce a molecule which is a natural insecticide that makes them resistant to aphids.* But, the rats that ate the potatoes didn't grow as large as normal rats and were less resistant to disease. Further research 70 showed that the added gene wasn't the only cause for concern: the genetic-engineering process itself was causing some serious problems in the development of organs such as the kidney and spleen. 75

G Some genetic modifications have been clearly beneficial. For example, one variety of maize has been genetically manipulated to produce a natural insecticide that protects it from the corn-borer moth. Scientists have also developed GM 80 soybeans which are not damaged by some common herbicides used to kill weeds. What is more, the rats that were fed GM potatoes may not have been harmed as a result of the genetic modification but possibly as a result of the way the potatoes were 85 grown; all in all, there are just too many variables to blame the genetic-engineering process alone. Still, some believe that the potential problems with gene modification are so well known that existing safeguards, in both America and the European 90 Union, can prevent them.

H Supporters of GM foods look on the bright side. According to the International Service for the Acquisition of Agri-biotech Applications (financed largely by biotechnology firms), the insect-resistant 95 maize has increased yields in fields where it is planted by 9%. And there might be an environmental advantage too. In 1997, 2.8 million hectares of this variety of maize were planted in the U.S. and farmers were able to avoid using $190 100 million worth of insecticide. Herbicide-resistant soybeans also needed less spraying, pumping between 20% and 40% fewer chemicals into the environment.

*a type of insect which feeds on plants

Questions 1–3

Using NO MORE THAN THREE WORDS OR A NUMBER from the passage, answer the following questions.

1   How much of the food Canadians buy contains GM ingredients? *75%*
 Many changes
2   What method did farmers use to improve the quality of crops before genetic modification became possible?
3   What chemical substances may be less necessary as a result of the genetic modification of agricultural products?

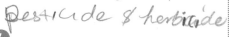

Pesticide & herbicide

Questions 4–7

The reading passage has eight paragraphs (A–H). Which paragraphs contain the following information? Write the appropriate letters (A–H) for each question.
NB You need only write ONE letter for each answer.

4   Genetic modification is the continuation of a traditional farming practice.
5   Scientific advances have sometimes had disastrous consequences.
6   The alarming results of one genetic modification.
7   The benefits to the environment of some GM crops. *H*

Questions 8–10

Complete the following statements (Questions 8–10) with words taken from the reading passage.
Write NO MORE THAN THREE WORDS for each answer.

8   Canadian consumers may be unaware that food has been genetically modified because it needn't be

 labelled

9   Genetic modification is expected to reduce global food

 shortages by increasing the *nutritional*
 content of food.

10 Undesirable side-effects of genetic engineering can be

 avoided by applying *dropping pesticide*

Questions 11–14

List the FOUR things mentioned in the reading passage which can damage crops and which crops can be protected from by genetic modification.
Write NO MORE THAN THREE WORDS for each answer.

11 *Pesticide*
12 *herbicide*
13 *Super weeds*
14 *Insects*

Question 15

From the list below choose the most suitable title for the whole of the reading passage. Choose the appropriate letter A–E.

A   The dangers of GM food *F*
B   The benefits of genetic engineering *Ga*
C   How crops are modified *C*
D   The debate about GM food *G*
E   GM food and the environment *H*

3 Follow-up

Speaking Module Part 3

In Part 3 of the speaking module you have to answer questions and discuss them with the interviewer. Work in pairs to ask and answer these questions.

Your taste
● Can you describe your perfect meal?
● Are there any types of food which we should not eat too much of?

Your attitude to food
● How important is it to be careful about what we eat?
● Do you think that the quality of food is better now, or not so good as in the past?

Estimated class time: *1 hour (Intermediate)*
                       50 minutes (Advanced)

🕑 Short of time? You could:
- give questions **8–15** for homework.
- do the follow-up activities in the following lesson.

1 Introduction *(10 minutes)*
- To help with Question **4** you can mention square tomatoes which are easier to pack in boxes and take up less space, or featherless chickens (which don't need plucking).
- Have some fun getting students to suggest other genetic modifications which would make life easier.
- If necessary, explain that 'tampering' means 'interfering'.

2 Reading *(5 minutes)*
Before dealing with the questions

This passage gives practice in *skimming*, *scanning* and *reading in detail*.
- *Skimming* involves reading the passage quickly to get a *general idea* of what it is about, but without working out the meanings of individual words or sentences as there may not be a question about them. Students gain a global view of the contents and some idea where to locate the information or answers when they come to the questions. (The article presents fairly balanced arguments for and against GM food, though the writer gives the impression of being in favour of it.)
- *Scanning* means reading the passage to locate *specific information* which may then require reading in detail in order to answer a particular question.

Advanced
- Ask your students to look at the 5 different types of question.
- Tell them that to answer the questions they may either have to *skim* the passage, or *scan* it and then read the relevant part quite carefully.
- Ask them which question-types will probably require *skimming* (Answer: Questions **4–7**) and which *scanning* followed by more careful reading (Answer: Questions **1–3**, **8–10** and **11–14**. Question **15** is a very general question which should not require further reading).

Questions 1–3 *(5–10 minutes)*

Tell your students to *scan* the passage to find where the answers are mentioned and then read those sections in detail.

Intermediate
- Students look at the instructions for Questions **1–3**. Point out that they must answer with words or a number from the passage. Ask them whether the answer to Question **1** will be a word or a number, and ask them to find the answer.
- Point out that to answer the other 2 questions they will have to scan and then read in detail. Give them 6 or 7 minutes.
- For Question **3**, some students may have chosen *fertilizers* as the answer. If so tell them to find what is said about fertilizers in the passage and ask them to find out why this is not a correct answer. (*It's only used as an example to show how unnatural traditional farming is anyway.*)

Advanced
Give your students just 2 or 3 minutes to do these questions.

ANSWER KEY
1. (about / around) 65% (line 14)
2. traditional selective breeding / selective crossbreeding / eliminating weaker varieties (lines 27–30)
3. herbicides (and) pesticides (line 53)

Questions 4–7 *(10 minutes)*

Point out that they should *skim* in order simply to locate the information.

Intermediate
If your students require more preparation:
- They can work in pairs and paraphrase what each of the sentences or phrases **4–7** means.
- Ask them if they remember what, roughly, was said in the article about each of these things.
- Ask them to skim quickly just to locate the information.

Advanced
To encourage an efficient skim-reading technique, give them a time limit of, say, 3 minutes.

ANSWER KEY
4 C   5 D   6 F   7 H

Questions 8–10 *(5 minutes)*

Intermediate
- For Question **8**, elicit from students a short explanation of *unaware* (*i.e. they don't know, they are not conscious*) and tell them to scan the passage for a word or phrase with that meaning. Ask them to answer the question.
- For Question **9**, tell them to scan the passage for where the world's hunger problems are mentioned and answer the question from there.
- For Question **10**, you may elicit synonyms for *undesirable* and *avoided*.

Advanced
- They will have to look for synonyms or similar meanings.
- When checking the answers, you may wish to discuss what *labelled*, *nutritional value* and *existing safeguards* mean.

ANSWER KEY
8 labelled (as such)   9 nutritional content   10 existing safeguards

Questions 11–14 *(5 minutes)*
- Ask your students to remember what the purposes of GM foods were.
- Elicit the idea of *resistant to* and *immune to* and tell them this may help them to find the answers.

ANSWER KEY
11 frost (line 35)   12 aphids (line 68)
13 (the) corn-borer moth (line 79)
14 (some common) herbicides / herbicide (line 82)   } in any order

Question 15 *(2 minutes)*
- Point out to students that if they are not sure which is the correct answer, they should eliminate wrong answers first.

ANSWER KEY
15 D

3 Follow-up

Speaking Module Part 3 *(10 minutes)*
- Before they speak, ask your students to study the questions and think of 2 or 3 other questions on the subject.
- Remind them that when they answer these questions, they should give quite long answers by giving reasons and examples.

Light Pollution

1 Introduction

Work in pairs. Discuss whether you agree or disagree with these statements. Why? Why not?

a   Bright lights at night can cause accidents.
b   Bright lights discourage criminals.
c   It is easier to see stars in the country than in the city.
d   Lights from streets and cities help aeroplane pilots to navigate at night.
e   Bad lighting is a cause of air pollution.
f   Many cities could save money by improving street lighting.
g   Lights are sometimes a danger to wildlife.

2 Reading

You will read an article about light pollution.
Before you read, look at the instructions for Questions 1–5 and answer these two questions.

● Will you have to read the whole article in order to answer the questions?
● Will you need all the headings?

Study the headings carefully so that you are familiar with them when you read the article.
Try to answer the questions without looking up difficult words, as you would do in the test.

Questions 1–5

The first six paragraphs of reading passage 1 are lettered A–F. Choose the most suitable headings for paragraphs A–F from the list of headings below.
NB There are more headings than paragraphs, so you will not use them all.

List of headings
i   Why lights are needed
ii   Lighting discourages law breakers
iii   The environmental dangers
iv   People at risk from bright lights
v   Illuminating space
vi   A problem lights do not solve
vii   Seen from above
viii   More light than is necessary
ix   Approaching the city

Example	Answer
Paragraph A	ix (Approaching the city)

1   Paragraph B ....
2   Paragraph C ....
3   Paragraph D ....
4   Paragraph E ....
5   Paragraph F ....

From *Instant IELTS* by Guy Brook-Hart © Cambridge University Press 2004   **PHOTOCOPIABLE**

Light Pollution Is a Threat to Wildlife, Safety and the Starry Sky

A ✪ After hours of driving south in the pitch-black darkness of the Nevada desert, a dome of hazy gold suddenly appears on the horizon. Soon, a road sign confirms the obvious: Las Vegas 30 miles. Looking skyward, you notice that the Big Dipper* is harder to find 5 than it was an hour ago.

B ✪ Light pollution—the artificial light that illuminates more than its intended target area—has become a problem of increasing concern across the country over the past 15 years. In the suburbs, where over-lit 10 shopping mall parking lots are the norm, only 200 of the Milky Way's 2,500 stars are visible on a clear night. Even fewer can be seen from large cities. In almost every town, big and small, street lights beam just as much light up and out as they do down, illuminating much more 15 than just the street. Almost 50 per cent of the light emanating from street lamps misses its intended target, and billboards, shopping centers, private homes and skyscrapers are similarly over-illuminated.

C ✪ America has become so bright that in a satellite 20 image of the United States at night, the outline of the country is visible from its lights alone. The major cities are all there, in bright clusters: New York, Boston, Miami, Houston, Los Angeles, Seattle, Chicago—and, of course, Las Vegas. Mark Adams, superintendent of the McDonald 25 Observatory in west Texas, says that the very fact that city lights are visible from on high is proof of their wastefulness. "When you're up in an airplane, all that light you see on the ground from the city is wasted. It's going up into the night sky. That's why you can see it." 30

D ✪ But don't we need all those lights to ensure our safety? The answer from light engineers, light pollution control advocates and astronomers is an emphatic "no". Elizabeth Alvarez of the International Dark Sky Association (IDA), a non-profit organization in Tucson, 35 Arizona, says that overly bright security lights can actually force neighbors to close the shutters, which means that if any criminal activity does occur on the street, no one will see it. And the old assumption that bright lights deter crime appears to have been a false 40 one: a new Department of Justice report concludes that there is no relationship between the level of lighting and the level of crime in an area. And contrary to popular belief, more crimes occur in broad daylight than at night.

E ✪ For drivers, light can actually create a safety hazard. 45 Glaring lights can temporarily blind drivers, increasing the likelihood of an accident. To help prevent such accidents, some cities and states prohibit the use of lights that impair night-time vision. For instance, New Hampshire law forbids the use of "any light along a 50 highway so positioned as to blind or dazzle the vision of travelers on the adjacent highway".

F ✪ Badly designed lighting can pose a threat to wildlife as well as people. Newly hatched turtles in Florida move toward beach lights instead of the more muted silver 55 shimmer of the ocean. Migrating birds, confused by lights on skyscrapers, broadcast towers and lighthouses, are injured, sometimes fatally, after colliding with high, lighted structures. And light pollution harms air quality as well: Because most of the country's power plants are 60 still powered by fossil fuels, more light means more air pollution.

G ✪ So what can be done? Tucson, Arizona is taking back the night. The city has one of the best lighting regulations in the country, and, not coincidentally, the highest 65 concentration of observatories in the world. Kitt Peak National Optical Astronomy Observatory has 24 telescopes aimed skyward around the city's perimeter, and its cadre of astronomers needs a dark sky to work with.

H ✪ For a while, that darkness was threatened. "We were 70 totally losing the night sky," Jim Singleton of Tucson's Lighting Committee told Tulsa, Oklahoma's KOTV last March. Now, after replacing inefficient mercury lighting with low-sodium lights that block light from "trespassing" into unwanted areas like bedroom 75 windows, and by doing away with some unnecessary lights altogether, the city is softly glowing rather than brightly beaming. The same thing is happening in a handful of other states, including Texas, which just passed a light pollution bill last summer. "Astronomers 80 can get what they need at the same time that citizens get what they need: safety, security and good visibility at night," says McDonald Observatory's Mark Adams, who provided testimony at the hearings for the bill.

I ✪ And in the long run, everyone benefits from reduced 85 energy costs. Wasted energy from inefficient lighting costs us between $1 and $2 billion a year, according to IDA. The city of San Diego, which installed new, high-efficiency street lights after passing a light pollution law in 1985, now saves about $3 million a year 90 in energy costs.

J ✪ Legislation isn't the only answer to light pollution problems. Brian Greer, Central Ohio representative for the Ohio Light Pollution Advisory Council, says that education is just as important, if not more so. "There are 95 some special situations where regulation is the only fix," he says. "But the vast majority of bad lighting is simply the result of not knowing any better." Simple actions like replacing old bulbs and fixtures with more efficient and better-designed ones can make a big difference in 100 preserving the night sky.

The Big Dipper: a group of seven bright stars visible in the Northern Hemisphere.

Source: the *Environmental Magazine*   © 2000 Earth Action Network, Inc. in association with The Gale Group and LookSmart. COPYRIGHT 2000 Gale Group

Questions 6–9

Complete each of the following statements (Questions 6–9) with words taken from reading passage 2.
Write ONE OR TWO WORDS for each answer.

6   According to a recent study, well-lit streets do not .... *decrease crime* .... or make neighbourhoods safer to live in.

7   Inefficient lighting increases ...... *accident* ...... because most electricity is produced from coal, gas or oil.

8   Efficient lights .... from going into areas where it is not needed.

9   In dealing with light pollution .... is at least as important as passing new laws.

Questions 10–13

Do the following statements agree with the information given in reading passage 2?
Write

YES   *if the statement agrees with the information.*
NO   *if the statement contradicts the information.*
NOT GIVEN *if there is no information on this in the passage.*

10   One group of scientists find their observations are made more difficult by bright lights.   T
11   It is expensive to reduce light pollution.   NOT GIVEN
12   Many countries are now making light pollution illegal.   T
13   Old types of light often cause more pollution than more modern ones.   T

3 Follow-up

Role play

You and your partners are the members of the town council responsible for the streets. Recently there has been a proposal to reduce light pollution in your town.
Today you have to discuss the proposal and decide what to do. You should each choose one of the roles below.

Role A: You are in charge of finance on the council and you believe that the council has enough money to change the street lighting in the town. Also you are a keen amateur astronomer and you find that the present lighting interferes with your hobby.

Role B: You are a member of the education committee, and you believe that it would be better to spend money on improving schools rather than changing the street lights which were only installed five years ago. Also, your house was recently burgled and you are concerned that less street lighting would lead to an increase in crime.

Role C: You are responsible for the town's parks. You would prefer to extend the street lighting to the town's parks so that people could use them safely at night. You are also the owner of a restaurant and you believe that good lighting encourages people to go out at night and enjoy themselves, so it benefits local businesses.

Role D: You are chairman of the council's environmental committee, and you believe that the present street lighting wastes energy and disturbs wildlife. Also, you believe the lighting installed at the moment is ugly. You are a light sleeper, and you find that the street lights outside your house prevent you from sleeping well at night.

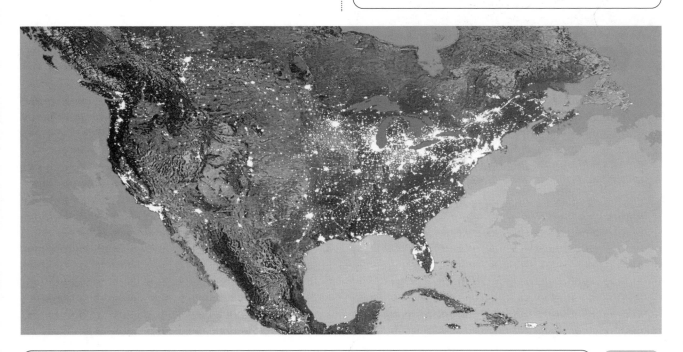

Estimated class time: 1 hour 5 minutes

🕐 **Short of time? You could:**
- give your students Questions **6–13** for homework.
- do the follow-up activity in the following lesson.

1 Introduction *(10 minutes)*

Students work in pairs to discuss the statements. Briefly get feedback from the whole class.

2 Reading

Questions 1–5 *(15 minutes)*

Before reading the passage, ask your students to answer the 2 questions in the Introduction *(Answer to both questions: no)*.
- Remind them that when questions come before the passage, they are expected to read the questions first.
- Tell them it is worth studying the list of headings carefully before starting reading, so that they are familiar with the questions.

Intermediate

Tell them to work in pairs and explain briefly what they would expect to find in a paragraph with these headings
e.g. for heading (i) a number of reasons why lights are necessary at night.

Advanced

Ask the students to work in pairs and paraphrase the meanings of the headings in order to familiarise themselves with what they will have to look for *e.g. for (i) reasons why lights are necessary*.

- Remind them that to do this type of question they may have to read some of the paragraphs more than once, they needn't answer the questions chronologically, and they should be ready to change their minds.
- Tell them to deal with the paragraphs and headings they find obvious first, thereby reducing the choice for the ones they find more confusing.

ANSWER KEY
1 Paragraph B   viii   **2** Paragraph C   vii   **3** Paragraph D   vi
4 Paragraph E   iv   **5** Paragraph F   iii

Intermediate

If they are unfamiliar with this type of question:
Tell them to look at the example and find the clues in the paragraph which give this answer *e.g. driving south … a dome of hazy gold suddenly appears.*
Ask them to look at paragraph **B**. Tell them the answer is either **i**, **v**, or **viii**. They should read the paragraph carefully and decide which is the best heading.
Ask them to work through the other 4 paragraphs alone, and then discuss their answers in small groups.

Advanced

Tell students that in the test they would have about 8 minutes to do these 5 questions, so they should try to do each question in about 1 minute leaving a couple of minutes at the end for checking.
An alternative way of working would be **not** to ask them to look at the list of headings first, but to read the passage and suggest their own headings for each paragraph.
They should think of headings of about 6 words maximum which summarise the general idea of each paragraph.
They then compare their headings.
Finally, they compare their ideas with the headings given in Questions **1–5** and do the exercise.

Questions 6–9 *(12 minutes)*

- Remind students that they will have to read the whole passage. The words they need will be together, not separate.

Intermediate

You can elicit explanations for *well-lit, inefficient, dealing, passing* (laws).
Elicit what type of word(s) will be needed in each space *e.g. nouns, verbs or adjectives*.

Advanced

Ask students to predict the approximate answers before they read the passage.

Tell them to check that their answers are grammatically accurate.

ANSWER KEY
6 deter crime   **7** (air) pollution   **8** block light   **9** education

Questions 10–13 *(12 minutes)*

A lot of students find the concept of 'NOT GIVEN' very difficult to grasp.
- Remind them that some of the sentences in the question are **not addressed** in the passage.
- When they think they have found a sentence that deals with the question, they need to read it very carefully and bear in mind that it may not express agreement OR disagreement.

Intermediate

Help them to identify the key words in the first question, then tell them to scan for key words.
Ask them to read the sentences they find carefully to see if they deal with the question.
Explain that scanning the passage like this will help them complete the task more quickly.

Advanced

Because the answers are given in chronological order, students can try to look for answers to 2 questions at a time.
If they find the answer to the second question, they should check back to make sure the first one is **NOT GIVEN**.
In the IELTS test, candidates would have 5–6 minutes for this part of the test, so to replicate test conditions, you could give them 6 minutes to complete the task.

ANSWER KEY
10 YES (line 69)   **11** NO (lines 88–91)   **12** NOT GIVEN
13 YES (lines 99–101)

3 Follow-up

Role play *(15 minutes)*

If necessary, discuss the situation with the class, for example, to decide what size the town is and what responsibilities the town council might have for the streets.
- Divide the class into groups of 4. If there are uneven numbers, students may share roles.
- Students gather their arguments before starting. To do this, you may ask people from different groups with the same role to work together.
- Allow them 5 or 10 minutes for the discussion, and then get feedback from each group on what they decided.
- Since each role represents a fairly inflexible position, you should not expect a very clear or unanimous solution.

1 Introduction

Work in groups of three or four and discuss the following points.

● What does the bar chart show?
● Interview each other and draw bar charts for other members of your group.

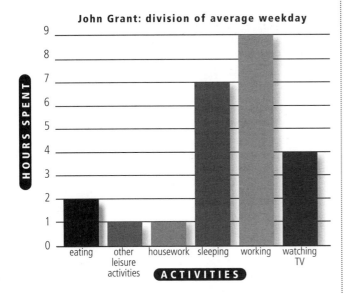

John Grant: division of average weekday

(bar chart: HOURS SPENT on vertical axis from 0 to 9; ACTIVITIES on horizontal axis)
- eating: 2
- other leisure activities: 1
- housework: 1
- sleeping: 7
- working: 9
- watching TV: 4

Now work with people from other groups and do the following:

● Present what you have found out about your colleagues.
● Draw conclusions for the whole class *e.g. men spend more time sleeping than women / students in this class spend an average of two hours a day watching television etc.*

2 Reading

You are going to read an article about addiction to television. Before you read, discuss with your group whether you think it is possible to be addicted to television. If so, what are the symptoms?

Now skim the passage to find out what it says about this. Do this in four minutes.

Television addiction is no mere metaphor

A **The term "TV addiction" is imprecise, but it captures the essence of a very real phenomenon.** Psychologists formally define addiction as a disorder characterized by criteria that include spending a great deal of time using the thing; 5 using it more often than one intends; thinking about reducing use or making repeated unsuccessful efforts to reduce use; giving up important activities to use it; and reporting withdrawal symptoms when one stops using it. 10

B All these criteria can apply to people who watch a lot of television. That does not mean that watching television, in itself, is problematic. Television can teach and amuse; it can be highly artistic; it can provide much needed distraction 15 and escape. The difficulty arises when people strongly sense that they ought not to watch as much as they do and yet find they are unable to reduce their viewing. Some knowledge of how television becomes so addictive may help heavy 20 viewers gain better control over their lives.

C The amount of time people spend watching television is astonishing. On average, individuals in the industrialized world devote three hours a day to the activity – fully half of their leisure time, 25 and more than on any single activity except work and sleep. At this rate, someone who lives to 75 would spend nine years in front of the television. Possibly, this devotion means simply that people enjoy TV and make a conscious decision to watch 30 it. But if that is the whole story, why do so many people worry about how much they view? In surveys in 1992 and 1999, two out of five adults and seven out of ten teenagers said they spent too much time watching TV. Other surveys have 35 consistently shown that roughly ten per cent of adults call themselves TV addicts.

D To study people's reactions to TV, researchers have undertaken laboratory experiments in which they have monitored the brain waves, skin 40 resistance or heart rate of people watching television. To study behavior and emotion in the normal course of life, as opposed to the artificial conditions of the laboratory, we have used the Experience Sampling Method (ESM). 45 Participants carried a beeper*, and we signaled them six to eight times a day, at random, over the period of a week; whenever they heard the beep, they wrote down what they were doing and how they were feeling. 50

E As one might expect, people who were watching TV when we beeped them reported feeling relaxed and passive. The laboratory studies similarly show less mental stimulation, as measured by brain-wave production, during viewing than during reading.

F   What is more surprising is that the sense of relaxation ends when the TV is turned off, but the feelings of passivity and lowered alertness continue. Viewers commonly report that television has somehow absorbed or sucked out their energy, leaving them exhausted. They say they have more difficulty concentrating after viewing than before. In contrast, they rarely report such difficulty after reading. After playing sports or doing hobbies, people report improvements in mood. After watching TV, people's moods are about the same or worse than before.

G   Within moments of sitting or lying down and pushing the "power" button, viewers report feeling more relaxed. Because the relaxation occurs quickly, people are conditioned to associate viewing with rest and lack of stress. The association is positively reinforced because viewers remain relaxed throughout viewing.

H   Thus, the irony of TV: people watch a great deal longer than they plan to, even though prolonged viewing is less rewarding. In our ESM studies the longer people sat in front of the set, the less satisfaction they said they obtained from it. When signaled, heavy viewers (those who consistently watch more than four hours a day) tended to report on their ESM sheets that they enjoy TV less than light viewers did (less than two hours a day). For some, a feeling of guilt that they are not doing something more productive may also accompany and reduce the enjoyment of prolonged viewing. Researchers in Japan, the U.K. and the U.S. have found that this guilt occurs much more among middle-class viewers than among less affluent ones.

I   What is it about TV that has such a hold on us? In part, the attraction seems to arise from our biological "orienting response". First described by Ivan Pavlov in 1927, the orienting response is an instinctive reaction to anything sudden or new, such as movement or possible attack by a predator. Typical orienting reactions include the following: the arteries to the brain grow wider allowing more blood to reach it, the heart slows down and arteries to the large muscles become narrower so as to reduce blood supply to them. Brain waves are also interrupted for a few seconds. These changes allow the brain to focus its attention on gathering more information and becoming more alert while the rest of the body becomes quieter.

*a beeper

Source: *Scientific American*, February, 2002

Questions 1–3

The list below gives some characteristics of addiction. Which THREE of the following are mentioned as characteristics of addiction to television? Circle the appropriate letters A–F.

A   harmful physical effects
B   loss of control over time
C   destruction of relationships
D   reduced intellectual performance
E   discomfort when attempting to give up
F   dishonesty about the extent of the addiction

Questions 4–8

Do the following statements agree with the information given in the reading passage?
Choose

YES   *if the statement agrees with the information.*
NO   *if the statement contradicts the information.*
NOT GIVEN   *if there is no information on this in the passage.*

4   One purpose of the research is to help people to manage their lives better.
5   Watching television has reduced the amount of time people spend sleeping.
6   People's brains show less activity while watching television than when reading.
7   There is a relationship between the length of time spent watching TV and economic status.
8   Pleasure increases in proportion to the length of time spent watching TV.

Questions 9–13

Write the appropriate letters A–D.

Classify the following feelings or mental states as generally occurring:

A   *before watching television.*
B   *while watching television.*
C   *after watching television.*
D   *both while and after watching television.*

 9   reduced anxiety and stress
10   increased fatigue
11   higher levels of concentration
12   less mental activity
13   worry about time wasted

From *Instant IELTS* by Guy Brook-Hart © Cambridge University Press 2004   **PHOTOCOPIABLE**

Questions 14–17

Complete the labels on the diagram.
Choose your answers from the box beside the diagram.

NB There are more words / phrases than spaces, so you will not use them all.

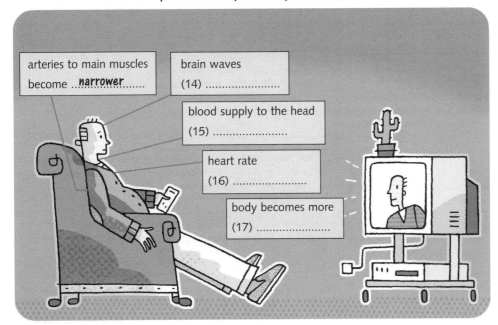

arteries to main muscles become ..**narrower**......

brain waves (14) ....

blood supply to the head (15) ....

heart rate (16) ....

body becomes more (17) ....

A relaxed
B accelerated
C increased
D lengthened
E reduced
F stopped momentarily
G widened
H regulated

3 Follow-up

Vocabulary

Match the words and phrases from the passage on the left with their explanations on the right.

Paragraph A
1 disorder
2 withdrawal symptoms
Paragraph D
3 monitored
4 at random
Paragraph F
5 alertness
Paragraph H
6 affluent
Paragraph I
7 predator

a animal which eats other animals
b checked regularly
c liveliness – being very awake
d not at regular times
e psychological problem or illness
f rich, well-off
g uncomfortable feelings experienced when giving up an addiction

Speaking Module Part 2

Work in pairs and choose one of the following topics.
- Spend a few minutes preparing what you are going to say, then give a short talk (one or two minutes) to your partner.
- After your partner has spoken, give feedback on what he / she did well and what he / she could improve.

Describe what you most enjoy doing in your free time.
You should say:
    why you enjoy it so much
    when you do it
    what the activity consists of
and explain how you took it up in the first place.

Describe your favourite television programme.
You should say:
    what type of programme it is
    what happens during the programme
    when you watch it
and explain why you enjoy it so much.

Estimated class time: 1 hour 20 minutes (Intermediate),
1 hour 15 minutes (Advanced)

1 Introduction *(10 minutes)*

> **ANSWER KEY**
> It shows the average number of hours John spends on different activities on an average weekday.

2 Reading

Before reading and skimming *(10 minutes)*

- Give students 2 or 3 minutes to discuss television addiction and its symptoms and then get feedback.
- Be strict with the time on skimming for an Advanced class. For an Intermediate class, you may allow 4 or 5 minutes.
- *Skimming* involves reading the passage quickly to get a *general idea* of what it is about, without working out the meanings of individual words or sentences. Students gain a global view of the passage and some idea where to locate the information they need.

Questions 1–3 *(5–10 minutes)*

If necessary pre-teach the vocabulary in the follow-up activity.

- Students should scan the passage for symptoms of addiction (not all of them are in the first paragraph).
- Warn them that there are more characteristics of television addiction described in the passage than are listed in the questions.

Intermediate

Ask students to paraphrase the alternatives in the question before reading e.g. 'harmful physical effects' may be rephrased as 'damage to one's body'.

Advanced

Set a time-limit for this question: in the test they would have about 4 minutes for the 3 questions.

> **ANSWER KEY**
> **1–3** B, D and E in any order

Questions 4–8 *(10 minutes)*

A lot of students find the concept of NOT GIVEN very difficult to grasp.

- Remind students that some of the sentences in the question are **not addressed** in the passage.
- When they think they have found a sentence that deals with the question, they need to read it very carefully and bear in mind that it may not express agreement OR disagreement.
- Tell them that the answers to Questions **4–8** will come in the same order in the passage.

Intermediate

Help your students to identify the key words in Question **4** and elicit possible synonyms e.g. *manage: deal with / control*.
Tell them to scan the passage quickly to see if they can find the key words or the synonyms.
Ask them to read carefully the sentences they find to see if they deal with the question.
Explain that scanning the passage like this will help them complete the task more quickly.

Advanced

Because the answers are given in chronological order, students can try to look for answers to 2 questions at a time. If they find the answer to the second question, they should check back to make sure the first one is **NOT GIVEN**.

> **ANSWER KEY**
> **4** YES (lines 19–21) **5** NOT GIVEN **6** YES (lines 53–56)
> **7** NOT GIVEN **8** NO (lines 78–80)

Questions 9–13 *(10 minutes)*

- Students should locate the paragraphs where they will find the answers (*Answer: paragraphs* **6–8**).
- Tell them that efficient reading techniques include locating which section of a passage to concentrate on when answering particular questions.
- Intermediate students could look for key words in the questions before scanning the passage. Elicit synonyms or explanations for the key words and ask them to look for these in the passage.
- Give Advanced students 6 minutes to find the answers.

> **ANSWER KEY**
> **9** B (lines 69–71) **10** C (lines 57–62) **11** A (lines 62–63)
> **12** D (lines 57–60) **13** D (lines 85–87)

Questions 14–17 *(10 minutes)*

Ask your students what the diagram shows (*Answer: Orienting response in the human body*).

- Tell them to locate the paragraph where this is dealt with (*Answer: paragraph 9*).
- Remind them that the words in the box will be synonyms of words or phrases from the passage.

Intermediate

You can elicit synonyms or explanations of the words in the box before they tackle the question.

Advanced

Give them 4 minutes to label the diagram.

> **ANSWER KEY**
> **14** F (lines 103–104) **15** C (lines 99–100) **16** E (lines 100–101)
> **17** A (lines 106–107)

3 Follow-up

Vocabulary *(5 minutes)*

Tell students to work in pairs and match the words from the passage in the left-hand column with the definition on the right. (Answers: 1e, 2g, 3b, 4d, 5c, 6f, 7a).

Speaking Module Part 2 *(15 minutes)*

Ask your students to choose which talk they are going to give, and then:

- Put students with the same talk in pairs to brainstorm some of the things they can mention.
- Give them 2 or 3 minutes to work alone and prepare some **brief** notes.
- Remix the class into new pairs, and ask them to give their different talks to each other.
- Tell the partners not giving talks to listen without interrupting and then give their partner feedback on what they did well with suggestions for improvements.
- If they wish, they may then repeat their 'improved' talk.
- Alternatively, you may choose 1 or 2 students to give their talk to the whole class and then invite feedback from the whole class.

1 🔊 Introduction

Listening

You are going to hear a lecturer on a social studies course talking about life expectancy. **Before you listen**
- look at the two tables below and say what they show.
- try to predict the dates, countries, continents and ages in each space.

Now listen and complete the tables by writing A WORD OR A NUMBER for each answer.

Canada – Life expectancy	
	Both sexes
1920	59
(1)	71
1990	**(2)** ....

Life expectancy 1998 by regions and countries	
	Both sexes
Africa	51
(3)	65
China	**(4)** ....
(5)	80
Hong Kong	**(6)** ....
Australia	**(7)** ....

Discussion

Work in small groups and briefly discuss these questions.
- Why do you think life expectancy is rising in most countries?
- Do you think human lifespans will rise much more? Why? Why not?

2 Reading

You are now going to read a passage about how life expectancy may increase in the future. First, skim the passage quickly to get a general idea of what it is about and answer the question:

Which paragraphs concentrate on scientific progress and which deal with people's opinions?

Now look at the questions which follow the passage and read the passage again to answer them. Try to answer the questions without looking up difficult words, as you would do in the test.

Life without death *by Duncan Turner*

A Until recently, the thought that there might ever be a cure for ageing seemed preposterous. Growing older and more decrepit appeared to be an inevitable and necessary part of being human. Over the last decade, however, scientists have begun to see ageing differently. 5 Some now believe that the average life-expectancy may soon be pushed up to 160 years; others think that it may be extended to 200 or 300 years. A handful even wonder whether we might one day live for a millennium or more.

B Behind this new excitement is the theory that the 10 primary cause of ageing lies in highly reactive molecules called free radicals, left behind by the oxygen we breathe. Free radicals react with the molecules in our bodies, damaging DNA, proteins and other cell tissues, and are known to be implicated in diseases as diverse as 15 cataracts, cancer and Alzheimer's. The body does its best to protect itself against free radicals by producing its own chemicals to prevent ageing, such as vitamins E and C, but it is always fighting a losing battle.

C A year ago Gordon Lithgow of the University of 20 Manchester discovered a way to help combat free radicals. Using one of these anti-ageing chemicals, he managed to increase the lifespan of one species of earthworm* by 50 per cent. Despite cautionary words from the scientists, many welcomed this as the first step 25 towards a drug which would extend life. Research involving the mutation of genes has also thrown up fascinating results: after identifying two of the genes that appear to control how long the earthworm lives, similar genes were found in organisms as various as fruit-flies, 30 mice and human beings. When one considers the vast evolutionary distances that separate these species, it suggests that we may have discovered a key to how ageing is regulated throughout the entire animal kingdom.

D In June last year a small American company called 35 Eukarion sought permission to carry out the first trials of an anti-ageing drug, SCS, on human beings. Although it will initially be used to treat diseases associated with old age, Eukarion said, that 'if the effect of treating diseases of old age is to extend life, everyone's going to be happy'. 40

E Some scientists, however, are quick to discourage extravagant speculation. 'There is no evidence whatsoever that swallowing any chemical would have an effect on mammals', says Rich Miller of the University of Michigan. 'And those people who claim it might need to 45 go out and do some experimenting'. Some research, moreover, has produced alarming results. As well as controlling ageing, these genes also partly control the hormones which regulate growth. The upshot of this is that although the lives of mutant mice can be extended 50 by up to 80 per cent, they remain smaller than normal.

F Quite apart from these sorts of horrors, the ethical implications of extending human lifespan are likely to worry many people. Even if the falling birth-rates reported in the world's developed nations were to be 55 repeated throughout the world, would this be sufficient to compensate for massively extended life-expectancy, and would we be willing to see the demographic balance of our society change out of all recognition? David Gems, the head of the Centre for Research into Ageing at 60 University College, London, is enthusiastic about the opportunities opened up by extended life, but even he observes, 'If people live much longer, the proportion of children would, of course, be very small. It strikes me that it might feel rather claustrophobic: all those middle-aged 65 people and very few children or young people.'

G The philosopher John Polkinghorne emphasises that any discussion of the merits of life-extending therapies must take into account the quality of the life that is lived: 'One would not wish to prolong life beyond the point it 70 had ceased to be creative and fulfilling and meaningful,' he says. 'Presumably, there would have to come a point at which life ceased to be creative and became just repetition. Clearly, there are only so many rounds of golf one would want to play.' 75

H But Polkinghorne, a member of the Human Genetics Commission, also observes that so far our experience of extended life-expectancy has not resulted in world-weariness. Throughout the last century, life-expectancy rose consistently, thanks to improved 80 diet, better hygiene, continuous medical innovation and the provision of free or subsidised healthcare. In 1952 the Queen sent out 225 telegrams to people on their 100th birthday; in 1996 she sent out 5,218. 'Consider also, the lives of our Roman and Anglo-Saxon ancestors,' 85 he says. 'By and large, the doubling of human lifespan we have seen since then has not been a bad thing. Life has not become frustrating and boring. 90 For example, we now live to see our children's children, and this is good.'

* *an earthworm*

Source: *The Spectator*, 9th February, 2002

Do the following statements agree with the information given in the reading passage?
Write

YES   *if the statement agrees with the information.*
NO   *if the statement contradicts the information.*
NOT GIVEN *if there is no information on this in the passage.*

1 Scientific predictions about how much it will be possible to lengthen human life vary greatly.
2 Research into extending life involves both new drugs and changes to genes.
3 Scientific experiments have not succeeded in making any animals live longer.
4 Most people in the future will decide not to have children.
5 Life expectancy has improved partly because people eat better.

 From *Instant IELTS* by Guy Brook-Hart © Cambridge University Press 2004 **PHOTOCOPIABLE**

Questions 6–9

Look at the following names of people or organisations (Questions 6–9) and the list of opinions (A–F).
Match each name with the opinion which the person or organisation expressed.

NB There are more opinions than names, so you will not use them all.

6 Eukarion
7 Rich Miller
8 David Gems
9 John Polkinghorne

A Increases in longevity may cause unwelcome changes in society.
B People will live longer but become tired of life.
C Past experience shows that people do not lose interest in life as a result of living longer.
D There is no scientific proof that any drug can prolong human life expectancy.
E One medicine we are developing may have a welcome benefit apart from its original purpose.
F Using drugs to treat the diseases of old age is only the beginning.

Question 10

Which TWO of the following are characteristics of free radicals?
Choose TWO letters A–E.

A They are a partial cause of certain diseases.
B They escape into the atmosphere when we breathe.
C They are present in two vitamins.
D They harm our body chemistry.
E They are produced by our bodies.

Questions 11–14

Complete the following summary of the scientific progress towards extending life expectancy.
Choose your answers from the box below the summary.
NB There are more words than spaces, so you will not use them all.

In one experiment using anti-ageing chemicals, the life of (11)......... was extended by half. (12)......... like the ones which control the ageing process in these animals have also been found in other species. Unfortunately, however, experiments on (13)......... have been less successful: while they live longer, the (14)......... controlling their growth are also affected with the result that they grow less.

A chemicals
B earthworms
C fruit flies
D genes
E hormones
F human beings
G mice
H organisms

3 Follow-up

Vocabulary

Find words or phrases in the passage which mean the same as the words listed below.

Paragraph A: ● ridiculous, absurd
  ● old and in poor condition
  ● a few
Paragraph B: ● different, varied
Paragraph C: ● fight
  ● has produced
Paragraph D: ● asked for
Paragraph E: ● worrying, frightening
  ● result
  ● not working properly, faulty
Paragraph G: ● advantages
  ● lengthen
Paragraph H: ● medical care

Discussion

Work in small groups and discuss how living to 160 might affect the following things:

education
marriage
work
leisure activities
our appearance
the age at which we do different things
our health
having children
our attitude to life

Estimated class time: 1 hour 10 minutes (Intermediate),
1 hour 5 minutes (Advanced)

🕐 Short of time? You could:
- give your students Questions **11–14** for homework, having talked through the advice in the teacher's notes.
- do the follow-up activities in the following lesson after checking their answers.

1 🎧 Introduction _(15 minutes)_

Listening

For the complete recording script, please see page 127.
Ask students to predict the type of information they will hear before doing the listening activity.

> **ANSWER KEY**
> **1** 1960 **2** 78 **3** Asia **4** 70 **5** Japan **6** 79 **7** 80

2 Reading

- This reading passage contains a summary of scientific progress in extending life, and a number of opinions. It provides an opportunity to train students in 3 reading skills: skimming to get a general overview of the passage, scanning to locate specific information, and intensive reading to answer specific questions.
- Students should try to answer the questions in spite of unfamiliar vocabulary, as in the test. If you feel your students would benefit, do the vocabulary exercise in the follow-up first.

Skimming _(Intermediate: 8 minutes, Advanced: 5 minutes)_
- Ask students to read the passage quickly (Intermediate students 5/6 minutes, Advanced students 3 minutes) to get a general idea of what the passage is about.
- To help them focus, ask them to answer the question before the passage.

> **ANSWER KEY**
> **Scientific progress:** the first 5 paragraphs.
> **People's opinions:** the last 3

Questions 1–5 _(10 minutes)_

A lot of students find the concept of NOT GIVEN very difficult to grasp.
- Remind your students that some of the sentences in the questions are **not addressed** in the passage.
- When they think they have found a sentence that deals with the subject of a sentence in the questions, they need to read it very carefully – it may not express agreement OR disagreement.

Intermediate
Help your students to understand the questions by asking them to paraphrase each statement _e.g. Q1: scientists give different figures for how long people will live._
Tell them that they should quickly scan for information.
Elicit what they should scan for:
Q1: figures
Q2: mention of drugs and genes
Q3: names of animals
Q4: children
Q5: a synonym of 'eat better' _e.g. improved diet._

Advanced
Students should scan for relevant parts of the passage then read that section carefully.
Tell them to work alone and answer the questions in 4 minutes.

> **ANSWER KEY**
> **1** YES (lines 6, 7 and 8)   **2** YES (lines 22, 50–51)
> **3** NO (lines 22, 50–52)   **4** NOT GIVEN
> **5** YES (lines 80–81)

Questions 6–9 _(6–8 minutes)_

Elicit from your students that they should scan for the names and underline them, then read carefully what each said.
- Point out that what is said may come before and after the name _e.g. Rich Miller_ or in another paragraph _e.g. John Polkinghorne_. They should look for the **meaning**, not exact words.
- Give Intermediate students 6 minutes to do this and Advanced students 4 minutes.

> **ANSWER KEY**
> **6** E (lines 39–40)   **7** D (lines 42–44)
> **8** A (lines 64–66)   **9** C (lines 89–90)

Question 10 _(5 minutes)_

Ask them to identify which paragraph deals with free radicals.
- They should work down the list ticking which meanings coincide with information in the paragraph.
- Remind students that the exact words will not be repeated, and that some of the sentences on the list may be deliberately confusing!

Advanced
Give your students a time limit of 3 minutes for this question.

> **ANSWER KEY**
> **10** A and D (lines 15–16 and 13–14)

Questions 11–14 _(10 minutes)_

Here, you can suggest a number of techniques:
- Putting the words in the boxes in categories _e.g. names of animals, words referring to chemicals, other words etc._ before they start.
- Looking for synonyms of particular words and phrases _e.g. by half (by 50 per cent), growing, growth, live more, live up to 80 per cent longer._
- Reading through the summary when they have finished and deciding whether it makes sense both for meaning and grammar.

You should give Advanced students a time limit of 5 minutes.

> **ANSWER KEY**
> **11** B (lines 23–24)   **12** D (lines 29–31)
> **13** G (lines 50–51)   **14** E (lines 48–51)

3 Follow-up

Vocabulary _(5 minutes)_

ridiculous, absurd – _preposterous_
old and in poor condition – _decrepit_
a few – _a handful of_
different, varied – _diverse_
fight – _combat_
has produced – _has thrown up_
asked for – _sought_
worrying, frightening – _alarming_

result – _upshot_
not working properly, faulty
   – _defective_
advantages – _merits_
lengthen – _prolong_
medical care – _healthcare_

Discussion _(10 minutes)_

Students discuss the implications of living to 160.

1 Introduction

- Work in pairs. Look at *one* of the charts and discuss what it shows. Describe the data shown on the chart.
- Work in groups of three with people who have worked on other charts. Explain your chart to the other people in your group. Listen to the other students' descriptions and suggest other things they could mention, or ways their descriptions could be improved.

Chart 1

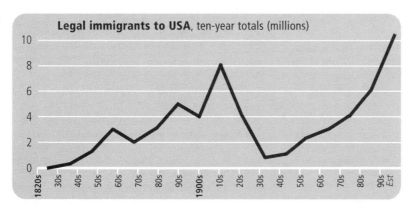

Chart 2

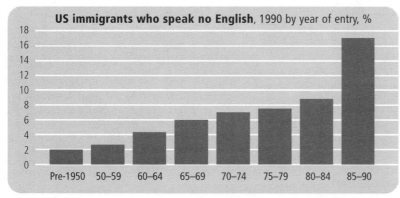

Chart 3

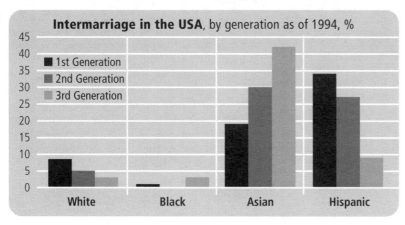

2 Reading

You are now going to read a passage about the history of migration. First, skim the passage quickly to get a general idea of what it is about and then answer this question:

The article concentrates on migration in certain parts of the world. Which parts of the world does the article give most attention to?

Now look at the questions which follow the passage and read the passage again to answer them. Try to answer the questions without looking up difficult words, as you would do in the test.

On the move

Economic analysis sheds light on the history of migration and on its future

A   DURING successive waves of globalisation in the three centuries leading up to the first world war, migration of labour was consistently one of the biggest drivers of economic change. Since 1945 the world has experienced a new era of accelerating globalisation, and 5 the international movement of labour is proving once again to be of the greatest economic and social significance. As a new study* by Barry Chiswick of the University of Illinois at Chicago and Timothy Hatton of the University of Essex makes plain, it is economic 10 factors that have been uppermost throughout the history of migration.

B   For many years after the discovery of America, the flow of free migrants from Europe was steady but quite small: transport costs were high, conditions harsh and 15 the dangers of migration great. In 1650 a free migrant's passage to North America cost nearly half a year's wages for a farm labourer in southern England. Slavery predominated until the slave trade was stopped in the first half of the 19th century. By around 1800, North 20 America and the Caribbean islands had received some 8m immigrants. Of these, about 7m were African slaves.

C   The first era of mass voluntary migration was between 1850 and 1913. Over 1m people a year were drawn to the new world by the turn of the 20th century. 25 Growing prosperity, falling transport costs and lower risk all pushed in the same direction. Between 1914 and 1945, war, global depression and government policy reduced migration. During some years in the 1930s, people returning to Europe from the United States, even 30 though comparatively few, actually outnumbered immigrants going the other way. After the second world war the cost of travel fell steeply. But now the pattern changed. Before long Europe declined as a source of immigration and grew as a destination. Emigration from 35 developing countries expanded rapidly: incomes there rose enough to make emigration feasible, but not enough to make it pointless. Many governments began trying to control immigration. Numbers, legal and illegal, surged nonetheless, as economics had its way. 40

D   Migration, it is safe to assume, is in the interests of (voluntary) migrants: they would not move otherwise. The evidence suggests that it is also very much in the overall interests of the receiving countries. But, as Mr Chiswick and Mr Hatton point out, there are losers in 45 those countries. The increase in the supply of labour means that the wages of competing workers may fall, at least to start with.

E   The economic conditions now seem propitious for an enormous further expansion of migration. On the face 50 of it, this will be much like that of a century ago. As before, the main expansionary pressures are rising incomes in the rich countries and rising incomes in the poor ones. (This second point is often neglected: as poor countries get a little less poor, emigration tends to 55 increase, because people acquire the means to move.) The study emphasises, however, two crucial differences between then and now.

F   One is that, in the first decade of the 20th century, the receiving countries needed lots of unskilled workers 60 in industry and farming. In the first decade of the 21st century, in contrast, opportunities for unskilled workers are dwindling. In the United States, wages of unskilled workers are falling. The fall is enough to hurt the workers concerned, but not to deter new immigrants.   65

G   And the other big difference between now and a century ago? It is that the affected rich-country workers are in a stronger position to complain, and get something done. The most likely result is that a trend that is already well established will continue: countries 70 will try to restrict the immigration of unskilled workers, giving preference to workers with skills.

H   This does help, in one way, quite apart from narrowing the rich countries' shortage of skilled workers: it reduces the pressure to make low wages even lower. 75 However, the idea has drawbacks too. It turns away many of the poorest people who want to migrate, which is hard to justify in humanitarian terms. Also, it pushes others from this group into illegal immigration, which exposes them to dangers, makes integration more 80 difficult and may even make the wages of low-paid workers even lower than if the same migrants entered legally. On top of all this is the loss of skilled workers in the sending countries. Already some of the world's poorest nations lose almost all the doctors they train to 85 jobs in Europe or North America. Money immigrants send home offsets some of that loss, but not all.

I   Today's migration, much more than the migration of old, poses some insoluble dilemmas. Belief in individual freedom suggests that rich countries should adopt more 90 liberal immigration rules, both for unskilled migrants and skilled ones. With or without such rules, more migrants are coming. And in either case, the question of compensation for the losers, in rich countries and poor countries alike, will demand some attention.   95

* International Migration and the Integration of Labour Markets. Forthcoming in an NBER conference volume, *Globalisation in Historical Perspective*.

Copyright © 1995–2001 The Economist Newspaper Group Ltd. All rights reserved.

From *Instant IELTS* by Guy Brook-Hart © Cambridge University Press 2004   **PHOTOCOPIABLE**

The History of Migration

Questions 1–5

Complete the sentences below.
Choose ONE OR TWO WORDS from the passage.

Until the early 19th century the majority of migrants to North America were (**1**).....................................

However, in the second half of the 19th century, (**2**)............. .... and cheaper travel meant that more people could afford to emigrate voluntarily.

At the beginning of the 20th century, immigrants to receiving countries found jobs as (**3**)..................................... in factories and on farms.

After the second world war there was a great increase in emigrants from (**4**)... .

Nowadays, receiving countries generally prefer immigrants (**5**)................................. .

Questions 6–11

Which paragraphs in the passage contain the following information? Write the appropriate letters (A–I).

NB You need only write ONE letter for each answer, so you will not need to use them all.

6 changing departure points and destinations for migrants
7 disadvantages of present immigration policies
8 the immigrants who rich countries find more acceptable
9 how earning more money affects migration
10 migration was mainly compulsory
11 changing the laws on immigration

Questions 12–13

Choose the appropriate letters A–D.

12 Pressure to migrate is increasing now because
   A economic conditions have become more desperate.
   B immigration restrictions are being relaxed.
   C people generally earn more.
   D there is a greater need for unskilled workers.

13 Lower incomes for unskilled workers in receiving countries have
   A encouraged countries to import skilled workers.
   B led to protests about immigration.
   C reduced the amount of money immigrants send home.
   D provided opportunities for immigrants in manufacturing and agriculture.

Questions 14–16

The list below gives some of the effects of immigration restrictions.
Which THREE effects are mentioned in the passage?

A It is more difficult for illegal immigrants to integrate.
B Jobs in sending countries become more secure.
C More unskilled workers immigrate illegally.
D Unskilled workers in receiving countries may become poorer.
E Workers in rich countries complain.
F Skilled workers may lose their jobs.

Questions 17–18

The list below gives reasons for relaxing immigration restrictions.
Which TWO reasons (A–E) are mentioned in the passage?

A Immigrants send money back to their country of origin.
B Immigration in greater numbers is inevitable.
C It would be ethically correct.
D It would ease population pressures in poor countries.
E Rich countries need more skilled workers.

3 Follow-up

Role play

Work in pairs or groups of three to prepare either Role A or Role B – you can use ideas from the passage or your own ideas.
When you are ready, do the role play with someone from another group.

Role A: You are a doctor in a developing country. For some time you have been thinking of emigrating to a richer country which will mean better opportunities for you professionally and for your family. On the other hand your country badly needs skilled professionals like you to stay and work there. For this reason you are hesitating about emigrating. You have just met a doctor from a rich country who has come to your country for a holiday. Discuss with him what you should do and ask for his advice.

Role B: You are a doctor from a rich country on holiday in a developing country. In your country there are plenty of job opportunities for doctors, and many medical workers are immigrants. However, while immigrant doctors find work without difficulty, they often have problems integrating into your society. Moreover, during your holiday you have noticed that the country you are visiting badly needs skilled workers to stay and not emigrate. You have just met a local doctor who is thinking of emigrating. Discuss the problem with him or her and offer him or her your advice.

Vocabulary

Scan the reading passage again and highlight any words or phrases you find which mean *increase* or *decrease*. You will find many of these useful when you do writing task 1.

Estimated class time: 1 hour 15 minutes (Intermediate)
1 hour 10 minutes (Advanced)

🕐 **Short of time? You could:**
- give your students Questions **12–18** for homework, having talked through the advice in the teacher's notes.
- do the role play and vocabulary follow-up in the following lesson.

1 Introduction *(15 minutes)*
- Tell students they are going to read a passage about the history of migration. Check that students know the difference between *immigrant*, *emigrant* and *migrant*. Elicit other words such as *immigration*, *emigration*, *migrate*, *emigrate*, *immigrate*, *receiving country* and *sending country*.
- Divide the class into pairs and ask each pair to look at **one** of the charts and decide what it shows.

ANSWER KEY
Chart 1 shows levels of immigration into the USA over the last 180 years,
Chart 2 shows the percentage of immigrants who have not learnt any English in the US.
Chart 3 shows how much different groups of immigrants marry people from other groups by generation.

Optional
- When they have finished, ask students to reform in groups of 3 with 1 student from each pair to describe the chart he or she has studied to the others.

2 Reading
Skimming *(3–6 minutes)*
You should give Intermediate students 6 minutes to do this, as the passage is very dense, and Advanced students 3–4 minutes.

ANSWER KEY
United States / North America and Europe.

Questions 1–5 *(10 minutes)*

Before answering these questions, elicit what parts of speech they will need to use in their answers *e.g. in Q1 either a noun / noun phrase or an adjective*.

Intermediate
- For Q1, ask your students which paragraphs deal with the 19th century. To do this, elicit that they should scan for dates between 1800 and 1900. (*Answer: B and C*).
- Ask them what the key words in Q2 are (*second half of the 19th century / cheaper travel*), and then ask them where they will find the answer.
- They should then do Qs **3–5** alone.

Advanced
- Ask them which paragraphs they will have to read to answer Qs **1–5**.
- To do this, elicit that each question deals with a different period of history, and they will then have to scan the passage to find where these periods are referred to (*Answer: Paragraphs B, C, F and G*).
- Give them 5 minutes to answer these questions.

ANSWER KEY
1 (African) slaves   **2** growing prosperity / rising incomes
3 unskilled workers   **4** developing countries   **5** with skills

Questions 6–11 *(10–15 minutes)*

Intermediate
- Tell them the answer to Q6 is **C** and ask them to find evidence in the paragraph which shows this *e.g. at the beginning it talks about immigration from Europe to America up to 1913.*
- Tell them the answer to Q7 is either **F** or **H**. Ask them to read the 2 paragraphs and then discuss in pairs which is the correct answer and why (*Answer:* **H**).
- Ask them to do Qs **8–11** alone and then discuss their answers in small groups.

Advanced
- Give them a time limit of 6 minutes.
- Ask them to work in pairs and make this exercise a race in order to encourage them to skim and scan effectively.

ANSWER KEY
6 C (lines 34–36)   **7** H (lines 76–87)   **8** G (lines 70–72)
9 E (lines 52–54)   **10** B (lines 18–22)   **11** I (lines 89–92)

Questions 12–13 *(5 minutes)*

- Students should look at the stems of Qs **12** and **13** and say if they will find the answers in the first or second half of the passage.
- Ask them to scan to find which paragraph(s) deal(s) with each of these points (Q**12**: paragraph E, Q**13**: paragraphs **F** and **G**)

ANSWER KEY
12 C (lines 54–56)   **13** B (lines 67–72)

Questions 14–18 *(10 minutes)*

Intermediate
- For Qs **14–16**, ask which paragraph deals with the effects of immigration restrictions (*Answer: paragraph H*) and get them to find the effects in pairs.
- These questions are tough, so ask them to paraphrase the alternatives *e.g. A: immigrants who don't have permission to enter the country may find it harder to find jobs, education for their children etc.*
- Repeat the procedure for Qs **17–18**.

Advanced
- Ask which paragraph deals with each of these sets of questions. Give them 5 minutes to find the answers.

ANSWER KEY
14 A (lines 80–81)   **15** C (lines 78–79)   **16** D (lines 81–82) in any order   **17** B (lines 89–90)   **18** C (lines 92–93) in any order

3 Follow-up

Role play *(10 minutes)*

Careful! Avoid doing this role play if you think opinions or attitudes may be expressed which some of your students will find upsetting or offensive.
- Remind your students that they are playing a role and therefore they can express ideas that do not reflect their personal opinions.

Vocabulary *(5 minutes)*

Your students should find these words and phrases:
accelerating, was steady, growing, falling, reduced, fell steeply, expanded rapidly, surged, increase (**n** and **v**), *are dwindling, declining, narrowing.*

1 Introduction

Work in pairs and discuss the following points.
- Briefly describe the people in the photos. Try to imagine and describe their ways of life.
- Put the points in box **A** in order from the ones which you think pose the greatest threat to indigenous peoples' ways of life to the ones which you think pose the least threat.
- Look at the titles in box **B** and briefly discuss how they can help to protect indigenous peoples and their cultures.

A

- [ ] television
- [ ] destruction of habitat
- [ ] disease
- [ ] exploitation of resources by multinational companies
- [ ] national education systems
- [ ] migration to cities
- [ ] the market economy

B

1 protected areas
2 accurate maps
3 a home-grown education system
4 government subsidies

2 Reading

You are now going to read a passage about making maps of indigenous communities. First, skim the passage quickly to get a general idea of what it is about and then answer this question:

Is the passage about the benefits or the problems of mapping indigenous communities?

Now look at the questions which follow the extract and read the passage again to answer them. Try to answer the questions without looking up difficult words, as you would do in the test.

Mapping
indigenous
communities

A We all were taught: the map is not the territory. However, recent attempts to secure land for indigenous peoples find the entanglement of maps and territories to be more complex. The map – or control of the map – sometimes makes the territory, especially when indigenous 5 people have been invaded by map-makers. "More indigenous territory has been claimed by maps than by guns," University of California geographer Bernard Nietschmann concludes from his field experience. "And more indigenous territory can be reclaimed and defended by maps than by guns." 10

B Mapping of common land – mapping of, by, and for the people – has been called "counter-mapping", "community-based mapping" or "participatory mapping". The mapping toolkit comprises everything from maps scratched on the ground to high-tech GPS,* and often assistance by outside 15 NGOs* or universities. Affordable equipment and access to a network of expertise provide communities with map-making capacities comparable to those formerly enjoyed only by nation-states and wealthy corporations.

C Official maps frequently misrepresent indigenous land, 20 treat it as uninhabited, or reveal ambiguous borders. Definite boundaries become the first line of defense against encroaching cattle farmers, timber companies, miners, road builders, and land speculators. But the mapping process also changes people's perceptions of themselves and their 25 territory, their resources, and their history. It can help political organizing and give them greater control of the resources on their land.

D Current projects range from making small maps of single communities to the Oxfam-sponsored effort to map all 1300 30 of Peru's Native Amazonian communities. Most projects work on a number of different levels – simultaneously applying inhabitants' terms, using their names, symbols, scales, and priorities (sometimes called "folkloric" maps), and converting these into conventional maps that will be 35 recognized by officials, accepted in court, and usable in negotiations. Neither folkloric nor orthodox maps are more "correct". Each represents a cultural interpretation of territory; each changes how residents and non-residents view their geography. 40

E A key, says Mac Chapin of the Center for the Support of Native Lands, is the level of local participation: the higher the level, the richer and more beneficial the outcome. Take a 1995–96 Native Lands project in Izoceno communities in Bolivia. Trained Izoceno surveyors armed with paper, colored 45

pencils, and notebooks conducted village censuses and – working with village leaders – drew sketch maps showing land-use activities (where people live, farm, hunt, practise ritual, gather medicinal plants and construction materials), as well as structures, resources, relationships, and physical landmarks.   50

F Cartographers used these maps to produce new 1:50,000 maps based on available military maps. Then the surveyors took the draft maps back to the communities for feedback and correction, while draftsmen checked exact locations using GPS and compass readings. Finally, the team produced a 55 1:250,000 map of the region and 1:75,000 zone maps.

G Some governments now accept many of these home-grown maps, acknowledging them as more accurate than their own. In Panama, government cartographers have participated from the beginning in recent projects. The maps 60 legitimize boundaries for protecting areas and document land use and occupancy for land-rights negotiations. They permit boundary monitoring with aerial or satellite photography, and setting priorities for managing and conserving the land.   65

H Just putting their own traditional names on folkloric maps gives people a spiritual ownership of the things named, says Mac Chapin. These maps also give birth to a sense of region. The Honduran Mosquitia, for instance, includes 174 communities; before mapping, each dealt individually with 70 cattle farmers and timber companies, unaware of others' arrangements. Mapping created a feeling of territory, leading to the organization of seven regional Miskito federations for collective action. Since most place names have historical origins, the mapping process also became the occasion for 75 communities to gather across generations, share stories and songs, and recollect their identity.

*GPS – Global Positioning Satellites
*NGOs – Non-governmental organisations

Source: *Whole Earth Magazine*, Fall, 1998

From *Instant IELTS* by Guy Brook-Hart © Cambridge University Press 2004   **PHOTOCOPIABLE**

Questions 1–5

Complete the summary below. Choose ONE OR TWO WORDS from the reading passage for each answer.

Nowadays maps are a more effective way of protecting native lands than (1)............................ . Moreover, because (2)............................ is available it has become possible for small communities to make their own maps with help from outside experts.

On official maps, native territory is often shown to be (3)............................ or its frontiers are not clearly defined. Maps showing (4)............................ can help to protect indigenous areas from outside exploitation. Also, map-making can alter the inhabitants' (5)............................ of their identity, their land and their culture.

Questions 6–9

Look at the following countries (Questions 6–9) and the list of characteristics of mapping projects (A–G).
Match each country with the characteristic of the mapping project which is mentioned in the passage.

NB There are more characteristics than countries, so you will not need to use them all.

6   Peru
7   Bolivia
8   Panama
9   Honduras

A   Every indigenous village in the region will be represented.
B   Indigenous communities make better use of the region where they live.
C   Local people have stopped using weapons to defend their territory.
D   Communities have become more aware of their culture as a result of mapping.
E   People from the local community were responsible for gathering the basic information.
F   The mapping received official support from the start.
G   The maps were made entirely by people from the community.

Questions 10–14

For Questions 10–14 complete the diagram on the right to show the process used for making maps in Bolivia. Use NO MORE THAN THREE WORDS from the passage for each answer.

(10)............. are carried out before drawing rough maps.

↓

Large-scale maps are made by (11)............. using sketch maps and army maps.

↓

These maps are then shown to villagers for (12)............. .

↓

Meanwhile (13)............. are confirmed by professional map-makers.

↓

Lastly, regional and (14)............. are issued.

Questions 15–17

The list below gives some uses of maps.
Which THREE of these are mentioned as uses of folkloric maps?

A   They are suitable for use in legal battles.
B   They enable local people to exploit their resources more efficiently.
C   They enable communities to remember their past.
D   They help outsiders find their way in the region.
E   They help people in the area to unite politically.
F   They show where local people carry out various activities.

3 Follow-up

Vocabulary

Scan the passage again to find these words and try to guess their meanings from the context. Then use the words to complete the sentences below.
comprises high-tech formerly outcome feedback monitoring

1   I'm pessimistic about the .... of these negotiations.

2   It's difficult to improve your service if you get no .... from your clients.

3   People flood to this region in search of jobs in .... industries.

4   Tax .... over 50% of the price of fuel.

5   This area was .... a desert, but now it has been converted to rich agricultural land.

6   We've been carefully .... your progress and you should be ready to leave hospital shortly.

Estimated class time: 1 hour 5 minutes (Intermediate)
1 hour (Advanced)

🕐 **Short of time? You could:**

- give your students Questions **10–17** for homework, having talked through the advice in the teacher's notes.
- do the vocabulary follow-up and discussion in the following lesson.

1 Introduction *(15 minutes)*

Ask your students to discuss the questions in pairs.

2 Reading

Skimming *(Intermediate 5 minutes, Advanced 3 minutes)*

- Ask them to skim the whole passage quickly to get a general idea of its contents.
- The question should help them to focus (*Answer: it's more about the benefits*).
- They should not spend time working on the meanings of individual words or sentences as there may not be a question about them.
- Give an Advanced class 3 minutes to do this, and an Intermediate class 5 minutes.

Questions 1–5 *(15 minutes)*

- One sentence in the summary may summarise the main idea of a whole paragraph from the passage. However, the words needed to fill the gaps **must** come from the passage.
- Students should highlight the key words and phrases from each sentence in the summary *e.g. in the first sentence* 'more effective' *and* 'protecting native lands'.
- They then scan to find where each of these ideas is dealt with in the passage.

Intermediate

To guide your students more:

- Ask them to look in the first paragraph and find a synonym for *protecting* (*defending*) and for *native lands* (*indigenous territory*).
- Elicit the answer to Q**1**.
- For Q**2**, ask them to read paragraph **B** and to identify the 2 things which have made it possible for small communities to make their own maps. Ask them which one is already mentioned in the summary (*outside experts*) and so, which one should they choose as their answer?

ANSWER KEY

1 guns **2** affordable equipment **3** uninhabited
4 definite boundaries **5** perceptions

Questions 6–9 *(Intermediate 10 minutes, Advanced 7 minutes)*

This is a matching exercise.
Elicit how to deal with these questions.

- Scan and find where each country is dealt with in the passage.
- Underline or highlight it.
- Then read carefully what is said about each.

Intermediate

- Ask them if they noticed the names of any countries mentioned in the first 3 paragraphs when they were answering Qs **1–5**.
- Tell them they should scan from paragraph **D** onwards (i.e. run their eyes quickly over the passage) until they find the name of one of the countries mentioned and then highlight it.
- If necessary, for Q**6**, tell them the answer is **A** and ask them to find the evidence in the passage which shows this.

Advanced

Give them 4 minutes to do this.

ANSWER KEY

6 A (lines 30–31) **7** E (lines 44–50) **8** F (lines 60–61)
9 D (lines 75–77)

Questions 10–14 *(5 minutes)*

These questions are a simple flowchart.

- Tell your students to work carefully through the 2 paragraphs on Bolivia.
- Elicit what sort of words will be needed in each space. (*Answers: nouns or noun phrases*).

ANSWER KEY

10 Village censuses **11** cartographers **12** feedback and correction
13 exact locations **14** zone maps

Question 15–17 *(10 minutes)*

Students should scan to find folkloric maps mentioned and then read carefully from there.

Intermediate

- Before they start, ask your students to study the 6 alternatives and underline the key words e.g. **A** *legal battles,* **B** *exploit resources etc.*
- Elicit synonyms or explanations for each.
- Then ask them to remember what each of the alternatives was without looking at the question page.
- Point out that it is worth spending time studying the question carefully so as to save time when reading for the answers.

Advanced

- Your students should read the 6 alternatives carefully. If you wish, ask them to study the alternatives for 30 seconds and then, with a partner, they try to remember what each of them was – they can then look back at the page and check what they were.
- Give them 4 minutes to scan the passage and find the answers.
- Tell them to underline or highlight words and phrases in the passage which gave them the answers, then check with the whole class.

ANSWER KEY

15 C (line 77)
16 E (lines 72–74) } in any order
17 F (lines 47–49)

3 Follow-up

Vocabulary *(5 minutes)*

This is an exercise which asks them to use some vocabulary from the passage which they might find useful when doing writing tasks.

ANSWER KEY

1 outcome
2 feedback
3 high-tech
4 comprises
5 formerly
6 monitoring

1 Introduction

Imagine you are going to visit a foreign country for the first time and you are particularly interested in problems of health and safety. Think of four or five questions you might ask. The two questions below are given as examples:

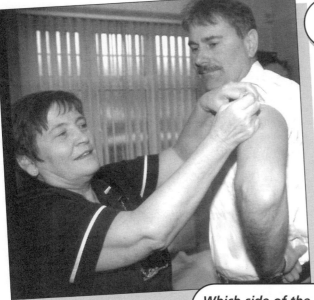

Is there much street crime?

Which side of the road do people drive on?

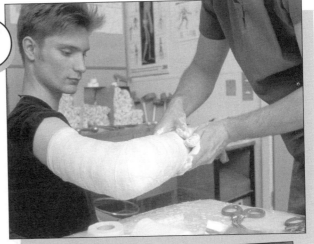

2 Reading

You will now read a leaflet giving advice and information to people who are thinking of visiting Australia.
Skim the passage on the next page quickly to see how many of your questions are answered in the leaflet.

After your first reading, try to answer the questions after the leaflet without looking up difficult words, as you would do in the test.

VISITING AUSTRALIA   Traveller's Tips

A   Quarantine Arrangements

Australia is a beautiful country free from many pests and diseases found elsewhere in the world. Quarantine helps keep it that way. When entering Australia, it's vital that you declare on your Incoming Passenger Card any food, live 5 plants and animals and any items made from wood, plants or animals. Quarantine officers use detector dog teams, X-ray machines and random baggage checks to detect undeclared quarantine items. If you conceal items of quarantine concern, you may receive an on-the-spot fine or 10 you could be prosecuted.

B   Health in Australia

Australia has a very high standard of hygiene and very safe food and drinking water. As a result special precautions are unnecessary. No vaccinations are required unless some time 15 has been spent in an infected country in the previous two weeks, although immunisation is always a good idea if your international itinerary is broad.

C   Health Services

Australia offers free service at public hospitals to its own 20 citizens and permanent residents and has universal health care under the Medicare system. This covers most or all of the cost of visiting a doctor. However, these services only extend to citizens of the United Kingdom and New Zealand. All visitors will have to pay in full and up-front for dental 25 treatment, ambulance charges and medicines. The cost of an unsubsidised, standard visit to a doctor is currently around A\$35, but serious illness can be much more expensive. Traveller's insurance covering medical care and medicines is therefore highly recommended. A personal basic medical kit 30 could also be a good idea.

D   Fire Bans

Respect fire bans (broadcast on the radio) and be careful with cigarette butts and broken glass which can ignite bush fires in hot, dry weather. If caught in a fire, head for a 35 clearing (avoid dense tree growths). If in a car get off the road, stay in the vehicle, get under the dashboard and cover yourself, preferably with a woollen blanket.

E   Bushwalking

If bushwalking or camping, be sure to leave an itinerary with 40 friends and go carefully prepared for the contingency of getting lost. Remember that nights can be freezing despite the daytime temperature.

F   Bite and Fright

When walking in the bush and rainforest, be sure to wear 45 boots, thick long socks and long trousers and be careful about putting your hand into holes. Ticks* and leeches* are common so check your body thoroughly after bushwalking. Ticks can be dangerous if not removed. They can be removed with kerosene or methylated spirits (don't break the head off inside your 50 body) and leeches can be removed with salt or heat.

G The chances of being attacked, stung or bitten by poisonous wildlife are extremely remote but, if a poisonous snake or spider should bite, try to stay calm, wrap the area in a tight bandage, keep very still and send for medical help. 55

H A similar procedure applies to poisonous marine life. Sea wasps are a deadly type of jellyfish which sting with their tentacles, causing telltale welt marks. Wash the wound with vinegar and don't remove the stingers. Do not swim in unprotected waters. Areas of danger – particularly those 60 involving sharks, crocodiles and stingers – have clearly marked signs. Even if your English is less than perfect, the signs have clear illustrations of the potential dangers of an area.

I   Australian Roads

There is a very clear division between inland and coastal 65 roads. The built-up coastal area from South Australia to Queensland (and the south western corner of Western Australia) is served by modern freeways and good quality sealed roads. The further inland the traveller goes, the worse the roads become. In the far west of Queensland, for 70 example, the roads can be unsealed and around the Gulf it is common for a road to only have a single width of tarmac. This means that if you come across a road train (they can be over 20 metres long) carrying cattle you have to head off the road. This is not a humorous suggestion. Road trains need all 75 the road and expect on-coming traffic to head for the hills. They have trouble deviating and will destroy a car rather than endanger their entire load.

*small animals which suck blood

Questions 1–6

The passage has nine paragraphs labelled A–I.
Which paragraphs contain the following information?
Choose the appropriate letters A–I.

1   a comparison between the interior and areas near the sea
2   a warning about luggage
3   advice about clothing
4   advice on litter
5   information on a problem which doesn't occur often
6   reassurance about what you can eat

Questions 7–13

Do the following statements agree with the information
given in reading passage 1?
Write

YES   *if the statement agrees with the information.*
NO   *if the statement contradicts the information.*
NOT GIVEN *if there is no information on this in the passage.*

7   If you try to bring things which are forbidden into
    Australia, you may be taken to court.
8   Under certain circumstances, vaccinations are obligatory
    for entry to Australia.
9   Only people with Australian nationality receive free
    medical treatment in Australia.
10 If you are trapped in a bush fire while driving, you should
    abandon your car.
11 Leech bites can cause dangerous infections.
12 Sea swimming is completely safe in protected areas.
13 If you meet a road train on a narrow road, leave the road.

Questions 14–18

Complete the following table with words taken from the
passage.
Use ONE OR TWO WORDS for each answer.

Problem or danger	Precaution or remedy
Medical costs	Obtain (**14**)................................ .
(**15**)........................	Find an open space away from trees.
Getting lost in the bush	Tell someone your (**16**).............................. in advance.
Ticks and leeches	Examine (**17**)................................... carefully after a walk.
Snake or spider bite	Put a (**18**)... around it.

3 Follow-up

Vocabulary

Find words or phrases in the passage which mean:

Paragraph A   ● isolation to prevent disease
                    ● immediate
                    ● taken to court
Paragraph B   ● places you are going to visit, route you
                       will take
Paragraph C   ● in advance
Paragraph D   ● prohibitions
                    ● go towards
Paragraph E   ● possibility
Paragraph F   ● carefully and completely
Paragraph H   ● possible
Paragraph I   ● approaching, coming in the opposite direction

Discussion

Work in pairs. Imagine you are giving advice to visitors to
your country. What traveller's tips would you give?
Mention:

● what you can or can't bring into the country.
● health – especially food, drink and immunisation.
● health services.
● particular dangers, especially for visitors on holiday.
● advice about the roads.

Estimated class time: 1 hour 5 minutes (Intermediate)
                          55 minutes (Advanced)

🕐 **Short of time? You could:**

- give your students Questions **7–18**, or **14–18** for homework, having talked through the advice in the teacher's notes.
- do the vocabulary follow-up for homework and the discussion in the following lesson.

1 Introduction (12 minutes)

Elicit more questions from your students *e.g. Is the water safe to drink? Can I get free health care if I have an accident?*

2 Reading

Skimming (Intermediate 5 minutes, Advanced 3 minutes)

- Skimming consists of reading quickly to get a **general** idea of what a passage is about. Ask students if they found any answers to their questions.
- They should try to answer the questions in spite of unfamiliar vocabulary, as they would have to in the test. If necessary you can pre-teach some vocabulary by doing the exercise in the follow-up first.

Questions 1–6 (Intermediate 12 minutes, Advanced 6 minutes)

The words in the questions will almost certainly not be the words in the passage, so they should look for synonyms. This will require them to scan the passage.

Intermediate

- Before reading, ask them in pairs to think of synonyms for the vocabulary in Questions **1–6** *e.g. areas near the sea: the coast / luggage: suitcases etc.*
- Tell them to scan to find the information i.e. run their eyes over the passage looking for the synonyms. When they find something which seems possible, they should read that part carefully to see whether it coincides with the ideas in the questions.
- Point out that they managed to answer the questions in spite of unfamiliar vocabulary.

Advanced

To encourage efficient, fast reading you could set a time limit of 5 minutes to answer Questions **1–6**.

ANSWER KEY
1 I   2 A   3 F   4 D   5 G   6 B

Questions 7–13 (Intermediate 15 minutes, Advanced 10 minutes)

- The answers to these questions occur in chronological order in the passage.
- Students should identify which section each question is answered in (by scanning) and then read that part more carefully.
  Many students find the concept of NOT GIVEN very difficult to grasp.
- Remind them that some of the sentences in the questions are **not addressed** in the passage.
- When they think they have found a sentence that deals with the question, they need to read it very carefully and bear in mind that it may not express agreement OR disagreement.

ANSWER KEY
7 YES (lines 9–11)   **8** YES (lines 15–17)   **9** NO (lines 22–24)
10 NO (lines 36–38)   **11** NOT GIVEN
12 NOT GIVEN   **13** YES (lines 73–75)

Intermediate

To help your students grasp the point of NOT GIVEN, ask them to say whether these underlined sentences are TRUE, FALSE or NOT GIVEN, according to the text:

- In Australia, eating ice-cream in public is illegal (ice-cream is not mentioned in the text, so, though it may be illegal, we must say NOT GIVEN).
- There are danger signs on all the beaches (danger signs are mentioned in the text, but in connection with 'areas of danger'. Nothing is said about signs on beaches – so, NOT GIVEN).
- Many cars are destroyed by road trains (it says that road trains will destroy cars rather than endanger their entire load, but it doesn't mention whether this happens much – so, NOT GIVEN).
- Ask them to check in pairs and find evidence to support their answers. If there is no evidence in the passage, they should choose NOT GIVEN.

Questions 14–18 (6 minutes)

- The main problem may be to identify which section deals with Question **15** (*clearing* and *open space*). However, the word *trees* should solve the problem.
- Since this is quite straightforward, give them a time limit of 3 minutes to answer all the questions.

ANSWER KEY
14 traveller's insurance   **15** Bush fires   **16** itinerary
17 your body   **18** tight bandage

3 Follow-up

Vocabulary (7 minutes)

If you do this in class, you may make it a little more communicative by asking your students to work in pairs and assigning each pair either paragraphs A–C, D–F or G–I. They find the answers for their paragraphs and then you remix the pairs into groups of 3 with 1 person from each pair and they tell each other the answers for their part of the passage.

ANSWER KEY
A quarantine, on-the-spot, prosecuted
B itinerary
C up-front
D bans, head for
E contingency
F thoroughly
H potential
I on-coming

Discussion (8 minutes)

- Ask your students to do this activity in pairs if they are all from the same country, and in groups of 3 or 4 if they are from different countries.
- If they are from the same country, get feedback by asking what they disagreed about. If from different countries, ask what they found surprising or very different from their country.
- If they are hoping to visit or emigrate to Australia, you may ask them what other things they would like to know about the country before they go.
- If the facilities are available, you could refer them to websites including http://walkabout.com.au, which this passage comes from.

1 Introduction

Work in pairs. Describe what you can see in each picture. What are the advantages and disadvantages of shopping in each?

Do you enjoy shopping? Why, or why not?

2 Reading

You will now read descriptions of six street markets in London from *Time Out*, a magazine about events in London.

Try to answer the questions without looking up difficult words, as you would do in the test.

Questions 1–10

Look at the six descriptions of London markets (A–F).
Answer the questions below by writing the letters of the appropriate descriptions A–F.

NB You may use any letter more than once.

1 It occasionally gets overcrowded. ....

2 It has a section based on a traditional activity in the area. ....

3 It has become more organised than before. ....

4 It has become more popular as a result of a film. ....

5 It is more traditional than in the past. ....

6 It offers typical British food as well as food from overseas. ....

7 It sells items which have always been expensive. ....

8 These TWO markets are typical places for Londoners to visit at weekends. .... and ....

9 These TWO markets sell hand-made items. .... and ....

10 These THREE markets are recommended for their prices. .... and .... and ....

LONDON'S MARKETS

A Brick Lane Market

The Spitalfields area has become much wealthier over the last few years, resulting in this chaotic, uncontrolled market becoming a lot more ordered. However, you'll still find a massive range 5 of goods on sale at this sprawling, ever-entertaining East End institution, including meat, fruit and vegetables, electrical goods, tools, bicycles, clothing, jewellery and household goods. A trip here is a quintessential Sunday morning out 10 in London: make sure not to miss it.

B Brixton Market

Running down Electric Avenue into two shopping arcades on either side of Atlantic Road, this thriving multicultural market has a community 15 feel. African and Caribbean produce and other exotic staples can be found, along with traditional fruit and veg and fish. There are also record stalls, second-hand clothes and bric-a-brac.

C Camden Market

London's fourth-biggest tourist attraction 20 stopped being progressive a long time ago, but continues to sell a wide variety of articles designed to appeal to youth culture. Street fashion and old-fashioned clothes dominate the main market, 25 while Camden Lock maintains its crafts heritage. It's usually busy and, at times, claustrophobic.

D Greenwich Market

Still going strong, Greenwich is less frenetic than Camden and Portobello and generally cheaper. 30

The covered section that makes up Greenwich Market proper is filled with arts and crafts that range from personal craftsmanship to uninspired tat. The nearby Village Market is funkier, with interesting second-hand clothing stalls, lots of 35 records and books, and some great '50s, '60s and '70s furniture. Sundays here are another London tradition.

E Petticoat Lane Market

While Brick Lane gets fashionable and Spitalfields 40 Market appeals to the ecological intentions of London's liberals, nearby Petticoat Lane remains resolutely traditional, and as East End as they come. But although much is unremarkable, there's a hell of a lot of it, and almost every type of 45 electrical goods can be found at bargain prices. Up on Cutler Street are gold and silver jewellery traders, a leftover from the gold and coin market that used to operate here.

F Portobello Road Market 50

Though now even more of a tourist attraction since the release of *Notting Hill*, Portobello still hasn't gone the way of Camden and given in to low quality. There's something for everyone at this lengthy street market; the choice of antiques is 55 huge, though prices have always been high, and you'll also find some of west London's cheapest fruit, veg and flowers. But it's probably most famous for its new and vintage clothes stalls.

© Time Out Group 2002. All rights reserved.

Complete the notes below.
Use ONE OR TWO WORDS from the passage for each answer.

> Brixton: recommended for its
> (11).................................. atmosphere
> Camden: good for clothes, crafts and things
> connected with (12)...............................
> Greenwich: look for used clothes at the
> (13)....................... (not far away)
> Petticoat Lane: good if you want to buy cheap
> (14)...
> Portobello Rd: a large selection of
> (15)...............................

3 Follow-up

Vocabulary

Find words or phrases with these meanings in the passage:
Brick Lane Market
disorganised .... typical ....
Brixton Market
lively and healthy .... cheap ornaments ....
Camden Market
uncomfortably crowded ....
Greenwich Market
busy .... things in bad taste ....
.... more unconventional ....

Discussion

Work in pairs or small groups. Imagine that your partner or the other students are visitors to your area. Describe the markets or shopping facilities in the area to them.

Estimated class time: 45 minutes

⏱ Short of time? You could:

- give your students Questions **11–15** for homework, having talked through the advice in the teacher's notes.
- give the vocabulary activity as homework if you didn't do it as a pre-reading task.
- do the follow-up activities in the following lesson.

1 Introduction *(10 minutes)*

If appropriate, also ask your students how shopping is different in their country from the impression given by the photos.

2 Reading

Your students should try to answer the questions in spite of unfamiliar vocabulary, as they would have to in the test. For this reason the vocabulary exercise is printed after the questions. If you feel your students will deal with the tasks with more confidence by doing the vocabulary exercise beforehand, do it now.

Questions 1–10 *(15 minutes)*

Explain to your students that this is a typical scanning activity, which they can expect to meet in sections 1 and 2 of the reading paper. They are expected to deal with each question in turn by looking at it and then scanning down the passage to find the answer. The answers will not appear in the passage in the same order as the questions.
Students should:

- study the questions carefully so they know what to look for in the text.
- highlight / underline key words in the questions and think what type of words they will need to look for in the text (they will be synonyms rather than the same words).
- run their eyes over the text to pinpoint the information.

Extra idea: You may give them 3 minutes to study the questions and then ask them in pairs to write down all the questions they remember.

Intermediate

- Warn your students that they will come across unfamiliar vocabulary, but that they shouldn't let this distract them from answering the questions.
- Tell them to scan the passage for the answer to each question in turn. If they find the answer to another question while they are looking, obviously they should note this down too.
- When they have finished, ask them to check their answers in pairs and to back up their choices with evidence from the passage.

Advanced

Give them 6 or 7 minutes to answer the questions, or:
Alternatively ask them to work in pairs to answer the questions and make the activity into a race (possibly with a prize for the pair which answers all the questions correctly most quickly).

ANSWER KEY

1 C (line 27) **2** E (lines 47–49) **3** A (lines 3–5)
4 F (lines 51–52) **5** C (lines 21–22) **6** B (lines 16–18)
7 F (line 56) **8** A, D (lines 10–11 and 37–38)
9 C, D (line 26 and 31–33) **10** D, E, F (lines 30, 46, 57)

Questions 11–15 *(5 minutes)*

The questions themselves tell your students where they will find the answers, so they only need to read those sections again carefully.

Intermediate

- Ask them to look at Q**11** before they start and say what type of word they should be looking for (*Answer: an adjective or the compound element of a noun*) as this will narrow their choice considerably.
- They should then do the same for Qs **12–15**.

Advanced

Give your students a time limit of 3 minutes to accustom them to working under pressure.

ANSWER KEY

11 community / multicultural **12** youth culture
13 Village Market **14** electrical goods **15** antiques

3 Follow-up

Vocabulary *(7 minutes)*

- You can make it a little more communicative by asking your students to work in pairs and assigning them 2 markets per pair.
- They find the answers for their markets and then you remix the pairs and they tell each other the answers for their part of the passage.

ANSWER KEY

Brick Lane: disorganised – chaotic / typical – quintessential
Brixton: lively and healthy – thriving / cheap ornaments – bric-a-brac
Camden: uncomfortably crowded – claustrophobic
Greenwich: busy – frenetic / things in poor condition or bad taste – tat / more unconventional – funkier

Discussion *(8 minutes)*

Students describe familiar markets and shopping areas to the rest of the group.

Distance Learning

1 🔊 Introduction

Listening

Work in small groups. Discuss:
- What do you think is meant by distance learning and learning face-to-face?
- What different types of distance learning can you think of?
- Brainstorm the advantages of distance learning, and the advantages of learning face-to-face in a classroom.
- Look at Questions **1–10** below and try to predict the information you will hear. Then listen to the conversation between two students on a teacher-training course and complete the notes.

Complete the notes below.
Write ONE OR TWO WORDS in each space.

Distance learning
- *You are geographically* (1).................
- *You can choose when to study.*
- *You can combine studying with* (2)........................
- *You can do it at* (3)........................
- *The quality of the teaching materials is very* (4)........................

Face-to-face
You are constantly in contact with other students and teachers which:
- *facilitates the* (5)........................ *of information*
- *stimulates* (6)........................
- *maintains your interest and* (7)........................
- *means your learning is closely* (8)........................

Also:
- *you get feedback and answers to queries in* (9).................
- *And you participate in the university's wider* (10).................

2 Reading

You are now going to read an extract from a booklet published by the Open University (OU) in Britain.

Try to answer the questions without looking up difficult words, as you would do in the test.

Questions 1–5

The reading passage has six paragraphs.
Choose the most suitable headings for paragraphs A–F from the list of headings below.

NB There are more headings than paragraphs, so you will not use them all.

Example	*Answer*
Paragraph C	vi

i   Not like last time
ii   Combining your studies with your personal situation
iii Making the most of the facilities
iv   Managing your time
v   The things you will miss
vi   Taking charge of your learning
vii The input from the Open University
viii The tutor's role
ix   What have I taken on?

1 Paragraph A ....
2 Paragraph B ....
3 Paragraph D ....
4 Paragraph E ....
5 Paragraph F ....

 From *Instant IELTS* by Guy Brook-Hart © Cambridge University Press 2004 **PHOTOCOPIABLE**

Supported Open Learning

A   Having decided to study towards a Master's degree with the Open University, you may now be wondering what it will entail and what commitment it will require from you. Let's start with explaining how the Open University will support your learning. 5

B   The method of study you will use with the Open University is called 'supported open learning'. This means that the course is carefully structured and you are taken through the components step by step. Each course is made up of a number of components, 10 and could include: written texts, study guides, set books (which you will have to buy before the course begins), readers, videos, audio tapes, computer software, and CD-ROM. You will be learning mostly on your own, in your own time, and in the space that 15 you have organized yourself, but with the support of your tutor and services from the Open University.

C   Supported open learning involves you in becoming an active learner, taking responsibility for motivating yourself, pacing your studies, and 20 managing your workload to suit your own circumstances. There are deadlines to meet such as assignment submission and exam dates, but matters such as how, when and where you study are very much up to you. In order to learn effectively from 25 this method, you need to become actively involved in your own learning process. This means both assessing what you have learned as you go, and testing out new ideas and concepts. One way of doing so is by keeping in regular contact with your 30 tutor letting him or her know if you are experiencing difficulties with your studies, or are having problems that may affect your ability to study.

D   Most of you will have gained a first degree already and may feel that studying for a Master's 35 degree will entail more of the same. However, besides differences between the two levels of study, it may be several years since you completed your first degree and it is important to realize that your circumstances may have changed radically from 40 when you were last a student. Your experience of being a student this time around may be very different. The majority of students studying for a Master's degree with the OU completed their first degree as a full-time student at a traditional 45 university. Studying was their main occupation. This time, things may be very different. You may be in full-time employment, possibly in a position of some responsibility, which entails working long hours and perhaps bringing work home with you. 50 You may have a family and other domestic responsibilities. What you will definitely have less of, is spare time.

E   Students studying at a distance are expected to be able to cope with increased independent learning, 55 and be able to use their tutor as a resource rather than a provider of knowledge. Many courses include project work, which means planning and executing a small piece of research. Although your tutor will expect to see the plan for your project, and may 60 check up on your progress, there may not be an opportunity for lengthy discussions or feedback as your project develops.

F   You will have to organize your time and motivate yourself to keep to your timetable, if you 65 want to avoid last minute panics. Likewise, the amount of secondary reading you do will be your own responsibility and, if time is scarce, it can be tempting to cut corners and miss out on some essential background reading. One of the 70 advantages of supported open learning is that it allows you to have more autonomy as a student, and gives you the flexibility to study how, where, and, to some extent, when you choose to do so. The reverse side of the coin, however, is that you need self- 75 discipline in order to meet deadlines and submit work on time – you are responsible for your own learning.

Source: *Learning with the Open University starts here, 1999*

Questions 6–7

The list below gives some study requirements.
Which TWO are requirements for students following the Supported Open Learning method?
Choose TWO letters A–E.

A self-motivation
B regular attendance at classes
C working entirely alone
D deciding when to do work
E buying computer software

Questions 8–9

The list below gives some tutor's functions.
Which TWO are functions of Open University tutors?
Choose TWO letters A–E.

A teaching students what they need to learn
B organising students' studies
C monitoring students' progress
D answering students' queries and study problems
E maintaining students' interest in the subject

Questions 10–11

List two things mentioned in the passage which may limit your study time.
Use NO MORE THAN THREE WORDS from the passage for each answer.

10 ....

11 ....

Questions 12–15

Complete each of the following statements (Questions 10–13) with the best ending A–G from the box below.

12 Being an active learner means ....

13 Most students doing a Master's degree at the Open

   University will not be ....

14 You will be required to do some investigation when

   ....

15 If you are short of time, you may make the mistake of

   not ....

A doing project work.
B attending tutorials.
C doing necessary reading.
D completing work within time limits.
E supervising your own learning.
F studying full time.
G preparing for exams.

3 Follow-up

Speaking Module Part 2

Work in pairs to practise Part 2 of the speaking module. Each of you should choose one of the prompt cards and speak for one to two minutes about the topic. You have one minute to prepare what you are going to say and make a few notes.

A

> Describe a particularly good student you have known.
> You should say:
>   when you met them
>   what they were studying
>   what they do now
> and explain why that person was such a good student.

B

> Describe an educational course you have done.
> You should say:
>   what kind of course it was
>   where you did it
>   why you did it
> and explain what you liked and disliked about the course.

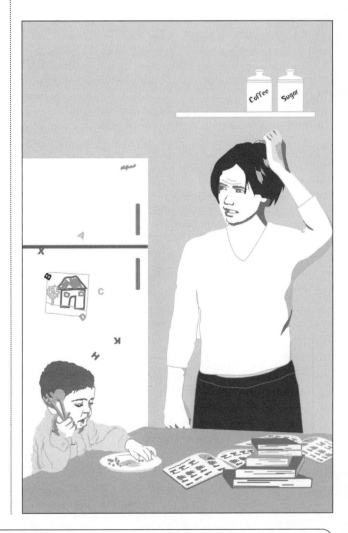

From *Instant IELTS* by Guy Brook-Hart © Cambridge University Press 2004 **PHOTOCOPIABLE**

Estimated class time: 1 hour 5 minutes

🕐 **Short of time? You could:**
- give your students Questions **11–16** for homework, having talked through the advice in the teacher's notes.
- do speaking module Part 2 in the following lesson.

1 ● Introduction *(20 minutes)*

Listening

For the complete recording script, see page 127.

Distance learning is when you study without normally meeting your teachers face-to-face: your input consists of such things as books, CD-ROM, materials delivered online and correspondence courses.
- After they have discussed and brainstormed the advantages and disadvantages in groups, get feedback from the whole class.
- Tell them they won't be able to predict the answers to all the questions on the recording. Where they can't predict the answer, they should try to predict the type of information required. Get feedback on this also, but don't give any indication of whether they have predicted correctly or not!

> **ANSWER KEY**
> 1 independent
> 2 other commitments / family life / job
> 3 any age
> 4 closely controlled
> 5 free flow
> 6 (more) ideas
> 7 motivation
> 8 supervised
> 9 real time / immediately
> 10 (educational) culture

- Finally, compare what they heard on the recording with what they brainstormed earlier.

2 Reading

Questions 1–5 *(20 minutes)*

When questions come before the passage, students are expected to read the questions first. It is worth studying the list of headings carefully before starting reading, so that they are familiar with the questions before looking for the answers.

Intermediate
- Elicit suggestions for the meanings of: *personal situation, taking charge, input* and *taken on*.
- Ask them to study the example and say why **vi** is the correct answer (line 19).
- Tell your students to work in pairs and explain briefly what they would expect to find in a paragraph with these headings *e.g. for heading (i) how studying will be different this time from the last time they did it.*

Advanced
- **Either:** As a memory game, you may ask them to study this for a minute and then ask them to write down all the headings they remember.
- **Or:** to sensitise them to how headings work, do **not** ask them to look at the list of headings first, but to read the passage and suggest their own headings of between 3 to 6 words for each paragraph.

- Tell them not to read the whole passage before starting on the questions, but to deal with the questions paragraph by paragraph.
- Point out that the headings are unlikely to repeat words from the passage, and they should concentrate on finding a heading which summarises the main idea of each paragraph.
- Encourage them to be flexible and change their minds if necessary.
- **A useful follow-up activity** to help your students understand how the passage is constructed is to ask them to **identify and highlight the topic sentence** in each paragraph – i.e. the sentence which carries the main idea or thrust of the argument in each paragraph *e.g. in paragraph **C** the first sentence.*

> **ANSWER KEY**
> **1** ix (lines 2–4)   **2** vii (lines 10–17)   **3** i (lines 41–43)
> **4** viii (lines 56–57)   **5** iv (lines 64–65)

Questions 6–11 *(10 minutes)*

For Question 6, students will have to scan the passage very quickly to identify where the Supported Open Learning method is explained *(Answer: paragraphs **B** and **C**)* and then read this part with care.

Intermediate
- Before they start, elicit suggestions for the meanings of *self-motivation, regular attendance* and *monitoring*.
- If you think your class needs it, ask them to explain all the alternatives in their own words.

Advanced
- You can point out that, when in doubt, a good technique is to eliminate the answers that are clearly wrong, thereby narrowing the choice.

> **ANSWER KEY**
> **6** A   **7** D in any order   **8** C   **9** D in any order
> **10** (full-time) employment   **11** family / domestic responsibilities in any order

- Elicit suggestions before they look for the exact answers in the passage *(they will be to do with work and home life).*
- Ask them to suggest a few synonyms for each of these, and then to scan the passage to find them.

Questions 12–15 *(5 minutes)*

Your students will still have to scan the passage to find where each of the questions is dealt with, and then read that section carefully.

> **ANSWER KEY**
> **12** E (lines 26–29)   **13** F (lines 43–53)
> **14** A (lines 57–59)   **15** C (lines 68–70)

3 Follow-up

Speaking Module Part 2 *(10 minutes)*

- Students should work in pairs and each student should take one of the prompt cards and prepare for about a minute before speaking.
- They then take it in turns to speak.
- Tell the partner whose turn it is to listen, to note down mistakes in his / her partner's English.
- When they have finished they should give each other feedback.
- They should also be ready to consult with you whether certain things are correct English or not.

1 Introduction

Below is some advice for people revising for exams. Work in pairs and sort the advice into things you should do and things you shouldn't do.

- give up your part-time job
- study in groups
- take plenty of notes
- do past exam papers
- work late at night
- continue your social life
- take a break every half hour

2 Reading

You will now read an article in which a university lecturer gives advice to students studying for history exams. Before you read, study Questions 1–7 so that you are familiar with them.

Try to answer the questions without looking up difficult words, as you would do in the test.

Questions 1–7

The passage on revising for exams has eight paragraphs (A–H).
Choose the most suitable headings for paragraphs B–H from the list of headings below. Write the appropriate numbers (i–xi) for each of them.

NB There are more headings than paragraphs, so you will not use all of them.

Example	Answer
Paragraph A	vii

i	Know when to stop	
ii	Make your studies amusing	
iii	Organise	
iv	Check your notes are accurate	
v	Read textbooks	
vi	Use various formats for your notes	
vii	Start early	
viii	Take mock exams seriously	
ix	Make sure you can answer every question	
x	Work out what to revise	
xi	Study with your colleagues	

1 Paragraph B ....

2 Paragraph C ....

3 Paragraph D ....

4 Paragraph E ....

5 Paragraph F ....

6 Paragraph G ....

7 Paragraph H ....

 From *Instant IELTS* by Guy Brook-Hart © Cambridge University Press 2004 **PHOTOCOPIABLE**

REVISING FOR EXAMS

The way to do well at History is to know which study techniques work best for you as an individual. Nevertheless here are some sensible guidelines that are worth following.

A Apply good study skills from the beginning of your 5 course, rather than seek magical solutions a few weeks before the exam. Ideally, every evening you should read through the notes you made that day, improving them and making sure they are useful. Then, every few months, go through all your notes – 10 this will make your final revision much easier. In this way, essential information will be committed to your long-term memory and will be readily recalled, even under stressful exam conditions. You will also avoid last-minute cramming, which is seldom useful. 15

B Make sure that you have a copy of the syllabus or course handbook. Check the format of your exam. How many papers? How many questions must be answered? Are there any compulsory sections? Sort out any external or personal problems that might 20 hamper your progress. If necessary talk with your tutor, student counselling service or doctor. From Easter cut out or cut down your weekend employment until after the exams.

C Listen to your teacher's advice on important areas or 25 likely questions. Select topics for revision. Decide what number you need to know about: for example if you are required to answer four questions, go through the papers of the last few years and make sure that you can answer five or six of them. If you 30 can answer them all, take care – you are probably working too hard.

D Do not work from poor material. Improve your notes by comparison with a friend's or read them alongside a textbook, making any additions and modifications 35 needed. Make sure that you understand them before you try to commit them to memory – if you don't the ideas simply will not stick. Underline, colour or highlight headings and key points.

E The more your notes are rewritten, the better you will 40 remember them. Summarise key information on each topic on one A4 page. Abbreviate again on small index cards: carry them round with you and learn them whenever you have a few spare minutes. If you are having difficulty remembering key quotes or 45 dates, write them out and put them in places around the house where you will see them frequently. Perhaps record them on tape. But remember to think actively about key issues as well as memorising information. Your aim should be to look at old, 50 familiar material in a new way.

F Working with a group (the right group for you) will enable you to share ideas, notes and books and can help alleviate boredom and stress. Revising in pairs is good, but working in groups of three or four is 55 better. The ideal is to meet for two or three hour sessions two or three times a week at home, school or college – look for a working environment with minimum distractions. Discuss questions or problems, do timed questions, read out answers for 60 group criticism, test each other, prepare outline answers.

G When your teachers give you practice exams to do in class time, enter into these wholeheartedly. They will help you assess your progress and familiarise you 65 with working under strict exam conditions. Afterwards, take note of the feedback you receive. Pinpoint the errors you made. Did you include too little information, misread the questions, run out of time? What does your mark tell you about your 70 revision techniques?

H Far more exams are failed because of too little work than too much. But often the brightest students work too hard at revision and worry unnecessarily. So take regular exercise, get plenty of sleep, maintain a 75 sensible social life. If you are an arch-worrier, then by all means carry on gentle revision until the last moment: you can't worry if your mind is occupied with something else. But remember that the aim is to reach your peak at the right time, so be sure not to 80 go into the exam room exhausted from overwork. Frenetic late-night cramming can be easily avoided by the sort of revision techniques outlined above.

Source: History Review, March 2001

Using NO MORE THAN THREE WORDS from the passage, answer the following questions.

8 When should you check what you have noted down earlier in the day?

9 Near the exam, what should you either reduce, or stop completely?

10 If you can answer all the questions from past exams, what is this often a sign of?

11 Where is a good place to write down brief notes?

12 What problems can be relieved by revising with other students?

Choose the appropriate letters A–D.

13 What is the main cause of poor performance in exams, according to the passage?

   A tiredness due to overwork

   B not studying enough

   C not getting enough exam practice

   D worrying about exams

14 According to the passage, when should you continue revising right up to the exam?

   A when you have not been working hard enough

   B if you suffer from exam nerves

   C when you cannot remember vital information

   D if your tutor advises you to do so

3 Follow-up

Vocabulary

Match the words from the passage in the column on the left with their synonyms on the right.

Paragraph A	1	go through	a enthusiastically
	2	cramming	b check, revise
Paragraph B	3	hamper	c evaluate, check
	4	cut out	d find exactly
	5	cut down	e information about how well you have done something
Paragraph F	6	alleviate	f make more difficult
Paragraph G	7	wholeheartedly	g your best performance
	8	assess	h read wrongly
	9	feedback	i reduce
	10	pinpoint	j relieve, reduce
	11	misread	k stop
Paragraph H	12	peak	l studying hard just before an exam
	13	overwork	m working too hard

Discussion

Work in groups of three or four. Discuss these questions:

● Which advice do you agree with?

● How would you advise someone to revise for language exams?

"I had all the right answers, but I had them in the wrong order."

Estimated class time: 55 minutes

🕐 **Short of time? You could:**
- give your students Questions **8–14** for homework, having talked through the advice in the teacher's notes.
- do the follow-up activities in the following lesson.

1 Introduction *(10 minutes)*

> **ANSWER KEY**
> **Possible answers:** Should do: everything on list except work late at night. It's OK to continue your social life at a sensible level.

2 Reading

- This passage provides an opportunity for intensive and detailed reading. Superficially, it will give students few problems, but particularly when answering Questions **1–7** they will have to read it very carefully indeed.
- Your students should try to answer the questions in spite of unfamiliar vocabulary, as they would have to in the test. For this reason the vocabulary exercise is printed after the questions. However, you can do the vocabulary exercise beforehand if you feel it will help your students to deal with the tasks with more confidence.

Questions 1–7 *(20 minutes)*

- Students should study the list of headings before they start reading. Even if the meanings of the headings seem obvious to them, ask them to work in pairs and paraphrase them in order to familiarise themselves with what they will have to look for.
- To do this type of question they may have to read some of the paragraphs more than once. They needn't answer the questions chronologically, and they should be ready to change their minds.
- They can deal with the paragraphs and headings they find obvious first, thereby reducing the choice for the ones they find more confusing.

Intermediate
- Ask them to read paragraph **A** (which is the example) and find all the clues in the paragraph which give **vii** (*Start early*) as the answer e.g. *from the beginning, rather than a few weeks ... before the exam, every evening, every few months, long-term memory, avoid last-minute cramming.*
- Ask them to work in pairs and look at paragraph **B**. Tell them the answer is either **iii**, **ix** or **x**. They should read the paragraph carefully and decide which is the best heading – **ix** may seem the best answer if they only look at the first 2 lines, so encourage them to look for the global meaning of the paragraph (*Why might they need to talk to their doctor, cut down part-time employment?*).
- Follow the same procedure for paragraph **C** – this time offer them just **ix** and **x** (if they choose **ix**, ask why it says, 'Listen to your teacher's advice').
- Ask them to work alone and choose a heading from the list for paragraph **D**. Get feedback from the whole class, but don't tell them the correct answer. Write their suggestions on the board (they will probably suggest **iv**, **v** and **vi**). Ask them to do the same for paragraph **E**, and ask them to decide whether this helps them to get the correct answer for paragraph **B**.
- Ask them to work through the final 3 paragraphs alone, and then discuss their answers in small groups.
- Get feedback from the whole class.
- Finally, if they have some answers wrong, tell them the correct answers and elicit from them why these answers are correct by finding evidence in the paragraphs.

Advanced
An alternative way of dealing with these questions in class in order to sensitise them to how headings work would be *not* to ask them to look at the list of headings first, but to read the passage and suggest their own headings for each paragraph.
- Tell them they should think of headings of 5 words maximum which will summarise the general idea or main point of each paragraph.
- When they have finished, you may discuss the relative merits of their suggestions.
- Finally, they can compare their ideas with the headings given in Questions **1–7** and do the exercise.

> **ANSWER KEY**
> 1 Paragraph B – iii (organise)
> 2 Paragraph C – x (work out what to revise)
> 3 Paragraph D – iv (check your notes are accurate)
> 4 Paragraph E – vi (use various formats for your notes)
> 5 Paragraph F – xi (study with your colleagues)
> 6 Paragraph G – viii (take mock exams seriously)
> 7 Paragraph H – i (know when to stop)

Questions 8–12 *(5 minutes)*

If they remember in which paragraph the information was mentioned, they should go straight there. Otherwise, scan to locate the information.

> **ANSWER KEY**
> 8 every evening (line 7)
> 9 (your) weekend employment (line 23)
> 10 working too hard (line 32)
> 11 small index cards (lines 42–43)
> 12 boredom (and) stress (line 54)

Questions 13–14 *(5 minutes)*

Questions 13 and 14 both deal with points in the last paragraph, so they do not need to read the whole passage again.
- Ask your students to paraphrase 'poor performance in exams' and, if they don't remember where it is dealt with, to scan for mention of it and then read in detail from there.
- Ask students what the key words in Question **14** are (*continue revising right up to the exam*) and to paraphrase these – they then scan if necessary and read in detail to answer the question.

> **ANSWER KEY**
> 13 B (lines 72–73)
> 14 B (lines 76–78)

3 Follow-up

Vocabulary *(10 minutes)*

> **ANSWER KEY**
> 1 b 2 l 3 f 4 k 5 i 6 j 7 a
> 8 c 9 e 10 d 11 h 12 g 13 m

Discussion *(5 minutes)*

Students work in groups of 3 or 4 to discuss the questions.

1 Introduction

Match the names of these animals with the pictures.

1 toad
2 beetle
3 wallaby
4 dingo
5 pheasant
6 bandicoot
7 flea
8 moth
9 mussel

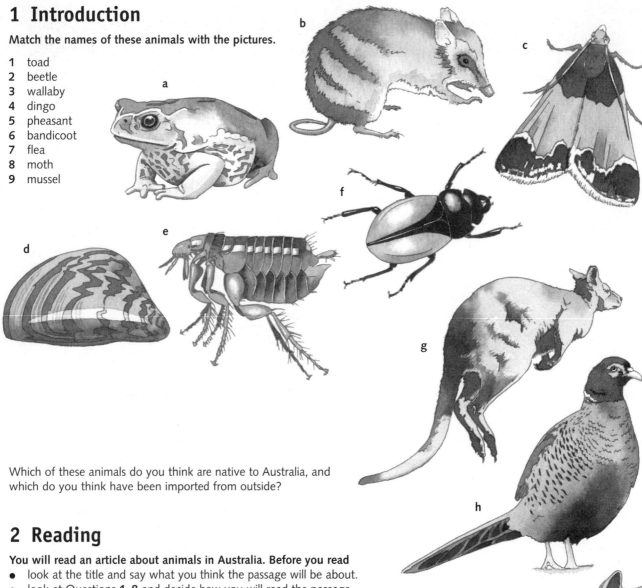

Which of these animals do you think are native to Australia, and which do you think have been imported from outside?

2 Reading

You will read an article about animals in Australia. Before you read
- look at the title and say what you think the passage will be about.
- look at Questions **1–8** and decide how you will read the passage to answer them: will you scan, skim or read in detail?

Try to answer the questions without looking up difficult words, as you would do in the test.

Questions 1–8

Classify the following animals as:

A native to Australia.
B introduced as a form of biocontrol.
C introduced for other reasons, or by accident.

Example	Answer
Rabbit	C

1 cane toad
2 quoll
3 dingo
4 pheasant
5 bilbie
6 Spanish flea
7 cactoblastis
8 zebra mussel

From *Instant IELTS* by Guy Brook-Hart © Cambridge University Press 2004 **PHOTOCOPIABLE**

Australia Fights Back Against Invader Species

1 The nearly one-foot, 10-pound cane toad might strike visitors to Australia as just one more example of the country's notoriously bizarre fauna. In reality, this amphibian is not native, but one of many human-introduced species currently ravaging the ecosystem 5 'down under'.

2 Originally from South America, the cane toad was introduced by the sugar industry in 1935 in a misguided attempt to control two sugarcane pests: the Grey Backed cane beetle and the Frenchie beetle. 10 Unfortunately, no one noticed that the toad doesn't generally eat these bugs, though it successfully devoured other native insects to the point of extinction. Moreover, the poisonous toad instantly kills any predator that attempts to eat it, particularly the quoll, 15 Australia's marsupial cat, and giant native lizards.

3 The cane toad is not an isolated incident for Australia, but disturbingly typical of the ecological problems on the island continent. Australia's native wildlife is almost entirely endemic, having evolved in 20 virtual isolation from the rest of the world. The fauna includes koalas, kangaroos, duck-billed platipi, wallabies – but no placental mammals. The first introduction by humans was probably dingoes, brought by early aborigines in the form of pets almost 25 7,000 years ago. Larger introductions began with European colonization in the mid-1800s. Colonists thought the ecosystem 'badly flawed' because it lacked the wildlife to which they were accustomed, and so stocked the country with deer, rabbit and 30 pheasant to provide favorite foods, foxes for hunting, and a wide variety of other species for sheer familiarity. The effort proved a disastrous success.

4 One notable disaster occurred in 1859 when British colonist Thomas Austin imported 24 rabbits 35 for sport hunting. The population quickly exploded to more than 200 million, devouring native grasses, brush and tree sprouts, and turning grassland and farmland into dusty desert. Cattle, goats and sheep exacerbated the problem with relentless grazing, 40 resulting in diminished food, and fewer hiding places for small marsupials such as the hare wallaby, the bilbie and the bandicoot. Their populations crashed.

5 Troubles continued from another introduced predator, the European Red Fox, which proved itself 45 highly effective, preying on native mammals too big to hide in the ground and too small to defend themselves, like wallabies and rat-kangaroos. Wherever foxes and rabbits have appeared, native mammals have vanished. 50

6 Many efforts have been undertaken to control these invaders, particularly the rabbits, which cause approximately $20 million annually in agricultural damage alone. Exclusion fences and poisoning require constant maintenance, however, and are often 55 overwhelmed by the rabbits' astronomical reproduction rates. In the 1950s, the government released a disease called Myxomatosis, which killed 90 percent of the animals it infected – an ideal solution until the rabbits recovered and developed a 60 resistance. Moreover, the disease carrier, a flea, can't survive in the arid conditions of much of the country, and so the Australian Animal and Plant Control Commission was forced to introduce an even hardier Spanish flea. 65

7 While larger animals may be the most obvious alien invaders, they are hardly alone. According to the Australian government, 'almost 10 per cent of all the plant life in Australia is alien to the country'. The most infamous example – the prickly pear cactus – 70 was brought over in the early 1900s as a hedging plant to keep livestock under control. It quickly ran wild, overtaking the Australian desert, but was eventually checked by the introduction of the Cactoblastis, a cactus-hungry Mexican moth. 75

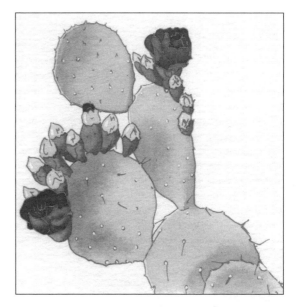

8 The European Zebra Mussel, which caused billions of dollars of damage to America's Great Lakes, has now shown up in two of Australia's ports, most likely transported there by foreign ships. The Australian government responded by chlorinating the 80 entire marina where the mussels were sighted. While it is still not clear if the chlorination killed all the Zebra Mussels, it did kill vast amounts of native coral, fish and marine invertebrates.

9 As long as wildlife still exists, some people may 85 wonder why we should care if one animal or plant replaces another? The answer is common sense: introduced wildlife often changes habitat and sets in motion negative long-term effects. It will ultimately mean extinction of Australia's exotic wildlife, and 90 destruction of a major ecosystem.

Source: *The Environmental Magazine, November, 2000*

Questions 9–12

Look at the following animals or plants and the list of problems below.
Match each animal or plant with the problem it has caused. Choose the appropriate letters A–G.

NB There are more problems than plants and animals, so you will not use them all.

9   cane toad
10 rabbit
11 fox
12 prickly pear cactus

A   causes illness in humans
B   destroys fertile land
C   eats native mammals
D   has made some native mammals extinct
E   has caused an increase in the numbers of sugar-cane pests
F   poisons its attackers
G   spreads across desert

Questions 13–16

Choose the best answer A–D.

13 Why did early British settlers consider the Australian environment imperfect?
  A   The native animals couldn't be eaten.
  B   The native animals were unfamiliar to them.
  C   Some native animals were dangerous.
  D   Native animals prevented successful farming.

14 How have farm animals caused a decline in the numbers of native mammals?
  A   They have destroyed their habitat.
  B   They have eaten all their food.
  C   They have attacked native mammals.
  D   They have spread disease.

15 What was the result of the appearance of the European Zebra Mussel?
  A   Harbours in Australia were damaged.
  B   It attacked other sea-life in the area.
  C   Other marine life was poisoned.
  D   Ships from other countries were disinfected.

16 What is the purpose of the article?
  A   To describe the animals living in Australia.
  B   To criticise early colonists' behaviour in Australia.
  C   To suggest people should be cautious about introducing new species to Australia.
  D   To explain how Australian animals are incompatible with modern agriculture.

3 Follow-up

Vocabulary

Find words in the passage which mean:

Paragraph 1
a   give people the impression of being
b   strange
c   causing great damage to
Paragraph 2
d   mistaken
e   eaten
f   animal which hunts other animals
Paragraph 3
g   unique to an area
h   imperfect
i   filled or supplied
Paragraph 4
j   significant
k   made worse
l   non-stop and intense
Paragraph 5
m   disappeared
Paragraph 6
n   defeated
o   tougher, stronger
Paragraph 7
p   foreign
q   worst
r   farm animals
Paragraph 8
s   appeared
t   seen

Speaking Module Part 2

Work in pairs to practise Part 2 of the speaking module.
● Look at the following prompt card and decide together what you can say (you can still do this even if you come from different countries, but your answers will be different). Make a few notes to help you.
● Speak for one or two minutes about the subject to a student from another pair, and also listen to what he / she says.
● Discuss what you find difficult about doing this speaking task, and what you could do to improve your performances.

Describe a serious environmental problem in your country. You should say:
  what the problem is
  what has caused it
  why it is serious
and explain what is being done about the problem.

Speaking Module Part 3

Discuss with your partner – give reasons and examples to support your ideas:
● Why is it important to protect native animals?
● Are some wild animals more important than others?

Estimated class time: 1 hour 30 minutes (Intermediate)
1 hour 25 minutes (Advanced)

⏱ Short of time? You could:
- give your students Questions **13–16** for homework, having talked through the advice in the teacher's notes.
- do the follow-up activities in the following lesson.

1 Introduction (5 minutes)

> **ANSWER KEY**
> 1a 2f 3g 4i 5h 6b 7e 8c 9d

2 Reading
- This passage provides useful opportunities for your students to improve their scanning skills by looking for particular pieces of information, and for reading in detail where appropriate.

Before reading (10 minutes)
- Ask them to discuss the title and predict what problem the passage will describe.
- Ask them if they know of instances in their own countries of problems caused by species introduced from outside. (In Britain, a well-known example is the North-American grey squirrel which has displaced the native red squirrel.)
- They then should look briefly at the questions which follow the passage and say what type of questions they are (*Answer: classification, matching and multiple choice*). When they do the test, the types of question should determine the way they read the passage.
- Elicit how Questions **1–8** should be answered (*by scanning for the names of the animals and then reading what is said about each of them carefully*). This will increase their confidence in their ability to deal with particular questions without struggling through the whole passage first.
- Use the example – ask them to scan to find where rabbits are mentioned in the passage and to say why **C** is the correct answer.

Questions 1–8 (12 minutes)
- Ask your students to spend 2 or 3 minutes finding and underlining where these animals are mentioned.
- Tell them **not** to try to answer the questions at this stage.
- Be strict about the time limit, and then ask your students to check what they have done in pairs.
- They read just the parts they have underlined carefully to classify the animals.
- After checking the answers, ask them how they feel about dealing with a passage in this way, and whether they think it is an efficient way of answering this type of question. Let them suggest other ways of doing it and discuss the merits of these with them.

> **ANSWER KEY**
> **1** B (lines 7–9) **2** A (lines 15–16) **3** C (lines 23–26)
> **4** C (lines 30–33) **5** A (lines 42–43) **6** B (lines 63–65)
> **7** B (lines 73–75) **8** C (lines 76–79)

Questions 9–12 (10–15 minutes)

Ask your students if they would deal with Questions 9–12 in a similar way.

Intermediate
They can look at the alternatives in the box and brainstorm ways of expressing the same ideas using other words e.g.

'Causes illness in humans' could be 'infects people'.
- Tell them to scan the passage for the names of the animals and then to read those sections carefully.

Advanced
- You can divide the class into those who say 'yes' when you ask if these questions should be dealt with in a similar way, and those who say 'no' and who have an alternative suggestion as to how to deal with them. Invite the 'yeses' to compete with the 'nos' to find who answers the questions more correctly (or more quickly if they all get the answers correct!).
- Point out to the 'yeses' that they should study the box of alternatives carefully before scanning the passage again.
- Give them a time limit of 4 minutes to do this.

> **ANSWER KEY**
> **9** F (lines 14–15) **10** B (lines 38–39) **11** C (lines 45–46)
> **12** G (lines 72–73)

Questions 13–16 (10 minutes)
- Remind your students that multiple-choice questions are dealt with chronologically in the passage, and that they will have to deal with the whole passage again.
- They will have to scan for synonyms of words in the stem – for example, *settlers* is not the word used in the passage. Ask them to look in the first 4 paragraphs and say what word is used (*Answer: colonists*).
- The correct alternative will not repeat the exact words of the passage either.
- If they are unsure which to choose, they should narrow the choice by eliminating alternatives they are sure are wrong.

> **ANSWER KEY**
> **13** B (lines 27–29) **14** A (lines 39–41) **15** C (lines 81–84)
> **16** C (lines 88–89)

After reading (5 minutes)
Point out to your students that if they have scanned the passage, they probably haven't read all of it carefully, but they have managed to answer the questions. If your students feel unsatisfied by this, they can read the whole passage again at home.

3 Follow-up

Vocabulary (10 minutes)

a strike visitors ... as	h flawed	o hardier
b bizarre	i stocked	p alien
c ravaging	j notable	q most infamous
d misguided	k exacerbated	r livestock
e devoured	l relentless	s shown up
f predator	m vanished	t sighted
g endemic	n overwhelmed	

Speaking Module Part 2 (15 minutes)
- Put students in pairs to brainstorm some of the things they can mention.
- Then give them 2 or 3 minutes to work alone and prepare some brief notes.
- Remix the class into new pairs and ask them to give their talks to each other.
- They should not interrupt each other but afterwards give feedback on what did or did not go well.

Speaking Module Part 3 (10 minutes)
- Students work in pairs to discuss the questions.

1 Introduction

Look at the pictures and answer the questions below.
- What do you think is happening in the two pictures?
- Why do you think people are so interested in Mars and other planets?
- Why do people want to know if there is life in other parts of the universe?

2 Reading

You will read an article which describes how many astronomers in the 19th century became convinced that there was life on Mars.
- Before you read, look at the question-types which follow the article and decide how you should read the article in order to answer them.
- Try to answer the questions without looking up difficult words, as you would do in the test.

From *Instant IELTS* by Guy Brook-Hart © Cambridge University Press 2004   **PHOTOCOPIABLE**

CANALS on MARS

A Popular interest in Mars, the 'Red Planet', is long-established, but has enjoyed two dramatic flowerings, one in the 1890s and the other a century later.

B Any speculation about life on Mars, then or now, is part of a long discussion on 'the plurality of worlds'. Pluralists believe that there are other worlds apart from ours which contain life – an idea that had its origins in classical Greece. In the 19th century, the new science of astrophysics suggested that large numbers of stars in the sky were similar to the sun in their composition – perhaps they too were circled by planetary systems. Nearer to home Mars, our neighbour in the solar system, seemed to offer the evidence the pluralists had lacked until then.

C The characteristics of Mars' orbit are such that its distance from Earth varies considerably – from 34.5 to 234.5 million miles. From an astronomer's standpoint it was particularly well-placed for observation in 1877, 1892 and 1909. Observations in each of these years intensified discussion about possible life on Mars.

D If life, intelligent or otherwise, were to be found on Mars then life on Earth would not be unique. The scientific, theological and cultural outcomes of such a discovery could be stupendous. In 1859, Fr. Angelo Secchi, director of the Vatican observatory and a confirmed pluralist, observed markings on the surface of Mars which he described as *canali*, 'channels'. The fateful word had been launched on its career, although there was little immediate development from Secchi's work.

E In 1877 another Italian, Giovanni Schiaparelli, one of Europe's most distinguished astronomers, also observed the *canali*, but he added the refinement that they appeared to be constituents of a system. Other astronomers observed features that might be continents or seas; Schiaparelli confirmed these findings and gave them finely sonorous classical names such as Hellas, Mare Erythraeum, Promethei Sinus.

F Although Schiaparelli was cautious in his public statements, recent research suggests that he was a pluralist. Certainly his choice of familiar place names for the planet, and his publicising of the *canali* network, encouraged pluralist speculation. Inevitably, *canali* was soon being translated into English as 'canals' rather than 'channels'. In 1882 Schiaparelli further fuelled speculation by discovering twin canals, a configuration which he named 'gemination'; he described no fewer than sixty canals and twenty geminations.

G Some of Schiaparelli's findings were confirmed by the astronomers Perrotin and Thollon at Nice Observatory in 1886. In 1888, however, Perrotin confused matters by announcing that the Martian continent of 'Libya' observed by Schiaparelli in 1886 'no longer exists today'. The confusion grew; two prestigious observatories in the US found in one case no canals, in another a few of them but no geminations, and no changes to Libya.

H While the observers exchanged reports and papers, the popularisers got to work. They were generally restrained at first. The British commentator Richard Proctor thought that the canals might be rivers; he was among the first to suggest that a Martian canal would have to be 'fifteen or twenty miles broad' to be seen from Earth. The leading French pluralist, Camille Flammarion, published his definitive *La Planète Mars* in 1892: 'the canals may be due ... to the rectification of old rivers by the inhabitants for the purpose of the general distribution of water ...'. Other commentators supposed the 'canals' might be an optical illusion, a line first advanced by the English artist Nathaniel Green, teacher of painting to Queen Victoria and an amateur astronomer.

I The canals debate might have levelled off at this point had it not been for the incursion of its most prominent controversialist – and convinced pluralist – Percival Lowell. Lowell, an eminent Bostonian, entered the astronomical argument after a career in business and diplomacy, mainly in the Orient. He may not have brought an entirely objective mind to the task. Even before he started observing he had announced that the canals were probably 'the work of some sort of intelligent beings'.

J The newly-arrived popular press was very willing to report Lowell's findings and views; canal mania grew apace. By 1910 Lowell had reported over 400 canals with an average length of 1,500 miles. He wrote plausibly about the Martian atmosphere and the means by which the canals distributed water from Mars' polar caps to irrigate the planet before evaporation returned moisture to the poles. This water cycle appealed to popular evolutionism which perceived Mars as an old, dying world trying to avert its fate by rational and large-scale engineering – this was, after all, an age of great canals: Panama, Dortmund-Ems, Manchester, Corinth.

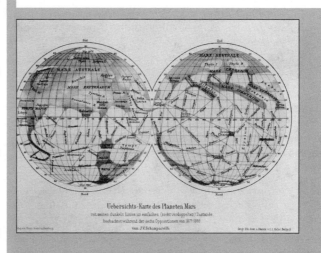

Schiaparelli's map of the canals of Mars

Source: *History Today*, July, 1998

Questions 1–2

Choose the appropriate letters A–D.

1 What do pluralists believe?
A There is life in other parts of the universe.
B Other stars have planets.
C There is life on Mars.
D There are many other stars like the sun.

2 What circumstance helped astronomers to study Mars in the late 19th century?
A A new science had developed.
B People believed that there was life on other planets.
C Mars was close to Earth on several occasions.
D There was popular interest in Mars at the time.

Questions 3–8

Look at the following lists of astronomers and thinkers (Questions 3–8) and ideas about Mars (A–I).
Match each astronomer with the idea or ideas he expressed.

NB There are more ideas than astronomers and thinkers, so you will not need to use them all.

3 Schiaparelli
4 Perrotin
5 Proctor
6 Flammarion
7 Green
8 Lowell

A A particular geographical feature of Mars has disappeared.
B People think they can see canals, but they do not really exist.
C Life on Mars has become extinct.
D Some *canali* are organised in pairs.
E The *canali* are used to carry water from colder areas to warmer areas.
F The canals must be extremely deep to carry so much water.
G The inhabitants of Mars are still building canals.
H The Martians have adapted natural features to meet their needs.
I The *canali* might be very wide and not artificial.

Questions 9–14

Do the following statements agree with the opinions expressed by the writer of the passage?
Write

YES if the statement agrees with the information.
NO if the statement contradicts the information.
NOT GIVEN if there is no information on this in the passage.

9 Discussion about whether there is life on Mars forms part of a long tradition.
10 The belief that life existed on Mars was encouraged by a translation error.
11 The limitations of 19th century technology encouraged the idea that there were canals on Mars.

12 All Lowell's statements about Mars were based on what he was able to see.
13 Lowell's investigations of Mars aroused little interest outside the scientific community.
14 Lowell's theory about how canals on Mars were used may have been inspired by fashionable ideas of the time.

3 Follow-up

Vocabulary

Match the words on the left from the passage with their definitions on the right.

1	apace (line 76)	a	controlled, unemotional
2	avert (line 83)	b	convincingly
3	fuelled (line 43)	c	encouraged
4	outcomes (line 22)	d	point of view
5	plausibly (line 78)	e	prevent
6	prestigious (line 50)	f	quickly
7	restrained (line 54)	g	results
8	standpoint (line 16)	h	with a good reputation

Discussion

What do you think? First, work alone and circle:
1 if you completely disagree with the statement.
2 if you disagree to some extent.
3 if you neither agree nor disagree.
4 if you agree to some extent.
5 if you completely agree with the statement.

1 There is life in other parts of the universe. 1 2 3 4 5
2 The Earth has, in the past, been visited by beings from outer space. 1 2 3 4 5
3 If there is life in other parts of the universe, we should try to make contact with it. 1 2 3 4 5
4 Discovering life in other parts of the universe could help us to understand our own origins. 1 2 3 4 5
5 Money spent on trying to discover life in other parts of the universe is money well spent. 1 2 3 4 5
6 If we find other inhabitable planets, we should try to colonise them. 1 2 3 4 5
7 If we discovered life on other planets, it would change the way we look at the world and the universe. 1 2 3 4 5

Now work in pairs and compare your opinions.

From *Instant IELTS* by Guy Brook-Hart © Cambridge University Press 2004 **PHOTOCOPIABLE**

Estimated class time: 1 hour 5 minutes

🕐 **Short of time? You could:**

- give your students Questions **9–14** for homework, having talked through the advice in the teacher's notes.
- do the follow-up activities in the following lesson.

1 Introduction *(5 minutes)*

The first picture shows a still from the film *The War of the Worlds* based on the novel by H.G. Wells in which Martians invade Earth. The second shows the Mars exploration rover, *Opportunity*.

2 Reading

Before reading *(7 minutes)*

Students should look at the question-types first. Elicit what types of reading techniques would be suited to each.
(Answers:1–2 reading in detail, 3–8 scan for names and then read in detail, 9–14 read in detail).

Questions 1–2 *(8 minutes)*

When the passage starts with multiple-choice questions, they should:

- Skim the passage quickly to get a general idea of the subject-matter.
- Return to the stem of the multiple-choice question, and scan the passage for where this is dealt with.
- Once there, they should read in detail in order to choose the correct answer.
- Give students between 3 minutes (Advanced) or 5 minutes (Intermediate) to skim the passage before dealing with the first 2 questions.

ANSWER KEY
1 A (lines 5–7)
2 C (lines 14–18)

Questions 3–8 *(15 minutes)*

- Before reading the passage, ask them to look at the list of ideas in the box and make sure they know what each of them means.
- Give students 2 minutes (for Advanced) or 3 minutes (for Intermediate) to scan and underline or highlight where the astronomers and thinkers are mentioned in the passage.
- Tell them **not** to try to answer the questions at this stage.
- Be strict about the time limit, and then ask your students to check what they have done in pairs.
- Once they have identified where each of the people is mentioned, they should read just those parts of the passage carefully in order to match the people with the ideas.

ANSWER KEY
3 D (lines 41–43)
4 A (lines 47–49)
5 I (lines 55–58)
6 H (lines 59–62)
7 B (lines 62–64)
8 E (lines 79–81)

Questions 9–14 *(10 minutes)*

- For these questions they will have to read through the entire passage again – the answers will come in the same order in the passage.

Intermediate

- Help students to identify the key words in the first sentence, then tell them to pass their eye quickly over the passage to see if they can find them.
- Ask them to read the sentences they find carefully to see if they deal with the subject of the sentence in the question.
- Scanning the passage like this will help them complete the task more quickly.

Advanced

- Because the answers are given in chronological order, students can try to look for answers to 2 questions at a time.
- If they find the answer to the second question, they should check back to make sure the first one is **NOT GIVEN**.

A lot of students find the concept of NOT GIVEN very difficult to grasp.

- Remind students that some of the sentences in the questions are **not addressed** in the passage.
- When they think they have found a sentence that deals with the subject of a question, they need to read it very carefully and bear in mind that it may not express agreement OR disagreement.

Advanced

In the IELTS test, students will have 5–6 minutes for this part of the test, so to replicate test conditions, you could give students 6 minutes to complete the task (or 1½ minutes per question).

ANSWER KEY
9 YES (lines 4–7)
10 NOT GIVEN
11 NOT GIVEN
12 NO (lines 72–74)
13 NO (lines 75–76)
14 YES (lines 81–82)

3 Follow-up

Vocabulary *(10 minutes)*

ANSWER KEY
1f 2e 3c 4g 5b 6h 7a 8d

Discussion *(10 minutes)*

If your students have difficulty discussing these points, you could try to stimulate them with some of these questions:

- What do you think are the chances of discovering intelligent life elsewhere in the universe?
- Do you think it would be friendly or hostile?
- What would be the advantages of colonising another planet?
- Have we benefited at all from space research so far?

1 Introduction

Discuss the following question in pairs.

How do university students in your country spend their money?

Put the following things in order from the one students spend most on to the one they spend least on.

accommodation ☐ children ☐

food, bills, household goods ☐ course expenditure ☐

essential travel ☐ entertainment ☐

non-essential travel ☐ other things ☐

2 Analysing the chart

Work in pairs. Look at the task and chart below.
1 Say what the chart shows.
2 Explain what changes have occurred.
3 Say what the general trend is.

> The chart shows student expenditure over a three-year period in the United Kingdom. Write a report for a university lecturer describing the information shown below. You should write at least 150 words.

Student expenditure (aged under 26 in higher education) United Kingdom*

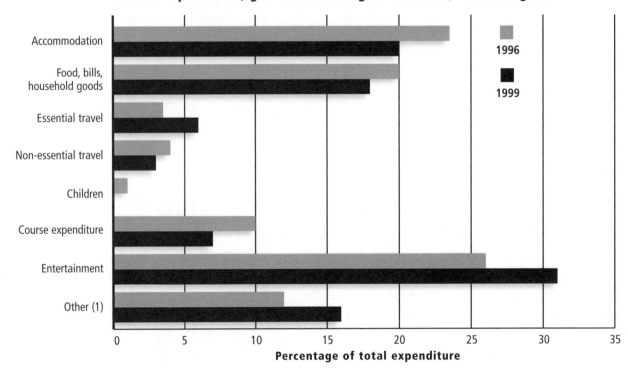

Percentage of total expenditure

(1) Includes non-essential consumer items and credit repayments
* Source: Student Income and Expenditure Survey, Department for Education and Employment

3 Describing trends

Study these three sentences and then write three similar sentences about other parts of the chart.

1 During the period 1996 to 1999, students <u>spent 3% less on</u> accommodation, which <u>fell from 23% to 20% of</u> total expenditure.
2 There was <u>a 3% decrease</u> in spending on accommodation, which <u>fell from 23% to 20%</u>.
3 Spending on accommodation <u>went down by 3% from 23% to 20%</u>.

 From *Instant IELTS* by Guy Brook-Hart © Cambridge University Press 2004 **PHOTOCOPIABLE**

4 Using prepositions

Complete the following sample report by putting a preposition in each space.

> A *The chart shows the changes which took place* **(1)** ....in....... *student spending in the United Kingdom* **(2)** .... *the three-year period from 1996 to 1999.*
>
> B *Students spent 3% less on accommodation, which fell* **(3)** .... *23%* **(4)** .... *20% of total expenditure, and there was a 2% decrease* **(5)** .... *spending on food, bills and household goods, which fell from 20% to 18%. At the same time course expenditure went down* **(6)** .... *3% from 10% to 7%. Children, who constituted 1%* **(7)** .... *students' expenditure in 1996, are not represented in 1999.*
>
> C *On the other hand, there was a 5% growth* **(8)** .... *spending on entertainment, which stood* **(9)** .... *26% of total expenditure in 1996 but rose* **(10)** .... *31% in 1999. Spending on other non-essential items and credit repayments grew* **(11)** .... *4% to make* **(12)** .... *16% of total expenditure. Spending on essential travel went up* **(13)** .... *3% while non-essential travel underwent a 1% fall.*
>
> D *Overall, with the exception of expenditure* **(14)** .... *travel, the most significant general change was a shift* **(15)** .... *spending on essential items* **(16)** .... *spending on non-essential items.*

Now read the sample report again and highlight any words or phrases which you think are useful when writing reports.

5 Structuring a report

Work in pairs. Study the sample report again. Say which paragraph each of these things is dealt with in. Write the paragraph letter in the boxes.

1 a detailed account of the changes in essential expenditure ☐
2 a detailed account of the changes in non-essential expenditure ☐
3 a generalisation about the trend illustrated in the chart ☐
4 mention of items which do not coincide with the trend ☐
5 the purpose of the chart ☐

6 Writing task 1

Do the following writing task.

> The table shows sources of student income over a ten-year period in the United Kingdom.
> Write a report for a university lecturer describing the information shown below.
> You should write at least 150 words.

Sources of student income (aged under 26 in higher education)

United Kingdom				Percentages
	1988/89	1992/93	1995/96	1998/99
Student loan	–	8	14	24
Parental contribution	32	26	22	16
Grant	38	38	23	14
Earnings	6	7	14	12
Other	24	21	27	34
All income (= 100%) (£ per student per year at July 1999 prices)	4,395	4,048	4,951	5,575

Source: Student Income and Expenditure Survey, Department for Education and Employment

You should:
a **make notes on:**
  ● what the table shows.
  ● the general trend.
  ● the differences in detail.

b **organise your notes so that your report will have a similar structure to the one in Activity 5.** (4 minutes)
c **write your report using words and phrases you highlighted in the sample report.** (14 minutes)
d **check what you have written.** (2 minutes)

Estimated class time: 1 hour 5 minutes

1 Introduction (5 minutes)

- Students' answers will vary, but accommodation and food are likely to be the greatest expenses for most.

2 Analysing the chart (10 minutes)

Question 1

This requires the title of the chart *and* the period it covers.

Intermediate

Ask your students to express the title in a grammatical sentence *e.g. The chart shows the expenditure of students under 26 in higher education in the United Kingdom during the period from 1996 to 1999.*
With a weak class write the sentence above on the board with the prepositions omitted and ask them to fill the gaps.

Advanced

Ask your students to do a bit more than repeat the vocabulary of the title.
For *student expenditure* elicit *the amount students spend.*
Elicit *items.*
Ask them to write down a suitable sentence *e.g. The chart shows changes in the amount students spent on different items between 1996 and 1999.*

Question 2

Be careful as your students may lose interest if more than 5 minutes is spent on this.

Question 3

They may have some difficulty in detecting a general trend. If so:
- ask them to put the items in the chart into 2 categories: necessary expenditure and unnecessary expenditure.
- ask them if they can draw a conclusion.

> **ANSWER KEY**
> The main trend is a shift in spending from essential expenditure to non-essential expenditure.

NB It is worth reminding them not to try to explain the trend. In the test they will only have to report the data presented to them.

3 Describing trends (10 minutes)

Ask your students to use these sentences as models and to write other similar sentences based on information from the chart.

Advanced

Elicit synonyms of *decrease*, *fell* **and** *went down*, **and antonyms where appropriate before they start writing.**

4 Using prepositions (15 minutes)

One of students' main difficulties in describing trends is the use of prepositions. If necessary, explain the following:
in – a change in (category) *e.g. a fall in living standards.*
of – noun + of + amount *e.g. a fall of 20%.*
by – verb + by + amount *e.g. it rose by 15%.*
at – a fixed number *e.g. the record stood at 250 kph.*

> **ANSWER KEY**
> **2** during / over **3** from **4** to **5** in **6** by **7** of **8** in
> **9** at **10** to **11** by **12** up **13** by **14** on **15** from/in **16** to

Intermediate

You can help them by:
- doing spaces **2–6** together as a whole-class activity.
- listing the prepositions they need on the board.

As an optional follow-up activity, you can
- ask them to highlight useful words and phrases which they can use in other writing tasks, then report back to the class some of the phrases they have highlighted.
- ask them to make a list of synonyms of *increase* and *decrease* (noun and verb) from the sample report. (*Answers: fell, went down, growth, rose, grew, went up, fall.*)

Intermediate

- Check they know the other forms of the irregular verbs: *fell, went down, grew, rose.*
You can extend your students' vocabulary here by:
- asking them to look up *constituted, underwent,* and *shift.*
- asking them to write sentences using these words in their notebooks.
- drawing their attention to *made up* and *stood at* and asking them to write sentences using these words.

Advanced

This is essential vocabulary for writing task 1. You can extend this work by:
- asking them to put the words into categories – noun and verb.
- pointing out to them that all the verbs here are intransitive and eliciting transitive equivalents *e.g. raise, reduce etc.*
For more work on this, please see *Words at Work,* Cambridge University Press (1996), pages 60–65.

5 Structuring a report (5 minutes)

Your students will gain marks in the test if their answer shows clear organisation and paragraphing.

Intermediate

If your students are uncertain about paragraphing you can:
- explain that written English should be divided into paragraphs to make it easy to read.
- tell them to start a new paragraph each time they move on to a new aspect of the subject they are writing about.

> **ANSWER KEY**
> **Paragraph 1** B **2** C **3** D **4** D **5** A

6 Writing task 1 (20 minutes)

- Do the first step in class. Ask your students to work in pairs or small groups and study the table. They should discuss how student income has changed over the ten-year period. Ask them to work out what the general trend in student income has been (*Possible answer: a general move from depending on grants and parental contributions towards more independence in the form of loans and earnings*).
- Elicit an overall plan for the task (*Possible answer: What the graph shows, sources of income which have fallen, sources of income which have risen, increase in total income, general trends*).
- Ask them to work in pairs to organise the information to fit their plan.

1 Introduction

Work in pairs and discuss the following questions:

1 Which partner in a marriage is more likely to do each of these household tasks in your country?
2 Why is this so?

Task	Males	Females
Cooking, baking, washing up		
Cleaning, house tidying		
Gardening, pet care		
Care of own children and play		
Maintenance, odd jobs, DIY		
Clothes, washing, ironing, sewing		

2 Analysing the chart

In the IELTS test it is important to show you understand the information in a chart, so take time to study it carefully.
Work in pairs and look at the task and chart below.

1 Say what the chart shows.
2 Explain what the differences are.
3 Say what, in general, men do more and what, in general, women do more.
4 Calculate how much time men spend on household tasks, and how much time women spend on household tasks in total and write a sentence comparing them.

> The chart shows the division of household tasks by gender in Great Britain.
> Write a report for a university lecturer describing the information shown below.
> You should write at least 150 words.

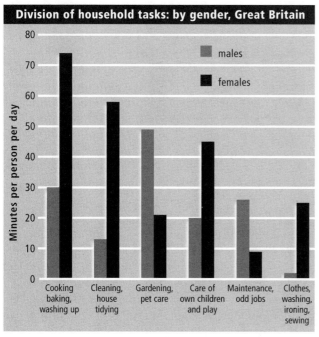

Division of household tasks: by gender, Great Britain

■ males
■ females

Minutes per person per day

Cooking, baking, washing up · Cleaning, house tidying · Gardening, pet care · Care of own children and play · Maintenance, odd jobs · Clothes, washing, ironing, sewing

Source: Office for National Statistics on behalf of the Controller of Her Majesty's Stationery Office.

3 Making comparisons

Study these three sentences and then write three similar sentences about other parts of the chart.

1 Women spend *over twice as much time* doing kitchen tasks *as* men.
2 Men spend 30 minutes a day doing kitchen tasks *whereas / while* women spend 74 minutes a day.
3 Women are *more active* in the kitchen *than* men (74 minutes a day for women *as opposed to* 30 minutes for men).

4 Sample report

Look at the following sample answer to the writing task. Write a word in each space.

The chart shows the average number of minutes per day men and women in Great Britain spend on jobs around the house.

In total, men spend just (1) ....*over*..... two-and-a-half hours on household tasks whereas women spend slightly (2) .... than four hours. Women spend more than (3) .... as much time doing kitchen tasks such as cooking and washing-up (4) .... men (74 minutes for women as opposed (5) .... 30 minutes for men). Women are also more active in cleaning the house – it takes 58 minutes of their day compared (6) .... minutes for men – and childcare, where women put in more than twice as (7) .... time as men.

On the other hand, men are (8) .... active in gardening and pet care, where they spend twice as (9) .... as women, and maintenance and DIY, on which they spend 14 minutes more (10) .... women. Women account for almost all the time spent on washing and ironing clothes. This takes them 25 minutes, (11) .... men spend just 2 minutes on this task.

Overall the figures show that women spend more time on routine domestic chores than men, (12) .... men do more household maintenance, gardening and pet care.

- Now, read the sample report again and highlight any words or phrases which you think are useful when writing reports.
- Does the report give any reasons or explanations for the information, or express any opinions?

5 Structuring a report

Look at the sample report again and decide the order in which each of these points is dealt with. Write a number in each box.

A a detailed explanation of the figures putting emphasis on men ☐

B a detailed explanation of the figures putting emphasis on women ☐

C a general statement of the types of tasks women do more of and men do more of ☐

D a statement about the total time men and women each spend on household tasks ☐

E the purpose of the chart ☐

6 Writing task 1

Do the following writing task.

> The chart shows the participation by young people in sports by gender in Great Britain. Write a report for a university lecturer describing the information shown below. You should write at least 150 words.

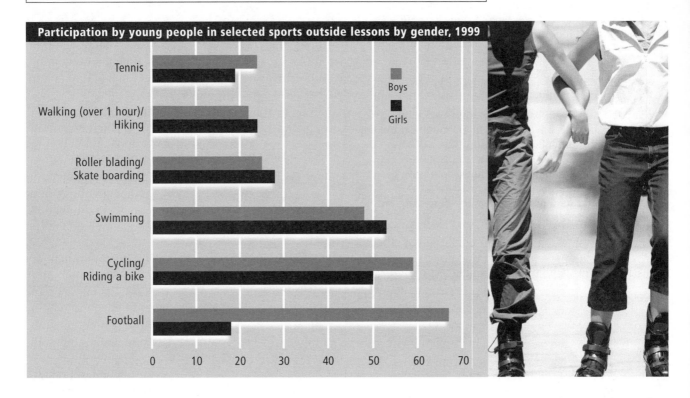

Participation by young people in selected sports outside lessons by gender, 1999

You should:

a make notes on:
- what it shows.
- the general trend.
- the differences in detail.

b organise your notes so that your report will have a similar structure to the one in Activity 5. *(4 minutes)*

c write your report using some of the words and phrases you highlighted in the sample report. *(14 minutes)*

d check what you have written. *(2 minutes)*

From *Instant IELTS* by Guy Brook-Hart © Cambridge University Press 2004 **PHOTOCOPIABLE**

Estimated class time: 1 hour

🕐 **Short of time? You could:**
- give Activities **5** and **6** for homework, and do the Optional activity in the following lesson.

1 Introduction *(10 minutes)*

Be careful about sexist remarks which may irritate some students. With a mixed-nationality class it may be interesting to tease out cultural differences – so if you think it is profitable, develop the activity into a class discussion.

2 Analysing the chart *(12 minutes)*

Question 1

Intermediate

- Ask them to express the title in a sentence *e.g. The chart shows the division of household tasks between males and females in Great Britain.*
- With a weak class write the sentence above on the board with the prepositions omitted and ask them to fill the gaps.

Advanced

- Ask them to do a bit more than repeat the vocabulary of the title.
- For *household tasks* elicit *jobs in the home* or *chores around the house.*
- Elicit *share* for *division.*
- Ask them to write down a suitable sentence *e.g. The chart shows how men and women share chores around the house in Great Britain.*
- By paraphrasing vocabulary they are showing they know what it means and will get higher marks in the test.

Question 2

Be careful as they may lose interest if more than 5 minutes is spent on this.

Questions 3–4

ANSWER KEY
3 Men spend more time on non-routine jobs which may require tools, such as maintenance and DIY, and on tasks outside the house, such as gardening and pet care whereas women spend more time on routine jobs within the home.
4 In total, men spend 138 minutes on household tasks per week and women 231 minutes.

As an oral follow-up, you can make obviously false statements and ask your students to correct them.

Intermediate

You can concentrate on simple comparisons of adjectives and adverbs. Say things like:
'Men do more work in the kitchen than women'. Your students should respond with either 'Women do more work than men', or 'Men do less work than women', or 'Men do not do as much work as women'.

Advanced

You can make more complex comparisons, e.g.:
'Men do far more cleaning than women',
'Women do not spend nearly as much time looking after clothes as men'.
These sentences are fairly complex so you may have to write them on the board.

3 Making comparisons *(10 minutes)*

Charts are an efficient way of presenting, contrasting and comparing information, which your students, when writing a report, will have to put into words. For this they will need to manage:
- comparison of adjectives and adverbs.
- other structures which express contrast.

You can explain to them that *while* is a synonym of *whereas* when you want to contrast 2 sentences which contain different, but not contradictory, facts.
For revision of comparison of adjectives and adverbs, please see *Advanced Grammar in Use*, **Units 88–89**.

4 Sample report *(15 minutes)*

Intermediate

Intermediate students may find this activity difficult in places. You can help them by:
asking them to look at the example (**Q1**) and the chart, so that they see how the report and the chart are connected.
doing Qs **2–6** together as a whole class, so that they realise the type of words or information required.
asking them to work in small groups to do the other questions.
If they suggest different answers for a question, write up the suggestions on the board without telling them which is correct and ask **them** to choose the correct answer.
You could also suggest alternatives for them to choose from – e.g. (**1**) over / above.

ANSWER KEY
2 less   3 twice   4 as   5 to   6 to / with   7 much   8 more
9 long   10 than   11 while / whereas   12 while / whereas

- When highlighting useful words and phrases, you can tell your students that they should be looking for language which may be useful to them when they have to do a writing task.
- Ask them to report back some of the phrases they have highlighted – this will help **all** your students realise what aspects / components of sample answers are useful when writing their own answers.

Intermediate

You can help by suggesting phrases such as *in total*, *women are more active in cleaning the house* (which provides a nice variation from *women spend more time cleaning ...*), and *account for.*

5 Structuring a report *(3 minutes)*

Your students will gain marks if their answer shows clear organisation and paragraphing as this makes it easier for the reader to follow. This task is designed to help them with their planning.

ANSWER KEY
1 E   2 D   3 B   4 A   5 C

6 Writing task 1 *(10 minutes)*

Your students could do this for homework.

1 Introduction

Work in small groups and discuss these questions for *your* country:

1   Is going to the cinema becoming more or less popular? Why?
2   Where are most of the films shown in your country made? Why do you think this is?
3   Are many of the films made in your country, or are they mostly imported?
4   What type of film is most popular?
5   Do people watch films in the original version or are they translated?

2 Analysing the charts

Look at the task below and the charts. Work in pairs and discuss your answers to these questions – you will not have to write the answers.

1   Say what the charts show.
2   Explain the main differences and similarities in market share between the two countries.
3   Say how the cinema market has evolved in the two countries during the period shown.
4   Say what the general trends are.

> The charts show the share of the Australian and British cinema markets in 2001
> and cinema admissions in Britain and Australia from 1980 to 2001.
> Write a report for a university lecturer describing the information.
> You should write at least 150 words.

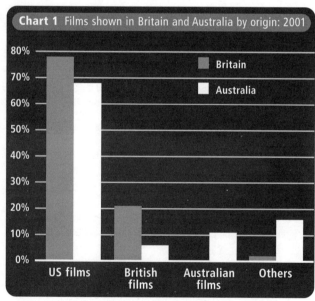

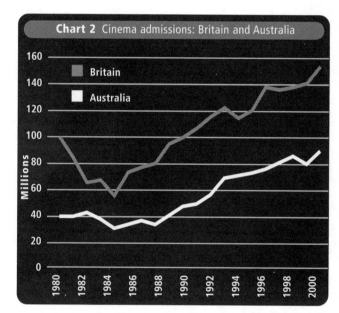

Various sources (both charts)

3 Giving accurate information

Each of these five points gives information which is not correct. Look at the charts again and rewrite the sentences to express correct information.

1   Whereas 67% of the films shown in Australia were made in Britain, 77% of the films shown in the United States were Australian.
2   Cinema admissions rose steadily in both Britain and Australia in the early 1980s. However, the increase was far more dramatic in Australia than in Britain.
3   The cinema projection industry recovered in both countries and by 2001 film admissions had reached more than 160 million in Britain and almost 80 million in Australia.
4   After the United States, Britain makes more films than any other country in the world.
5   The cinema has always been more popular in Britain than Australia.

4 Vocabulary in the report

Read this sample report and fill each space by choosing one of the words in the box.

| accounted | compared | dropped | stood | fell |
| increased | opposed | predominated | recovered | |

Chart 1 shows the cinema industry's share of the Australian and British cinema market by origin in 2001. In both countries, films made in the USA **(1)** .... with 77% of the market in Britain **(2)** .... to 67% in Australia. British films **(3)** .... for 21% of the British cinema market and 6% of the Australian market. On the other hand, while 11% of the films shown in Australia were Australian, no Australian films were shown in Britain. Films from other countries had 16% of the market share in Australia as **(4)** .... to just 2% in Britain.

Chart 2 shows cinema admissions in Britain and Australia since 1980. In both countries cinema admissions **(5)** .... in the mid-1980s. In Australia admissions **(6)** .... from just under 40 million in 1980 to about 30 million in 1984–6 while in Britain the decrease was far more dramatic (from 100 million in 1980 to less than 60 million in 1984). Since then, however, the industry has **(7)** .... in both countries. In 2001, cinema admissions in Britain **(8)** .... at over 150 million, whereas in Australia they reached 90 million.

Overall, the charts show that the cinema has **(9)** .... in popularity in both countries over the last 15 years, but that the origins of the films projected in Australia are more diverse than in Britain.

Now read the sample report again and highlight any words or phrases which you think are useful when writing reports.

5 The structure of the report

Look at the sample report again and decide which paragraph deals with each of these points. Write a number in each box (first paragraph = 1, second paragraph = 2, 3rd paragraph = 3).

A   a general view of what both charts show ☐

B   a comparison of the evolution of the cinema market in Britain and Australia ☐

C   a comparison of the world cinema industry's share of the Australian and British markets ☐

6 Writing task 1

Do the following writing task. You should spend about 20 minutes on this task. You should:

1   analyse the charts – decide what they show, the general trend and the differences in detail. Make notes while you are doing this and organise your notes so that your report will have a similar structure to Activity 4. (4 minutes)

2   write your report using the sample report as a model. (14 minutes)

3   check what you have written. (2 minutes)

> The charts show the number of people using the Internet from 1995 to 2002 and Internet users in the world in 2003.
> Write a report for a university lecturer describing the information below.
> You should write at least 150 words.

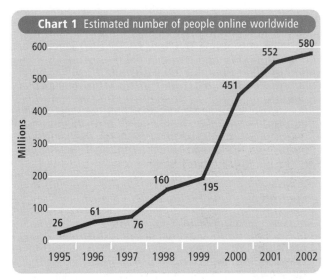

Chart 1 Estimated number of people online worldwide

Source: Nua Internet survey, 2003

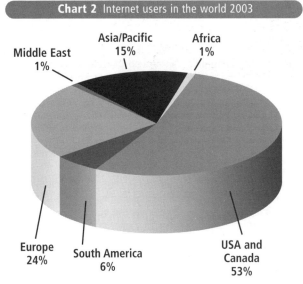

Chart 2 Internet users in the world 2003

Source: Nua Internet survey, 2003

Estimated class time: 1 hour 20 minutes

🕐 **Short of time? You could:**
- ask students to complete steps 2 and 3 of the writing task for homework.

1 Introduction (10 minutes)

If you have a mixed nationality class, you can ask them to compare the cinema market between countries.

2 Analysing the charts (15 minutes)

Question 1

This requires the titles of the charts *and* the period they cover.

Intermediate

Ask your students to express the titles in grammatical sentences e.g.:
- *Chart 1 shows the origin of films shown in Britain and Australia in 2001.*
- *Chart 2 shows cinema admissions in Britain and Australia from 1980 to 2001.*
- With a weak class write the sentence above on the board with the prepositions omitted and ask them to fill the gaps.

Advanced

Ask your students to do more than repeat the vocabulary of the title.
- For Chart 1 elicit *where the films shown in Britain and Australia were made.*
- For Chart 2: *the evolution of the cinema market in Britain and Australia from 1980 to 2001* or *ticket sales in Britain and Australia from 1980 to 2001.*

Question 2

Elicit that they should concentrate on Chart 1.

ANSWER KEY

Main similarities: the dominance of US-made films.
Main differences: US films were even more popular in Britain than Australia, while Australians watched British films, no Australian films were shown in Britain. Australians watch more films from other parts of the world.

Question 3

Elicit that they should concentrate on Chart 2.

ANSWER KEY

Cinema attendance fell in both countries in the early 80s (more dramatically in Britain) to reach a low point in 1984, and has since risen in both countries.

Question 4

In the actual report, answering this question will fulfil the function of providing a brief general summary at the end. They should look at both charts to answer the question.

ANSWER KEY

The origins of films shown in Australia are more diverse than in Britain, and after a fall in the early 80s, the cinema has increased in popularity in both countries.

3 Giving accurate information (15 minutes)

Students should be careful with Questions 4 and 5.
- Neither chart shows which countries make the most films.
- Neither chart shows the popularity of the cinema – it may be that the population of Britain is higher than Australia.

Students should only report what the graphs show and not offer reasons or interpretations.

Intermediate

Elicit:
- the meanings of: *rose steadily, increase, dramatic* and *recovered.*
- the opposites of *rose* and *increase – fell* and *decrease.*
- the infinitives and past participles of *rose* and *fell.*

Advanced

Write *rose, increase* and *steadily* on the board and ask them to brainstorm and list other words which can be used to describe trends or changes in their notebooks.

ANSWER KEY
Possible answers:
1 Whereas 67% of the films shown in Australia were made in the United States, 77% of the ones shown in Britain were from / made in the United States.
2 Cinema admissions fell in both Britain and Australia in the early 1980s. However, the decrease was far more dramatic in Britain than in Australia.
3 The cinema projection industry recovered in both countries and by 2001 film admissions had reached more than 150 million in Britain and over 80 million in Australia.
4 After the United States, British films were the most popular, both in Britain and Australia.
5 Cinema admissions have always been higher in Britain than Australia.

4 Vocabulary in the report (15 minutes)

Before they complete the sample report, ask them to work in pairs and read it carefully while looking at the charts. Tell them to point out to each other how the report reflects the charts.

Intermediate

Ask them to look up the words in the box before completing the report.

ANSWER KEY
1 predominated **2** compared **3** accounted **4** opposed / compared
5 dropped / fell **6** fell / dropped **7** recovered **8** stood **9** increased

5 The structure of the report (5 minutes)

Students will gain marks in the test if their reports have a clear structure. Point out that the final paragraph which describes general trends acts as a summary and conclusion.

ANSWER KEY
A 3 **B** 2 **C** 1

6 Writing task 1 (20 minutes)

Do step 1 in class.
- Elicit *online* i.e. *connected to the Internet.*
- Ask them to decide on a structure for the report *e.g. What Chart 1 shows, what Chart 2 shows, overall trend for each.*

1 Introduction

Discuss in small groups:

1 Which is your favourite advert?
2 Which do you hate most?
3 Have you ever bought anything as a result of advertising?
4 Why do you think advertising is so effective?
5 How do you think adverts for newspapers and magazines are produced?

2 Understanding the task

Work in pairs and look at the task below and the diagram.
- Discuss how you would describe the process of producing an advertisement.
- As you work, write brief notes **on each stage of the diagram**.

> The diagram shows the process by which advertisements are produced.
> Write a report for a university lecturer describing the information shown below.
> You should write at least 150 words.

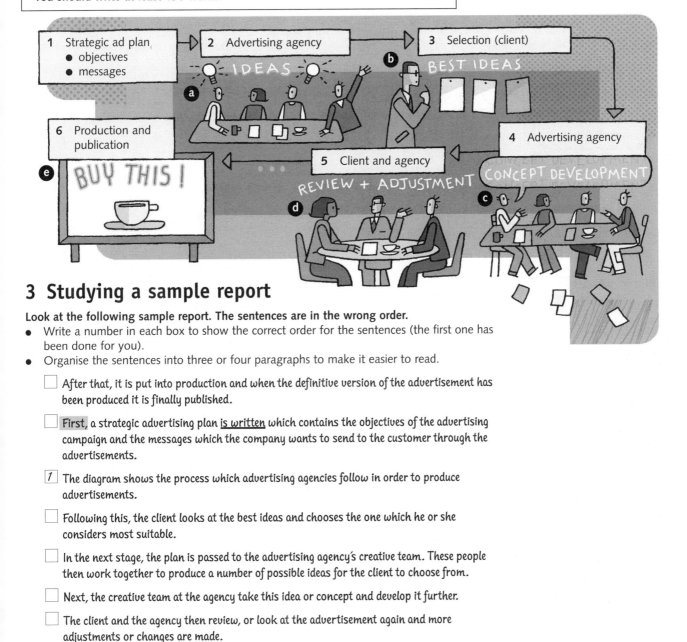

3 Studying a sample report

Look at the following sample report. The sentences are in the wrong order.
- Write a number in each box to show the correct order for the sentences (the first one has been done for you).
- Organise the sentences into three or four paragraphs to make it easier to read.

☐ After that, it is put into production and when the definitive version of the advertisement has been produced it is finally published.

☐ First, a strategic advertising plan is written which contains the objectives of the advertising campaign and the messages which the company wants to send to the customer through the advertisements.

☐1 The diagram shows the process which advertising agencies follow in order to produce advertisements.

☐ Following this, the client looks at the best ideas and chooses the one which he or she considers most suitable.

☐ In the next stage, the plan is passed to the advertising agency's creative team. These people then work together to produce a number of possible ideas for the client to choose from.

☐ Next, the creative team at the agency take this idea or concept and develop it further.

☐ The client and the agency then review, or look at the advertisement again and more adjustments or changes are made.

4 Studying the language

Read the sentences from the sample report again and:
- highlight or underline the verbs in the passive (the first has been done for you as an example).
- highlight in a different colour or circle the words or phrases used to show the order in which things are done (the sequencers). The first has been done for you as an example.

5 Using the passive

The passive is often used in reports which explain processes, especially when the process is more important than the people who carry out the process. If you feel confident about using the passive, you should use it in the IELTS test.
Rewrite the paragraph on the right by putting the verbs into the passive.

> Before they publish advertisements, advertising agencies test them on small groups of people. When they have done this, they analyse the results of the tests. They then adjust the advertisements and finally they send them for publication.

6 ⏺ Listening

Listen to a university lecturer explaining to graduate students one way in which the process of research is carried out. Complete the diagram below by writing ONE OR TWO WORDS in each space.

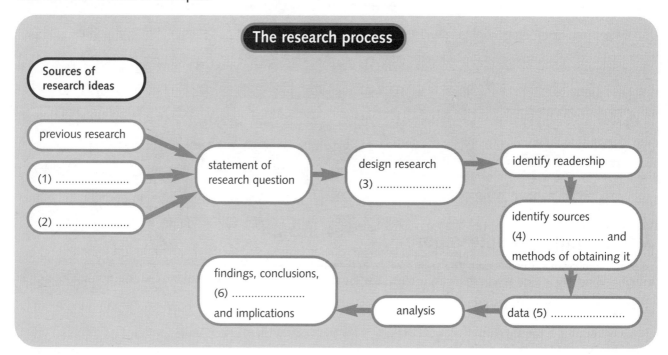

The research process

- Sources of research ideas
- previous research
- (1) ....
- (2) ....
- statement of research question
- design research (3) ....
- identify readership
- identify sources (4) .... and methods of obtaining it
- data (5) ....
- analysis
- findings, conclusions, (6) .... and implications

7 Writing task 1

Do the following writing task. You should spend about 20 minutes on this activity. You should:
- study the diagram – decide what it shows and how you will put the steps into words. (4 minutes)
- refer to the sample report in Activity 3, and use the 'sequencers' you highlighted there, and some verbs in the passive.
- write your report using the sample report as a model. (14 minutes)
- check what you have written. (2 minutes)

> The diagram in Activity 6 shows one process by which research is carried out. Write a report for a university lecturer describing the information shown. You should write at least 150 words.

 From *Instant IELTS* by Guy Brook-Hart © Cambridge University Press 2004 **PHOTOCOPIABLE**

Estimated class time: 1 hour 15 minutes

🕐 **Short of time? You could:**
- give Activity **7** for homework.

1 Introduction *(10 minutes)*

If your class is mixed nationality, they can answer Questions 1 and 2 by describing advertisements from their own countries.

2 Understanding the task *(15 minutes)*

Intermediate

You can help your students to get started by:
- eliciting the meanings of *strategic ad plan*, *objectives* (the aim of the advertisement) and *messages* (the message the advertiser wants people to receive).
- For step 2, you can ask: *What do you think a creative team is?* (Answer: people who work together to produce / create ideas).
- For step 3, elicit *choose* as a synonym of *select*. Then ask who does it (*the client*) and then elicit the complete sentence: *The client then chooses the best idea.*

Advanced

- Before they start, ask your students to look briefly at the diagram and brainstorm vocabulary which may be useful *e.g. advertising campaign, image, consumer, target audience etc.*
- When they start to explain the steps of the diagram, ask them to paraphrase the vocabulary rather than repeat it.
- To do this, give an example: *The strategic advertising plan outlines the aims which the advertising campaign hopes to achieve.*
Your students will get higher marks in the test if they use their own words rather than just repeating words lifted from the diagram.

3 Studying a sample report *(10 minutes)*

ANSWER KEY
2 First, a strategic...
3 In the next stage, the plan... (**paragraph 2**)
4 Following this, the client...
5 Next, the creative team... (**paragraph 3**)
6 The client and the agency...
7 After that, it is put... (**paragraph 4**)

Intermediate

If your students are uncertain about paragraphing you can:
- explain that written English should be divided into paragraphs to make it easy to read.
- Each time they move on to a new aspect of the subject they are writing about, they should start a new paragraph.
- As a rule-of-thumb, the first paragraph in this case can be one sentence, but most paragraphs should contain 2–4 sentences.
- Since this particular report is one continuous process, the paragraph divisions will be fairly arbitrary.
They will get higher marks in the test if their writing is clearly paragraphed.

Advanced

Optional extra activity
With a confident class which produced good ideas for vocabulary in Activity 2, you can:
- compare the words and phrases they thought of with the ones in these sentences.
- ask them to rewrite the sentences using their vocabulary, where they think it will improve the report *e.g. First a strategic advertising plan is written outlining the aims which the advertising campaign hopes to achieve.*

4 Studying the language *(5 minutes)*

Point out to your students that they should not use the passive excessively in this type of writing or it becomes tiresome to read. However, the style of a written report should be moderately formal and impersonal, so the passive is often suitable.

Intermediate

The aim of this and the following exercise is to remind students of the passive form. If necessary, see *English Grammar in Use* – **Units 41–44.**

Advanced

- Draw your students' attention to the sequencers and point out that these are in many cases different from the linkers used in discursive writing. Encourage them to copy them into their notebooks.
- Ask your students to look at the verb tenses – they will see that the present simple is used mainly, but elicit why a present perfect is used in the last sentence (*for something done at an unspecified time before the present*).

ANSWER KEY
Verbs in the passive: is put into production / has been produced / it is ... published / is written / the plan is passed;
Sequencers: After that / finally / first / Following this / In the next stage / then / Next / then

5 Using the passive *(10 minutes)*

Advanced

If you think your students would benefit from more advanced work on passives than this, see *Advanced Grammar in Use* **Units 31–32.**

ANSWER KEY
Before advertisements are published, they are tested on small groups of people. When this has been done, the results of the tests are analysed. The advertisements are then adjusted and finally they are sent for publication.

6 🎧 Listening *(15 minutes)*

For the complete recording script see page 127.
This listening activity should put the writing task which follows in context and help your students to understand the diagram and process.

ANSWER KEY
1 personal experience   2 curiosity   3 methodology
4 of information/data   5 collection   6 recommendations

7 Writing task 1 *(10 minutes)*

This task can be done for homework but the following preparation can be done in class:
- Ask students to work in pairs and talk through the diagram.
- Remind them that they only have to report the information in the diagram and not the extra information in the listening activity.

1 Introduction

Look at the pictures and discuss the questions in pairs.

- What aspects of childhood are shown?
- How has childhood changed in the last 100 years?

2 Analysing the question

Work in pairs or groups of three.
- Read the following writing task and underline the key words and phrases.
- Answer the two questions below.

> Modern lifestyles mean that many parents have little time for their children. Many children suffer because they do not get as much attention from their parents as children did in the past.
> To what extent do you agree or disagree?
> You should write at least 250 words.

- What is the idea you are expected to discuss in your answer?
- What should you do if you completely agree with the question?

3 Brainstorming ideas

Work in pairs.
- Brainstorm your arguments and examples.
- List as many ideas as you can think of.

4 Studying a sample answer

Read the following sample answer.
- Look at the words or phrases in capitals. Choose the word or phrase which sounds more formal by underlining it (as in the example).
- Rewrite the final paragraph in a more formal style.

Example	Answer
1	SAY/ARGUE

1 People who (1) SAY/ARGUE that nowadays parents give less attention to their children than in the past are (2) FREQUENTLY/OFTEN looking back to a (3) SHORT/BRIEF period of time in the twentieth century when (4) MOTHERS/MUMS in middle-class families (5) REMAINED/STAYED at home to look after their children. What these people are (6) SUGGESTING/ SAYING is that women nowadays should not go out to work.

2 (7) THE FACT OF THE MATTER IS THAT/ACTUALLY in (8) MOST/THE MAJORITY OF families in the past both parents worked (9) MUCH LONGER HOURS/MORE than they do nowadays. What has changed is that now in most countries their children (10) ATTEND/GO TO school rather than also working themselves. In that sense they may (11) SEE LESS OF/HAVE LESS CONTACT WITH their parents.

3 Nowadays, as a result of (12) ACQUIRING AN EDUCATION/ GOING TO SCHOOL, children come into contact with teachers who (13) NATURALLY/OF COURSE have to explain why some of their students are failing. What teachers come up with are (14) LOTS OF/ FREQUENT stories of parents who are (15) SIMPLY/ JUST too busy for their (16) CHILDREN/ KIDS. And (17) IF CHILDREN ARE NOT SUPERVISED BY THEIR PARENTS/IF PARENTS DON'T KEEP AN EYE ON THEIR CHILDREN, they will often (18) DO BADLY/ UNDERPERFORM at school. However, (19) FAILURE AT SCHOOL/ACADEMIC FAILURE is nothing new even when one or both parents are at home. If children (20) ARE NEGLECTED/DON'T HAVE ATTENTION GIVEN TO THEM by their parents, they will suffer.

4 I guess children probably had more problems in the past when they and their parents had to work non-stop just to get by. These days, the law looks after children and they can go to school, so children have lots more chances than they ever had before.

5 Analysing the sample answer

Read the sample answer again and complete these notes. This will give you a plan for the sample answer.

> *Paragraph 1: idea that parents had time for children in past mistaken —*
> (1) ....
> *Paragraph 2: (2) .... — now children go to school — not work*
> *Paragraph 3: parental neglect noticed nowadays by teachers because*
> *children in contact with teachers —*
> (3) ....
> *Paragraph 4: children suffered more in past*
> (4) ....

6 Emphatic language

Look at these two sentences from the sample answer.

What	these people	are suggesting	is that	women nowadays should not go out to work.
What	teachers	come up with	are	frequent stories of parents who are too busy for their children.

These are emphatic ways of saying:
- These people are suggesting that women nowadays should not go out to work.
- Teachers come up with frequent stories of parents simply too busy for their children.

Using this structure makes your arguments sound more convincing to the reader.

Rephrase these sentences in the same way to make them more emphatic:
1 Adults enjoy complaining about the behaviour of their children.
2 Parents often demand that schools take responsibility for bringing up their children.
3 Schools discover that many people make very poor parents.
4 Teachers think that they should just teach children their subject.
5 Parents find that badly-behaved children are often given lower marks.

7 Writing task 2

Do the following writing task. You should spend about 40 minutes on this task. You should:
- analyse the question. (1–2 minutes)
- brainstorm as many ideas as you can. (2 minutes)
- make a plan for the answer. Decide how many paragraphs you will need and choose ideas from the list you have just brainstormed. In your plan, note down examples you want to use as well. (2 minutes)
- write your answer following your plan. While writing your answer, try to use some conditional sentences and the type of emphatic language you looked at in Activity 6. Keep the sample answer in front of you as a model. (30 minutes)
- check your work carefully for mistakes. (4 minutes)

> People nowadays work hard to buy more things. This has made our lives generally more comfortable but many traditional values and customs have been lost and this is a pity.
> To what extent do you agree or disagree?
> You should write at least 250 words.

Estimated class time: 1 hour 10 minutes

Short of time? You could:
- give Activities **6** and **7** for homework.

1 Introduction (10 minutes)
Encourage your students to concentrate on the second question.

2 Analysing the question (5 minutes)
- It is important to analyse the question beforehand – candidates lose marks if they don't answer the question **exactly**.

ANSWER KEY
They should underline: Many children suffer because they do not get as much attention from their parents as children did in the past.

---

3 Brainstorming ideas (10 minutes)
Brainstorming is an essential part of preparing to write an answer. Many answers fall down because candidates run out of ideas. To practise this:
- Tell them to think of as many ideas as possible.
- Tell them not to discuss or evaluate ideas at this stage – just list them. Give them 5 minutes to do this.
- Get feedback from the whole class and put all their ideas on the board.

Intermediate

You can ask them 1 or 2 questions to get them started e.g.:
Did both parents generally work in the past?
What do people do now which takes up so much time?

Advanced

When they have finished brainstorming you can go a stage further and ask them to list vocabulary connected with their ideas.
To get them started, for how children suffer elicit:
juvenile delinquency
underperformance at school

---

4 Studying a sample answer (15 minutes)
A more formal academic register will improve your students' marks in the test.

Intermediate

You can simply point out that longer, less familiar words are often more formal.
NB In 'Latin' countries students will often find Latin-derived words more familiar and in English these are more formal.

Advanced

You can point out that generally (but by no means always):
longer words are more formal than short ones *e.g. frequently vs often*.
less usual words are more formal than more common words *e.g. brief vs short*.
single words are more formal than colloquial phrases or phrasal verbs *e.g. underperform vs do badly*.
contractions are less formal (and therefore to be avoided in this type of writing).

ANSWER KEY
Suggested answers:
1 argue **2** frequently **3** brief **4** mothers **5** remained
6 suggesting **7** The fact of the matter is that **8** the majority of
9 much longer hours **10** attend **11** have less contact with

---

12 acquiring an education **13** naturally **14** frequent **15** simply
16 children **17** if children are not supervised by their parents
18 underperform **19** academic failure **20** are neglected
Suggestion for final paragraph:
In my opinion, children probably suffered more in the past when the whole family was obliged to work long hours just to survive. Nowadays children are protected by the law. Moreover access to education means that they have greater opportunities than ever before.

---

5 Analysing the sample answer (10 minutes)
Your students should express their opinion clearly. Their answer must have a clear and logical structure so that the reader knows *what* the writer thinks and *why* he / she thinks this. To do this, they should:
- make notes before writing.
- divide their ideas clearly into paragraphs.

Intermediate

To make the structure more explicit, ask:
Which paragraphs talk about the situation in the past? *(Paragraphs 2 and 4)*
Which paragraph analyses the thinking behind the question? *(Paragraph 1)*
Which talks about how education has changed the way we see the situation? *(Paragraph 3)*
Which paragraphs clearly express the writer's opinion? *(All, especially 4)*

Advanced

In addition to the steps given for Intermediate students elicit how the task could be done giving a 'balanced' answer *e.g. introduction, arguments for, arguments against, conclusion.*

ANSWER KEY
Suggested answers:
1 mid-20th century middle-class mothers stayed home (short period of time)
2 in past parents worked longer hours
3 children do badly at school often from parental neglect
4 now protected by law and have more opportunities

---

6 Emphatic language (10 minutes)
Point out that:
- emphatic structures are more persuasive – used sparingly (once or twice in the answer).
- a variety of complex sentence structures appropriately used will win marks in the test.

ANSWER KEY
1 What adults enjoy is complaining about the behaviour of their children.
2 What parents often demand is that schools take responsibility for bringing up their children.
3 What schools discover is that many people make very poor parents.
4 What teachers think is that they should just teach children their subject.
5 What parents find is that badly-behaved children are often given lower marks.

---

7 Writing task 2 (10 minutes)
You can give the writing task for homework. It is a good idea to do the first 3 steps in class time with Intermediate students.

1 Introduction

Work in small groups and discuss the following questions.

a What is a multinational company?

b What are the names of each of these companies, and what do they do?

c Have you ever bought their products?

d Do you think having companies like these operating in your country has improved life, made life worse, or not had any effect?

2 Analysing and brainstorming

Work in pairs.

● Look at the following writing task title and underline the key words and phrases.

● Then answer the points below.

> In most countries multinational companies and their products are becoming more and more important. This trend is seriously damaging our quality of life.
> To what extent do you agree or disagree?
> You should write at least 250 words.

Which of these could your answer include?

a Why multinational companies are becoming more and more important.

b Suggestions of measures we as individuals can take to reduce the power of multinationals.

c Examples of how Western consumer culture is invading the rest of the world.

d How multinational companies and their products are affecting our quality of life.

e Whether you agree or disagree with the statement.

Work in pairs or small groups with people who share your opinion and brainstorm your arguments and examples.

3 Studying a sample answer

Read the following sample answer.

● What reasons does the writer give for agreeing with the statement in the question?

● The writer has tried to avoid repeating the same words too often in the answer. Read the sample again and find synonyms or phrases later in the answer with similar meanings to the underlined words.

Example:	Answer
easy	convenient

1 Multinational companies nowadays find it _easy_ both to market their _products_ all over the world and set up _factories_ wherever they find it convenient. In my opinion this has had a _harmful_ effect on our quality of life in three main areas.

2 The first area is their products. Supporters of globalisation would argue that multinational companies make high-quality goods available to more people. While this may be true to some extent, it also means that we have less choice of products to _buy_. When powerful multinational companies invade local markets with their goods, they often _force_ local companies with fewer resources to go out of business. In consequence, we are obliged to buy multinational products whether we like them or not.

3 This brings me to my second point. It is sometimes said that multinational companies and globalisation are making societies more open. This may be true. However, I would _argue_ that as a result the human race is losing its cultural diversity. If we consumed _different_ products, societies _all over the world_ would be more varied. This can be seen by the fact that we all shop in _similar_ multinational supermarkets and buy identical products wherever we live.

4 Thirdly, defenders of multinational companies often point out that they provide _employment_. Although this is undoubtedly true, it also means that we have become more _dependent_ on them, which in turn makes us more vulnerable to their decisions. When, for example, a multinational decides to move its production facilities to another country, this has an adverse effect on its workers who lose their jobs.

5 All in all, I believe that if we as voters pressured our governments to make multinational companies more responsible and to protect local producers from outside competition, we could have the benefits of globalisation without its disadvantages.

4 Completing the plan

The notes below are incomplete. Read the sample answer and complete the notes.

> *Paragraph 1 – Introduction: multinationals find it easy to operate – harmful*
> *Paragraph 2 – Less choice of products because* ....
> *Paragraph 3 –* ....
> *Paragraph 4 –* ....
> *Paragraph 5 –* ....

5 Functions

Here are some functions and examples of how the function can be expressed. Find and highlight other phrases in the sample answer which express the same functions.

Presenting other people's ideas
● It is often argued...

Disagreeing with ideas just stated
● However, I think this is a false argument because...

Presenting evidence
● This is shown by...

6 Second conditional sentences

Look at this example of a conditional sentence from the sample answer:

If we consumed different products, societies all over the world would be more varied.

● This sentence refers to an imaginary or hypothetical situation. Find one other second conditional in the sample answer.
● Express the ideas below by writing a second conditional sentence.

1 Television companies buy foreign programmes because they do not have enough money

to make their own. ....

2 People would like to watch locally-made programmes. Local television companies don't

make them. ....

3 Local television companies do not make programmes because they cannot sell them in

other countries. ....

7 Writing task 2

Do the following writing task. You should spend about 40 minutes on this task. You should:
● analyse the question. (1–2 minutes)
● brainstorm as many ideas as you can. (2 minutes)
● make a plan for the answer. Decide how many paragraphs you will need and choose ideas from the list you have just brainstormed. In your plan, note down examples you want to use as well. (2 minutes)
● write your answer following your plan. While writing your answer, try to use a second conditional and some of the functions you have looked at in this unit. Keep the sample in front of you as a model. (30 minutes)
● check your work carefully for mistakes. (4 minutes)

> In many countries television shows many foreign-made programmes. The dominance of imported entertainment is harmful to the cultures of these countries.
> To what extent do you agree or disagree?
> You should write at least 250 words.

Estimated class time: 1 hour 10 minutes

🕐 **Short of time? You could:**
- give Activities **6** and **7** for homework.

1 Introduction *(10 minutes)*

> **ANSWER KEY**
> **Suggested answers: a** a company which operates in a number of different countries **b** Haagen-Dazs produce 'luxury' ice-cream, British Petroleum produce oil and related products, McDonald's is a chain of fast-food restaurants, Ford produce motor vehicles and Puma produce sportswear and equipment

2 Analysing and brainstorming *(10 minutes)*

It is important to analyse the question beforehand. Candidates will lose marks if they don't answer the question exactly.

> **ANSWER KEY**
> **They should underline:** This trend is seriously damaging our quality of life. Do you agree or disagree?
> **a** this may be briefly mentioned but it is not central
> **b** this may be touched on, perhaps in the conclusion
> **c** only brief examples to back up other points
> **d** yes, especially how it is damaging / improving our quality of life
> **e** Yes, depends on the student

Brainstorming is an essential part of preparing to write. Many answers fall down because candidates run out of ideas. To practise this, tell them:
- to think of as many ideas as possible.
- not to discuss or evaluate ideas at this stage – just list them in 5 minutes.

> **Intermediate**
> Help them get started by suggesting *People stop buying local products* and ask them to:
> consider the consequences of this.
> think of similar ideas.

> **Advanced**
> When they have brainstormed ideas, ask them to list useful vocabulary with the help of dictionaries.

3 Studying a sample answer *(15 minutes)*

When they have read the answer, you can ask them to discuss which points they agree and disagree with. You can point out that:
- When writing in English, it's considered good style to avoid repeating the same words too often. They will get higher marks in the test by showing a range of vocabulary.
- When they do writing tasks for homework, they can use a dictionary of synonyms to extend their vocabulary.

> **Intermediate**
> To help them look for synonyms:
> Write these words on the board: *goods, production facilities, wherever we live, vulnerable, adverse.*
> Ask them to find them in the sample answer and match them with underlined words.
> Then ask them to do the others alone or with a partner.

> **ANSWER KEY**
> products – goods; factories – production facilities; harmful – adverse; buy – consume, shop; force – are obliged; argue – point out; different – varied; all over the world – wherever we live; similar – identical; employment – jobs; dependent – vulnerable

4 Completing the plan *(5 minutes)*

Ask your students to complete the plan within the space provided to keep it brief.

> **ANSWER KEY**
> **Suggested answer:**
> **Paragraph 2** – local companies go out of business
> **Paragraph 3** – loss of cultural diversity *e.g. everyone drinks cola*
> **Paragraph 4** – multinationals provide employment but we are vulnerable to their decisions
> **Paragraph 5** – conclusion: pressure governments to make multinationals more accountable

When they have completed their plans, elicit the structure of the sample answer by asking, *In which paragraph does the writer...*
- *give his opinion?* (In the first paragraph, and throughout)
- *express ideas he doesn't agree with?* (At the beginnings of paragraphs 2, 3 and 4)
- *put his counter-arguments?* (In paragraphs 2, 3, and 4, directly after summarising the arguments he doesn't agree with)
- *suggest what can be done about multinationals?* (Briefly in the final paragraph)

5 Functions *(10 minutes)*

> **Intermediate**
> When they have highlighted the phrases, ask your students to write their own sentences using the functions.

> **Advanced**
> Elicit other ways of expressing the same functions.

> **ANSWER KEY**
> **Presenting other people's ideas:** Supporters of globalisation would argue that, It is sometimes said that, Defenders of multinational companies often point out that...,
> **Disagreeing with ideas just stated:** While this may be true to some extent, it also means that..., This may be true. However, I would argue that..., Although this is undoubtedly true, it also means that...
> **Presenting evidence:** This can be seen by the fact that...

6 Second conditional sentences *(10 minutes)*

Encourage your students to use more complex sentences in their answers.

> **ANSWER KEY**
> **Suggested answers:**
> **1** If television companies had more money, they would make their own programmes / they wouldn't buy foreign programmes.
> **2** People would watch locally-made programmes if local television companies made them.
> **3** If local television companies could sell their programmes in other countries, they would make them.

7 Writing task 2 *(10 minutes)*

Students can complete the writing task for homework. The first 3 steps can be done in class.
- Encourage students to use the sample answer in Activity 3 as a model and to use some conditional sentences in their answers.

Alternative Writing Task:

If your students disagreed with the ideas expressed in the sample answer, you can suggest they write 4 or 5 paragraphs presenting their views. If they decide to do this, tell them to follow the same procedure as outlined in writing task 2 and try to answer some of the points in the sample answer in Activity 3.

1 Introduction

Discuss these questions in small groups.
- What rule or regulation does each of these pictures represent?
- Which do you think should be a rule and which do you think should be just advice?
- Do you think laws about these things should be made stricter or more relaxed?

2 Analysing and brainstorming

Read the following writing task question and underline the key words and phrases. Then check what you have done with another student.
- Work in pairs and brainstorm ideas for the writing task.
- Note down your ideas in two columns: 'For' and 'Against'.

> Governments make rules to protect people from danger, for example by making people wear seat belts in cars or not allowing smoking in public buildings. However, many people believe there are too many rules nowadays.
> To what extent do you agree or disagree?
> You should write at least 250 words.

3 Studying a sample answer

Study the following answer to the writing task and:
- check which of the ideas you brainstormed have been used in the answer.
- answer Questions a–f below the sample answer.

One of the duties of governments is to make society safe. This includes protecting us from other people's antisocial behaviour and discouraging us from pursuing dangerous activities such as smoking or driving too fast.

However, many people maintain that governments should make fewer rules about these things and they give three main arguments for this. Firstly, they argue that we should have the freedom to decide whether we want to take risks such as smoking or driving fast. However, I disagree with this point of view. I think that risky behaviour is costly for everyone because the public health service has to pay for the treatment of diseases caused by smoking, or injuries resulting from traffic accidents. Secondly, they assert that rules and regulations stop people enjoying themselves or having excitement. I think this idea is acceptable as long as no one else is put at risk. However, when such pursuits endanger other people, they should be banned. Finally, these people suggest that instead of legislating, governments should inform people about the dangers of habits such as smoking or riding a bicycle without a helmet. They should then permit people to make their own decisions about these things. Although this position sounds attractive, experience shows that many people do not pay attention to warnings, and that passing laws is a more effective way of protecting them.

a Does it answer the question?
b Does it have a clear, logical structure and is it organised in paragraphs?
c Is the writer's opinion clear?
d Is it the right length?
e Does the writer give examples?
f Does it use linking words and expressions?

4 Writing the final paragraph

The answer in Activity 3 is missing a concluding paragraph.
Below are five possible final paragraphs.
Work in pairs.
- Decide what are the good and bad points of each.
- Match them with the teacher's comments on the right.
- Choose the most suitable paragraph for the answer.

Final paragraphs

1 To sum up, I believe that rules are essential to protect the majority of people from the selfish and antisocial activities of the minority.

2 All in all, I believe that though it is desirable to allow as much individual freedom as possible, this should never be at the expense of other people's safety. Moreover, governments have a responsibility to keep us safe from the consequences of our own actions.

3 Finally, governments do not always protect us and sometimes start wars and expect people to do military service and risk their lives fighting.

4 To conclude, on the one hand people should have freedom to decide how they live, but on the other hand this can create problems for the rest of us.

5 In conclusion, I believe that government interference in our lives should be reduced. People should be encouraged to take risks, even if this occasionally puts them in danger or leads to accidents, because taking risks makes society more dynamic, and dynamic societies progress further.

Teacher's comments

a This is a good final paragraph which makes clear what your opinion is and the general reasons why you hold this opinion.

b This is a very good point, but not in the conclusion, because you are expressing new ideas here which you haven't mentioned earlier in your answer.

c This is not really a summary – you are just repeating one of the reasons you gave earlier in your answer. What you should do is pick out the main reasons for your opinion and summarise those as a reason for agreeing or disagreeing with the question.

d This paragraph seems to contradict the opinions you have expressed earlier in your answer and support the ideas I understand you don't agree with.

e Yes, but what is your opinion? I want to know what you think, not just what the arguments are!

5 Analysing the sample answer

Read the sample answer again and complete these notes.

Paragraph 1 – introduction – duty of government: protect people (crime, defence etc.), (1) ....
though some think there should be fewer rules

Paragraph 2 – individuals have right to decide about risks BUT (2) ....

Paragraph 3 – dangerous activities often fun BUT
(3) ....

Paragraph 4 – government should inform not oblige BUT
(4) ....

Paragraph 5 – conclusion – freedom but respecting freedom of others – (5) ....
....

6 Writing task 2

Do the following writing task. You should spend about 40 minutes on this task. You should:
- analyse the question. (1–2 minutes)
- brainstorm as many ideas as you can. (2 minutes)
- make a plan for your answer. Decide how many paragraphs you will need and choose ideas from the list you have just brainstormed. In your plan, note down examples you want to use as well. (2 minutes)
- think of vocabulary you might use before you start – use a dictionary where necessary. (Take extra time for this!)
- write your answer following your plan. (30 minutes)
- check your work carefully for mistakes. (4 minutes)

**Parents and teachers make many rules for children to encourage good behaviour and to protect them from danger. However, children would benefit from fewer rules and greater freedom.
To what extent do you agree or disagree?
You should write at least 250 words.**

Estimated class time: 1 hour 5 minutes

🕐 **Short of time? You could:**
- ask your students to do Activity **6** for homework.

1 Introduction (10 minutes)

After your students have answered the questions, you can:
- elicit other laws or rules governments make to protect us from ourselves *e.g. prohibiting the use of mobile phones while driving / wearing crash helmets when on a motorcycle.*
- develop the discussion by asking how much governments should interfere in people's lives, and what the function of government is.

2 Analysing and brainstorming (15 minutes)

- It is important to analyse the question beforehand – candidates lose marks if they don't answer the question exactly.

> **ANSWER KEY**
> **They should underline:** too many rules

- After analysing the question, put your students in small groups to discuss briefly whether they agree or disagree with it and then ask students who agree with each other to work in pairs to **brainstorm**.
- Tell them to think of as many ideas as possible.
- Tell them not to discuss or evaluate ideas at this stage – just list them in 5 minutes.

Intermediate
You can get them started by writing in the '_For_' column
Too many rules means less freedom.
and in the '_Against_' column
Other people are put at risk by dangerous behaviour.

Advanced
When they have finished brainstorming ideas, you can:
- Tell them to think of examples to support their arguments.
- Brainstorm words connected with:
danger; prohibit; allow; protect.

3 Studying a sample answer (15 minutes)

Intermediate
Ask them to:
- reread the answer and find vocabulary connected with:
danger; prohibit; allow; protect; argue.
- guess the meanings of unfamiliar vocabulary from the context.

Advanced
Ask them to:
- check for vocabulary they brainstormed in the previous exercise, and to add it to the list.
- highlight useful words and phrases in the sample.

> **ANSWER KEY**
> **a** Yes – you can stress that they will lose marks in the test if they don't answer the question exactly.
> **b** The structure is clear and logical, but the 2nd paragraph is too long and needs to be divided. Also it lacks a conclusion. You can ask them to divide the 2nd paragraph into shorter paragraphs (new paragraphs should start at 'Secondly...' and 'Finally...').
> **c** Yes.
> **d** It is too short (230 words) – tell your students that they will lose marks if they don't write enough in the test but that they should not count their words one by one – they won't have time.

e Yes – here you can ask students to say what examples are given and how suitable they think they are. Can they think of other better examples?
f Yes.

Intermediate
Suggest they divide paragraph 2 into 3 separate paragraphs.
- Paragraphs make the answer easier to read and understand.
- Each paragraph deals with a different aspect of the subject.
- Paragraphs normally contain several sentences, but should not be too long.
- They will gain marks in the test by using paragraphs correctly.
Ask them to summarise the *writer's* **arguments. To do this, they should:**
- read the arguments again and then,
- without looking back at the passage, explain the ideas in pairs.

Advanced
- Ask students to divide paragraph 2 into 3 paragraphs and to summarise the main point of each.
- Ask them to highlight the phrases the writer uses to:
  – introduce his ideas or arguments.
  – introduce the ideas or arguments he doesn't agree with.

4 Writing the final paragraph (10 minutes)

Many answers are spoilt by a poor final paragraph – the candidate has run out of time, or has not been thinking clearly. These examples, whilst well written, highlight some of the problems.

Intermediate
Before they start the exercise, elicit from them what the final paragraph should contain. (*The writer's opinion and a summary of the main points which have produced that opinion.*)

Advanced
You can ask them to make their own comments first *before* **they look at the 'teacher's comments', and then compare them.**

> **ANSWER KEY**
> **Suggested answers: 1**c **2**a **3**b **4**e **5**d
> paragraph 2 offers the most suitable conclusion

5 Analysing the sample answer (5 minutes)

The answer in Activity 3 provides an alternative structure for a discursive essay:
Paragraph 1: Introduction
Paragraph 2: 1st argument & refutation
Paragraph 3: 2nd argument & refutation
Paragraph 4: 3rd argument & refutation
Paragraph 5: conclusion with writer's opinion

> **ANSWER KEY**
> **Suggested answers: 1** prevent dangerous / antisocial activities
> **2** dangerous behaviour costly – health service costs
> **3** can put other people in danger i.e. reduce their freedom
> **4** people don't react to information – obligation more effective
> **5** government's responsibility to keep us safe

6 Writing task 2 (10 minutes)

You can give the writing task for homework. Intermediate students would benefit from doing the first 3 steps in class.

1 Introduction

Discuss in small groups.

- Which of these things would annoy you most in restaurants? Put these things in order from the ones which would annoy you most (**1**) to the things which would annoy you least (**7**).
- Discuss why you would find them annoying and what you could do about it.

a the service isn't quick enough ☐

b the food isn't good enough ☐

c there are too many people ☐

d the other customers are too noisy ☐

e the waiters aren't very friendly ☐

f the restaurant isn't very clean ☐

g there's a mistake in the bill ☐

- Which of these things would be worth writing a letter of complaint about? Can you suggest other problems at a restaurant which would be worth writing to complain about?

2 Analysing and brainstorming

Work in pairs.

- Read the following exam task and highlight or underline the key words and phrases.

> You eat at your college cafeteria every lunchtime. However, you think it needs some improvements. Write a letter to the college magazine. In your letter:
> - explain what you like about the cafeteria.
> - say what is wrong with it.
> - suggest how it could be improved.
> Begin your letter as follows: 'Dear Sir / Madam,'
> You should write at least 150 words.

- Quickly brainstorm ideas for the letter in five minutes. Think of:
  - three things you like about the college cafeteria.
  - three things you don't like about the college cafeteria (these shouldn't be too strong because you eat there every day!).
  - three suggestions for how the cafeteria could be improved.

3 Completing the sample letter

The sample letter contains eight gaps. Complete it by putting a word or phrase from the box below in each space.

Dear Sir / Madam,

I normally eat lunch at the college cafeteria because it is reasonably priced, convenient and it has a friendly atmosphere.

There are, however, a number of deficiencies which I think should be (1) .... Firstly, although the staff try to keep the tables clean, there are not (2) .... workers at peak times to do this adequately. Moreover, since the cafeteria is self-service, students are supposed to clear their tables themselves when they have finished eating. (3) .... , some students do not bother to do this. Also, there are a number of students who do not wait in the queue to be served, which is very (4) .... for the majority of us. Finally, I think the cafeteria could have better ventilation as it gets (5) .... , especially in the summer.

I think it would be a (6) .... if more signs were put around the cafeteria asking students to put their dirty plates and cutlery on the trolleys provided and to throw away their leftovers and rubbish. Also, I think we (7).............. tell students when they are being anti-social and jumping the queue. Finally, (8).............. we please have a few windows open when things get too hot?

Yours faithfully,

annoying	put right
could	should
enough	unfortunately
good idea	too hot

4 Analysing a sample letter

Work in pairs. Read the sample letter and answer the questions below.

a   How many paragraphs does the letter have?
b   What is the subject of each paragraph?
c   What does the writer like about the cafeteria?
d   What does the writer not like?
e   How many suggestions does the writer give to improve the cafeteria?

5 Functions

Saying what is wrong

- Highlight or underline phrases in the second paragraph of the letter which show that the writer doesn't like certain things in the cafeteria.

Making suggestions

- Highlight or underline phrases in the third paragraph which introduce suggestions.

6 Writing task 1

Do the following writing task. Although in the exam you will have 20 minutes for this task, you should treat this as an exercise and spend about 40 minutes doing it.
Before you write, you should:

- analyse the question. (1 minute)
- read the sample letter in Activity 3 again carefully and use it as a model. (5 minutes)
- brainstorm as many ideas as you can. (2 minutes)
- prepare the vocabulary (use your dictionary if necessary) (10–15 minutes)
- make a plan for the letter. Decide how many paragraphs you will need and choose ideas from the list you have just brainstormed. (1 minute)
- write the letter following your plan. (14 minutes)
- check your work carefully for mistakes. (2 minutes)

You normally go shopping in the area where you live. However, you think some of the facilities for shoppers could be improved.
Write a letter to your local newspaper. In your letter:
- say in general what you like about shopping in your area.
- say what is wrong with the facilities.
- suggest how they could be improved.
Begin your letter as follows: 'Dear Sir / Madam,'
You should write at least 150 words.

Estimated class time 1 hour 10 minutes

🕐 **Short of time? You could:**
● give Activities **5** and **6** for homework.

1 Introduction *(10 minutes)*

After they have discussed the questions, elicit what the purpose of a letter of complaint is.

> **ANSWER KEY**
> **Possible answers:** you could complain about any of the issues apart from the noisiness of the customers; normally, people complain to improve a situation or to get their money back.

2 Analysing and brainstorming *(15 minutes)*

Candidates lose marks in the test if they do not answer all the elements in the question.

> **ANSWER KEY**
> **They should underline:** what you like, what is wrong and how it could be improved

Brainstorming is essential as many students run out of ideas and therefore lose marks.

> **Intermediate**
> **Start them brainstorming by suggesting:**
> ● for things you like: *It's not expensive.*
> ● for what is wrong with it: *It's too crowded.*

> **Advanced**
> **Ask them to brainstorm more advanced vocabulary** e.g. instead of '*cheap prices*', '*reasonably priced*', instead of '*too hot*', '*the atmosphere is stuffy*'.

3 Completing the sample letter *(5 minutes)*

> **ANSWER KEY**
> **1** put right **2** enough **3** Unfortunately **4** annoying **5** too hot
> **6** good idea **7** should **8** could

4 Analysing a sample letter *(10 minutes)*

● Before doing this activity, check your students know when to use 'Yours faithfully' (*when the letter begins: Dear Sir / Madam*) and when to use 'Yours sincerely' (*with Dear Mr Smith etc.*).
● Students gain marks in the test by:
– covering all the points in the question.
– organising them clearly into paragraphs.

> **Intermediate**
> **If your students are not clear about paragraphing, you can point out that:**
> ● each paragraph deals with a different aspect of the subject.
> ● normally paragraphs have several sentences, but the first paragraph of a letter is often just one sentence.
> **As an extra activity, ask them to underline unfamiliar words and guess their meanings from the context.**

> **Advanced**
> **As an extra activity ask your students to:**
> ● compare the vocabulary they brainstormed with the vocabulary used in the sample.
> ● highlight words they think are worth remembering and copy them into their notebooks.
> ● suggest improvements to the vocabulary if they want to.

> **ANSWER KEY**
> **a** 3
> **b** **Paragraph 1:** what the writer likes about the cafeteria
> **Paragraph 2:** what is wrong with it
> **Paragraph 3:** how it could be improved
> **c** reasonably priced, convenient, friendly
> **d** dirty tables, queue-jumpers, too hot
> **e** 3

5 Functions *(10 minutes)*

Your students will gain marks by using functions correctly in the test.
Saying what is wrong
When your students have finished highlighting, you can
● point out or elicit *too* and *enough* as ways of making complaints.
● elicit how the writer feels (*which is very annoying for the majority of us*).
● elicit *supposed* as a way of expressing what they should do and what they don't do.
● ask students to write similar sentences to complain about a hotel.

> **ANSWER KEY**
> **They should underline:**
> **Saying what is wrong**
> a number of deficiencies
> not enough workers... to do this adequately
> Students are supposed to...
> However, some students do not bother to do this...
> which is very annoying...
> too hot
> **Making suggestions**
> I think it would be ...
> Also I think we ...
> Finally, ... we please ...

> **Intermediate**
> **If necessary, you can revise** *too* and *enough* **by using** *English Grammar in Use*, **Unit 102.**

When they have finished, ask them to write other suggestions for improving a hotel.

6 Writing task 1 *(20 minutes)*

If this is the first time your students have done an example of a writing task 1, it would be a good idea to do the first five steps in class, if time permits. Otherwise, encourage them to be independent and to do it for homework, but to follow all the steps.

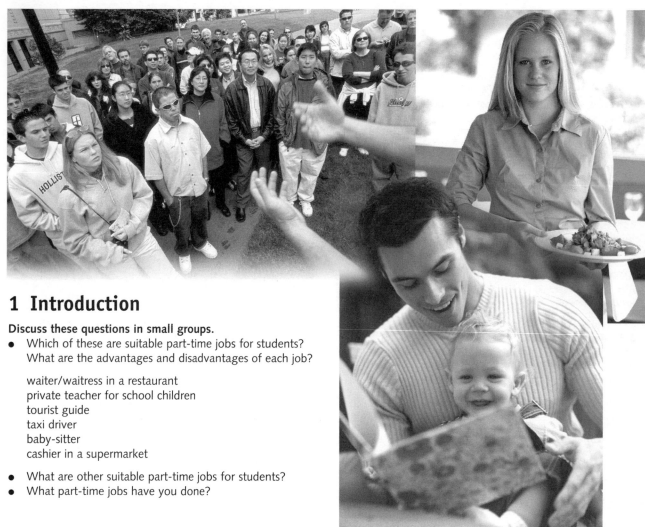

1 Introduction

Discuss these questions in small groups.

- Which of these are suitable part-time jobs for students? What are the advantages and disadvantages of each job?

  waiter/waitress in a restaurant
  private teacher for school children
  tourist guide
  taxi driver
  baby-sitter
  cashier in a supermarket

- What are other suitable part-time jobs for students?
- What part-time jobs have you done?

2 Analysing the question

Work in pairs.

- Read the exam task and underline the key words and phrases.
- Then discuss whether the statements are true or false. (You will not have to write the letter.)

You are looking for a part-time job. Write a letter to an employment agency. In your letter:
- **introduce yourself.**
- **explain what sort of job you would like.**
- **say what experience and skills you have.**
Begin your letter as follows: 'Dear Sir / Madam,'
You should write at least 150 words.

True or false?

You should:

a   say what you are doing at the moment.
b   describe your physical appearance and your personality.
c   give a detailed description of yourself.
d   give a detailed description of the type of job you want.
e   say how much money you expect to earn.
f   say when you are available to work.
g   briefly mention other jobs you have done in the past.
h   mention what languages you can speak, if you have a driving licence and if you know how to use a computer.
i   write the letter in a formal style.
j   use contractions.

3 Sample letter

Read the following sample letter.
1 Put the verbs in brackets into the correct form.
2 Find and correct nine spelling mistakes in the letter.

> Example   Answer
> Univeristy   University

Dear Sir / Madam,

I am a Polish national from Warsaw and at present I (study) for a Master's degree in Bussiness Administration here at the <u>Univeristy</u> of Hobart, where I (be) for the last two months.

I (look) for a part-time job and I (wonder) if you can help me. Preferibly, I would like an office job, perhaps working as a secretery, office administrator or tipist. I can only work during the afternoons and at weekends as my university studys (occupy) most of the day. I would be ready to start inmediately.

As you can see from my curiculum vitae, I have a degree in marketing from the University of Warsaw, I am a competant typist and I am computer-literate. Also, I speak Polish, and German fluently and I (learn) English for the past three years. While I (study) for my degree I worked as a part-time office manager for an import-export firm in Warsaw. In recent years I also (have) temporary sumer jobs as a hotel receptionist in Kiel, Germany.

I (look) forward to (hear) from you,

Yours faithfully,

Aniela Kwasniewski

5 Functions

Highlight or underline phrases in the letter which:
- describe Aniela and her experience and skills.
- explain the reason for writing the letter.
- explain the sort of job Aniela would like.

6 Writing task 1

Do the following writing task. Although in the exam you will have 20 minutes for this task, you should treat this as an exercise and spend about 40 minutes doing it.
Before you write, you should:
- analyse the question. (1 minute)
- read the sample letter in Activity 3 again carefully and use it as a model. (5 minutes)
- brainstorm as many ideas as you can. (2 minutes)
- prepare the vocabulary (use your dictionary if necessary) (10–15 minutes)
- make a plan for the letter. Decide how many paragraphs you will need and choose ideas from the list you have just brainstormed. (1 minute)
- write the letter following your plan. (14 minutes)
- check your work carefully for mistakes. (2 minutes)

> You would like a temporary job working in a summer camp which runs sports and outdoor activities for children and young people next summer.
> Write a letter to the organisers of the summer camp.
> In your letter:
> - explain what sort of job you would like to do.
> - describe your personality.
> - say what experience and skills you have.
> You should write at least 150 words.

4 Analysing the sample letter

Match these descriptions of the content of each paragraph with each paragraph number.

Paragraph 1   a Aniela describes her educational background, her work experience and her skills.

Paragraph 2   b Aniela says the type of job she wants and when she can work.

Paragraph 3   c Aniela says where she's from and what she's doing.

　　　　　　　　d Aniela gives the reason for writing the letter.

Estimated class time: 1 hour 15 minutes

🕐 **Short of time? You could:**
● give Activities **5** and **6** for homework.

1 Introduction *(10 minutes)*

Before starting this activity, elicit the difference between a full-time and a part-time job.

2 Analysing the question *(10 minutes)*

Candidates lose marks in the test if they do not answer all the elements in the question.

> **ANSWER KEY**
> **Students should underline:** introduce yourself, explain what sort of job you would like and say what experience, and skills you have

> **Intermediate**
> **Before they do this:**
> ● elicit an explanation for *employment agency*, *experience* and *skills*.
> ● ask them to give examples of experience and skills.
> ● elicit what is meant by *introduce yourself*.

> **ANSWER KEY**
> **a** True – this is part of introducing yourself
> **b** False – this wouldn't be an appropriate way to introduce yourself
> **c** False – a brief description of essential details, such as age nationality etc. is enough
> **d** False – a brief general description only is required
> **e** False – this wouldn't be appropriate in this type of letter
> **f** True – afternoons, evenings or weekends
> **g** True – the question asks you to say what experience you have
> **h** True – depending on the job you're applying for e.g. computer skills are not essential for a babysitter
> **i** True
> **j** False

Optional extra activity

Some of your students may never have applied for a job before and be uncertain what sort of things they should mention as skills and experience. In this case:
● ask them to talk to a partner and introduce themselves, their skills and their experience.
● discuss these points with the whole class if appropriate.

3 Sample letter *(15 minutes)*

The first task is intended to remind students of suitable tenses. If necessary, do some revision of tenses here. The second task is to remind them of the importance of checking for mistakes in their writing.

> **ANSWER KEY**
> **1** am studying / have been / am looking / wonder / occupy / have been learning / was studying OR studied / have also had / look / hearing
> **2** Business / Preferably / secretary / typist / studies / immediately / curriculum / competent / summer

> **Intermediate**
> Ask your students to read the letter again and guess the meanings of unfamiliar vocabulary from the context. Where necessary, elicit explanations for:
> *degree; grant; curriculum vitae.*

> **Advanced**
> As an optional extra activity ask them to brainstorm 2 lists of words:
> ● words connected with studying.
> ● words connected with work.

4 Analysing the sample letter *(10 minutes)*

● Before doing this activity, check your students know when to use 'Yours faithfully' *(when the letter begins: 'Dear Sir / Madam')* and when to use 'Yours sincerely' *(with 'Dear Mr Smith' etc.).*
● Your students will gain marks in the test by:
  – covering all the points in the question.
  – organising them clearly into paragraphs.
● A common error in this type of letter is for the student to write: *Dear Sir / Madam, My name is Aniela ...* It is worth pointing out that they should not do this.

> **Intermediate**
> If your students are not clear about paragraphing, you can point out that:
> ● each paragraph deals with a different aspect of the subject.
> ● normally paragraphs have several sentences, but the first paragraph of a letter is often just one sentence.

> **ANSWER KEY**
> **1**c **2**d & b **3**a

5 Functions *(10 minutes)*

Your students will gain marks by using functions correctly in the test.

> **ANSWER KEY**
> **Phrases describing Aniela:** I am a Polish national from..., at present I am studying ..., I have a degree in ..., I am a competent..., I speak..., While I was studying for my degree, I worked as a..., In recent years I have also had...
> **Reason for writing the letter:** I am looking for a part-time job
> **The sort of job:** I would like an office job, perhaps working as ...

> **Intermediate**
> If your students are particularly weak, ask them to imagine that they are in Aniela's situation. Ask them to copy Aniela's letter but to change the details so that they describe themselves instead.

6 Writing task 1 *(20 minutes)*

If this is the first time your students have done a writing task 1, it would be a good idea to do the first five steps in class. Otherwise, encourage them to do it for homework, but to follow all the steps.

Letter Giving Advice

1 Introduction

Work in pairs and discuss:
Which of these things would you recommend visitors to do in your town or region? Explain in more detail what the activities would consist of for a visitor.

- go sightseeing
- visit museums and art galleries
- eat in good restaurants
- go to the sea-side
- enjoy the countryside or mountains
- do adventure sports
- visit a theme park
- see animals in their natural habitat

2 Analysing the question

Read the following exam task and underline the key words and phrases. Then in pairs discuss the questions below. (You will not have to actually write the letter.)

> An English-speaking friend wants to spend a two-week holiday in your region and has written asking for information and advice. Write a letter to your friend.
> In your letter:
> - offer to find somewhere to stay.
> - give advice about what to do.
> - give information about what clothes to bring.
> Begin your letter as follows: 'Dear .... ,'
> You should write at least 150 words.

a What details about your friend will you have to invent before you answer the question?
b What place(s) to stay could you offer to find?
c How many pieces of advice about what to do should you give in your letter?
d What things should you consider when giving information about what clothes to bring?
e Should you use contractions?
f Should you use formal, neutral, or colloquial language?

3 Sample letter

Read the following sample letter. Write one word or phrase from the box in each space. You can use the same word or phrase more than once. You needn't use them all.

> although   and   as   because   but   if   since   so
> so that   that   when   where   which   who

> Dear Soo-in,
> I'm delighted (**1**) .... you are coming to Valencia next month. I think it would be great (**2**) ....
> you stayed with me and my family, (**3**) .... send you their best wishes. Otherwise, if you prefer, I can easily book you a cheap but comfortable hotel near the beach (**4**) .... you can be more independent.
>   There are lots of things to do in my city. If I were you, I'd spend some days on the beach relaxing (**5**) .... one or two days sightseeing in the city. There are several interesting museums and art galleries (**6**) .... I'm sure you will enjoy. One place you really should visit is an enormous aquarium called the Oceanographic Park, (**7**) .... you'll want to spend the whole day. Also, you ought to go to our excellent theme park, (**8**) .... is about an hour away by bus.
>   You don't need to bring a lot of clothes (**9**) .... the weather is normally warm and sunny at this time of year. In the evening it's a bit cooler, (**10**) .... you may need a jersey and a jacket.
>   Please let me know exactly (**11**) .... you're coming (**12**) .... I can meet you at the airport. It'll be great to see you again so we can get up-to-date with all our news!
>
> Love
> Manolo

4 Analysing the sample letter

Work in pairs and answer these questions:
1 How many paragraphs does the letter have?
2 What is the subject of each paragraph?
3 How many places does Manolo suggest Soo-in can stay and what reasons does he give for suggesting them?
4 How many activities does Manolo suggest for Soo-in to do? Does he give a reason for each activity?
5 How many details does Manolo give about the weather and clothes?
6 What does he offer to do at the end of the letter?

5 Functions

Highlight or underline phrases in the letter which:
● offer to do something.
● give advice.
● give information and reasons for it.

6 Writing task 1

Do the following writing task. Although in the exam you will have 20 minutes for this task, you should treat this as an activity and spend about 40 minutes doing it. Before you write, you should:
● analyse the question. (1 minute)
● read the letter in Activity 3 again carefully and use it as a model. (5 minutes)
● brainstorm as many ideas as you can. (2 minutes)
● make a plan for the letter. Decide how many paragraphs you will need and choose ideas from the list you have just brainstormed. (2 minutes)
● prepare the vocabulary (use your dictionary if necessary). (10–15 minutes)
● write the letter following your plan. (14 minutes)
● check your work carefully for mistakes. (2 minutes)

> An English-speaking friend is coming to study in your town next year and has written asking for information and advice.
> Write a letter to your friend. In your letter:
> ● offer to find a place for him / her to live.
> ● give advice about how to find a part-time job.
> ● give information on where they can learn your language.
> Begin your letter as follows: 'Dear .... ,'
> You should write at least 150 words.

From *Instant IELTS* by Guy Brook-Hart © Cambridge University Press 2004 **PHOTOCOPIABLE**

Estimated class time: 1 hour 15 minutes (Intermediate)
1 hour 20 minutes (Advanced)

🕐 **Short of time? You could:**
● give Activity **6** for homework.

1 Introduction *(10 minutes)*

Obviously this will take less time if your students come from the same town.

2 Analysing the question *(10 minutes)*

> **ANSWER KEY**
> **They should underline:** offer to find a place for him / her to stay, give advice about finding something to do and give information on what clothes to bring.

Advanced

After they have answered the questions, you can ask them to brainstorm and note down:
● alternatives for places to stay.
● advice about what to do.
● reasons for suggesting these things.

> **ANSWER KEY**
> **Suggested answers:**
> **a** You should decide whether the friend is male or female, how old, and his or her economic status, as your advice and suitable accommodation may depend on this. Also, how close a friend he or she is, as this will determine the style you write in.
> **b** Your students may have a number of ideas about this ranging from their own homes to youth hostels and cheap hotels.
> **c** 3 would be sufficient
> **d** The weather / climate, activities you are going to do etc.
> **e** Yes
> **f** Between neutral and colloquial, depending on how confident you are writing in a colloquial style and how well you know the friend.

3 Sample letter *(15 minutes)*

Intermediate

Students will get higher marks in the test if they use complex sentences. When they have done the activity, you can take this opportunity to revise relative pronouns. Ask them to:
● highlight the sentences containing relative clauses.
● say when you use *who*, *which* and *where*.
● suggest other relative pronouns (*whose, that, when*) and ask them to write a sentence containing each.
● **If necessary see** *English Grammar in Use*, **Units 91–95**.

Advanced

Remind them that they will get higher marks in the test if they use more complex sentences. You can ask them to find the following in the sample:
● conditional sentences
● relative clauses
● clauses expressing a reason
● time clauses

> **ANSWER KEY**
> **1** that **2** if **3** who **4** so / so that / where **5** and / before **6** which / that **7** where **8** which **9** as / because / since **10** so **11** when **12** so / so that

4 Analysing the sample letter *(10–15 minutes)*

Your students will gain marks in the test if they:
● divide the letter into suitable paragraphs

● write at least 150 words
● cover all the points of the question
● write in a suitable style

Intermediate

If your students are not clear about paragraphing, you can point out that:
● each paragraph deals with a different aspect of the subject.
● normally paragraphs have several sentences, but the first paragraph of a letter is often just one sentence.

Advanced

As an optional extra activity, elicit from them examples of informal style and vocabulary in the letter e.g.:
● contractions
● words such as *great, lots of, a bit*
● friendly declarations such as *I'm longing to see you again, Love*
● very personal style with *I* and *you* – no passives!
● use of exclamation mark

> **ANSWER KEY**
> **1** 4
> **2** **Paragraph 1** offers to find accommodation, **paragraph 2** gives advice about what to do, **paragraph 3** gives information about the weather and clothes to bring, and **paragraph 4** offers to meet the friend at the airport.
> **3** 2 (Manolo's home because his family will make her very welcome, or a hotel where she can be independent.)
> **4** 4 or 5 and he doesn't give a reason for all of them.
> **5** Very general details and a little advice about clothes – not a complete list of what Soo-in will have to pack.
> **6** Meet her at the airport.

5 Functions *(10 minutes)*

When your students have highlighted the structures in the letter, ask them to work in pairs and write sentences offering / advising / giving information and reasons for a friend who is going to visit *their* country.

> **ANSWER KEY**
> **Offering:** I think it would be great if you..., If you prefer, I can...
> **Giving advice:** If I were you, I'd..., One place you really should visit is..., you ought to go..., you may need ...
> **Giving information and reasons:** You don't need to... because..., In the evening it's a bit cooler, so you...

Intermediate

You may take this opportunity to revise second conditionals with them.
● Point out: *It would be great if you stayed with me and my family*, and *If I were you, I'd spend some days on the beach relaxing...*
● Elicit what the structure consists of (If + past tense – would + infinitive).

Advanced

Ask them to work in small groups and brainstorm other ways they know of:
● offering to do something e.g. *Would you like me to..., If you like, I'll...*
● giving advice e.g. *You'd better..., Why don't you...?*
Ask them to write examples of each.

6 Writing task 1 *(20 minutes)*

If this is the first time your students have done a writing task 1, it would be a good idea for them to do the first five steps in class.

Bei Heng Lang is a 28-year-old agronomist from Hunan, China. She is going on a one-month training course in Christchurch, New Zealand.

1 Introduction

Work in pairs and discuss:
- Which of these types of accommodation do you think would be most suitable for her? Give reasons for your answers.

☐ flat on her own

☐ room in a flat with other students

☐ room in a family house

☐ room in a student residence

☐ room in a hotel

2 Analysing the question

Work in pairs.
- Read the following exam task and underline or highlight the key words and phrases.
- Then with a partner discuss whether the points below are true or false.
- When you have finished, read the sample letter in Activity 3 and check whether your answers are correct.

> You are going on a short training course at a college in Christchurch, New Zealand. You need somewhere to live while you are there.
> Write a letter to the accommodation officer at the college. In your letter:
> - explain your situation.
> - describe the accommodation you require.
> - say when you will need it.
> Begin your letter as follows: 'Dear Ms Walker,'
> You should write at least 150 words.

True or false?

a You must deal with the points in the letter in the order in which they appear in the question.

b You can choose which of the points in the question you want to deal with. You needn't mention them all.

c When you explain your situation, you only need to repeat that you are going to do a short training course at a college in New Zealand.

d It is not necessary to give a complete description of the type of accommodation you need – just your basic requirements in order to orientate the accommodation officer.

e You should give the dates when you will need the accommodation.

3 Sample letter

Read the following sample letter and put one word in each space.

Dear Ms Walker,

I am a 28-year-old agronomist (1) .... Hunan Province in The People's Republic of China, and I have been accepted to (2) .... a one-month training course at Christchurch University College starting next January.

    I would be grateful (3) .... you could either find me accommodation for the month or give me a list of addresses (4) .... I could write to. I would like, if possible, to (5) .... a room in a family house because I would like the (6) .... to practise my English at the same time. I will need a room with a bed and a table (7) .... that I can study there also. If (8) .... , I would prefer a room near the college since I will (9) .... be in Christchurch for a short time and I will not have time to learn my way around.

    I will need the accommodation (10) .... five weeks from 28th December to the 3rd February as I would like to arrive a few days before the course begins.

    Could you also (11) .... tell me how much accommodation of this kind will cost and whether the price (12) .... meals?

    I look forward to (13) .... from you,

Yours sincerely,
Bei Heng Lang

4 Functions

Highlight or underline phrases in the letter which Bei Heng Lang uses to:
- describe herself.
- make requests.
- explain what she needs and give reasons.

5 Writing task 1

Do the following writing task. Although in the exam you will have 20 minutes for this task, you should treat this as an exercise and spend about 40 minutes doing it.
Before you write, you should:
- analyse the question. (1 minute)
- read the sample letter in Activity 3 again carefully and use it as a model. (5 minutes)
- brainstorm as many ideas as you can. (2 minutes)
- prepare the vocabulary (use your dictionary if necessary). (10–15 minutes)
- make a plan for the letter. Decide how many paragraphs you will need and choose ideas from the list you have just brainstormed. (1 minute)
- Write the letter following your plan. (14 minutes)
- Check your work carefully for mistakes. (2 minutes)

> You are going to take a short holiday in Sydney, Australia and you want to rent a holiday flat while you are there.
> Write to the tourist information office. In your letter:
> - explain what you need.
> - say when you will need it.
> - ask for information about prices.
> Begin your letter as follows: 'Dear Ms Narayan...'
> You should write at least 150 words.

Darling Harbour, Sydney, Australia

Sydney skyline, Australia

Estimated class time 1 hour 10 minutes–1 hour 15 minutes

⏱ **Short of time? You could:**
- give Activity **4** for homework.

1 Introduction *(5 minutes)*

With an unimaginative class you can stimulate them by suggesting they consider price, whether she might be lonely, and problems of finding her way around in a strange city.

2 Analysing the question *(15 minutes)*

Candidates lose marks in the test if they do not answer all the elements in the question.

> **ANSWER KEY**
>
> **Students should underline:** a short training course; explain your situation; describe the accommodation you require; say when you need it.
>
> **a** False – you can deal with them in any order, though the question is not designed to confuse students and the points are put in what seems a logical order.
>
> **b** False – you will lose marks if you don't deal with all the points as you will be considered not to have answered the question completely.
>
> **c** False – you must give (or invent) more details about yourself.
>
> **d** True – but take the opportunity to show some of the vocabulary you know.
>
> **e** True

Optional extra activities *(5 minutes)*

> **Intermediate**
>
> After reading the sample letter you can ask them:
> - to say what the subject of each paragraph is.
> - if the letter covers all the points in the task.
> - what extra details the writer gives to explain her situation.
> - what details of accommodation and reasons the writer gives.

> **Advanced**
>
> Ask your students to work in small groups and to talk about their experiences of writing letters in real life, both in English and in their own language.
> Ask them to discuss what the difficulties are in writing this type of letter e.g.:
> - using the right style when writing to someone you don't know.
> - making sure you can be clearly understood.
> - avoiding mistakes which create a bad impression.

3 Sample letter *(15 minutes)*

This activity is intended to extend your students' vocabulary a little and to revise / raise awareness of a number of language points such as relative pronouns and prepositions.

> **Intermediate**
>
> If they find this exercise hard, write the following words on the board and tell them they are some of the answers: *do, hearing, if, includes, opportunity, please, rent, so, want, which.*
> **You can also point out:**
> - the importance in English of using *please.*
> - the phrase *I look forward to hearing from you.* Tell them *to* is a preposition, and therefore followed by the *-ing* form.

> **Advanced**
>
> When they have done the exercise, point out that the letter is written in a polite style. Ask them to identify phrases which are especially polite, e.g.:
> - *I would be grateful if you could...*
> - *I would like...* (as opposed to *I want*)
> - *If possible, I would prefer...*
> - *Could you also please tell me...*
> - *I look forward to hearing from you.*
> Ask why the letter is phrased so politely. (*Because the writer is requesting things from someone she doesn't know.*)

> **ANSWER KEY**
>
> **1** from **2** do / take / complete **3** if **4** which / that **5** have / rent / take / find **6** opportunity / chance **7** so **8** possible / available **9** only **10** for **11** please **12** includes **13** hearing

> **Intermediate**
>
> Before going on to the next activity, check your students know when they should use *Yours faithfully* (**after** *Dear Sir / Madam*) and *Yours sincerely* (**after** *Dear* + *the name of the person*).

4 Functions *(15 minutes)*

When your students have highlighted the structures in the letter, ask them to work in pairs and write sentences to describe themselves (briefly), make requests and explain needs.
They will gain marks in the test if they use functions correctly in the letter.

> **ANSWER KEY**
>
> **Describe herself:** I am a 28-year-old agronomist etc.
> **Make requests:** I would be grateful if you could..., I would like, if possible, to rent..., Could you also please tell me...?
> **Explain what she needs and give reasons:** I will need a room with... so that..., I would prefer a room... since..., I will need the accommodation... as I...

> **Intermediate**
>
> They will need extra help with the structure:
> *I would be grateful if you could...* + infinitive.
> Point out that it is polite **written** English.
> Ask them to write 2 or 3 more requests using this structure.
> **You can also work on:**
> *If possible, I would like* + noun / infinitive,
> *I would prefer* + noun / infinitive.
> Tell them they should vary their structures when making requests to avoid repetitiveness.

> **Advanced**
>
> Point out the sentence: *Could you also tell me how much accommodation of this kind will cost and if the price includes meals?*
> Elicit why it is not *how much will accommodation of this kind cost* etc.
> If necessary, explain embedded questions or use *Advanced Grammar In Use*, **Unit 33**.
> Brainstorm other ways of making requests which contain embedded questions e.g.:
> *I wonder if you could tell me...*
> *I would be grateful if you could inform me...* (very formal) etc.
> Ask them to write other sentences using these words.

5 Writing task 1 *(20 minutes)*

If this is the first time your students have done a writing task 1, you should try to do the first five steps in class. Otherwise, encourage them to be independent and to do it for homework.

1 Introduction

Work in pairs.
- Look at sentences **1–6**, where people describe their neighbours and match each sentence with one of the adjectives from the box below.
- Which describe your neighbours?
- Write a sentence to describe what sort of neighbour you are.

1 'I'd like to keep them at a distance. I don't like the way they're always watching me!'

2 'She's always coming round asking to borrow things. I wish she'd make a proper shopping list! And her house is a mess!'

3 'They interest me. I'd like to get to know them better.'

4 'They keep themselves to themselves. Very unfriendly.'

5 'They're so noisy. Sometimes I feel like phoning the police to complain.'

6 'We're in and out of each other's houses all day. Yesterday I helped him fix his car, and last week he helped me paint the kitchen.'

> chaotic helpful inconsiderate intriguing
> nosy reserved

2 Analysing the question

Work in pairs.
- Look at the following writing task title and underline the key words and phrases.
- Then decide whether the statements in the next column are true or false.

> In general, people do not have such a close relationship with their neighbours as they did in the past. Why is this so, and what can be done to improve contact between neighbours?
> **You should write at least 250 words.**

True or false?

In your answer you should:
a say how neighbours can help.
b explain how relationships with neighbours have changed.
c explain what problems neighbours can cause.
d give reasons why people don't have so much contact with their neighbours.
e suggest how to make contact between neighbours better.

3 Brainstorming ideas

Work in small groups.
- Brainstorm ideas for the writing task title.
- Note down your ideas under two headings, **Causes of situation** and **Suggested solutions**, as you talk.

4 Studying a sample answer

Read this sample answer.
- Which of the ideas you brainstormed are mentioned in the answer?
- Choose the correct sentence from the box below for each space in the answer and write the letters in the gaps provided.

In the past, neighbours formed an important part of people's social lives and <u>they</u> helped <u>them</u> when <u>they</u> had problems. Nowadays, people often do not even know their neighbours and in consequence they live much more isolated lives.

(1)..
Firstly, our lifestyles are more mobile. <u>This</u> means people may change the area where they live quite frequently and this causes their relationships with their neighbours to be more superficial. Secondly, nowadays people often live and work in different places. <u>This</u> leads to people forming closer relationships with work colleagues than <u>the ones</u> they have with their neighbours. Finally, modern lifestyles make us spend more time inside our houses watching television, and when we go out, we travel by car. Consequently, we do not speak to the people in our neighbourhood so much.

(2)..
First of all, local authorities can provide communal areas such as playgrounds for children and community halls so that there are places where neighbours can meet and make friends. Next, I think that when new neighbours come to a street, the people living <u>there</u> ought to introduce themselves and welcome <u>them</u>. Lastly, people living in a street or small district should form neighbourhood associations and meet regularly to discuss the things which affect <u>them</u>.

(3)..
However, they will help our relationships with our neighbours to become more useful and valuable.

a In conclusion, these suggestions will probably not make neighbours as important in our lives as they were in the past.
b There are a number of reasons why we have less contact with our neighbours.
c There are a number of ways in which I think contact between neighbours can be improved.

5 Using reference devices

Look at the words and phrases which are underlined in the sample answer. These reference devices are used to avoid repeating the same word or phrase and to express the argument using fewer words.

- Say what each of them refers to. For example: 'they' (line 2) refers to 'neighbours'.
- Reduce the repetition in these sentences by replacing the underlined words with a reference device.

Example
Students have to get high marks to pass their courses. Having to get high marks puts them under considerable stress.

Answer
Students have to get high marks to pass their courses. *This* puts them under considerable stress.

---

1 Growing numbers of students suffer from stress and stress sometimes leads to depression.

2 Stress can also cause certain students to underperform and the students who underperform are the students who lose out in exams.

3 Many students work long hours. The students who take exercise undoubtedly manage to reduce their stress.

4 Taking exercise is a good way of controlling stress. Taking exercise can be done at any time of the day.

6 Expressing causes

Look at this extract from the sample answer.

This means people may change the area where they live quite frequently and this causes their relationships with their neighbours to be more superficial.

- Read the sample answer again and highlight other words and phrases which express causes.
- Complete the following sentences by putting a word or a few words in each space to express a cause.

1 For many students, competition .... them perform better.

2 Excessive stress may .... some students to lose sleep.

3 Lack of sleep in turn often .... to feelings of stress.

4 Students often don't study enough and this .... them to fail.

5 Poor study techniques .... to students failing.

7 Writing task 2

Do the following writing task. You should spend about 40 minutes on this task. You should:
- analyse the question. (1–2 minutes)
- brainstorm as many ideas as you can. (2 minutes)
- make a plan for the writing task. Decide how many paragraphs you will need and choose ideas from the list you have just brainstormed. In your plan, note down examples you want to use as well. (2 minutes)
- brainstorm ideas for each paragraph. In your plan, note down examples you want to use as well. (2 minutes)
- do the writing task following your plan. While writing, concentrate on using reference devices well, and expressing causes. Keep the sample in front of you as a model. (30 minutes)
- check your work carefully for mistakes. (4 minutes)

Life nowadays is generally much more stressful than in the past. Give some reasons why people suffer more from stress nowadays, and say what they can do to reduce it.
You should write at least 250 words.

From *Instant IELTS* by Guy Brook-Hart © Cambridge University Press 2004 **PHOTOCOPIABLE**

Estimated class time: 1 hour 5 minutes

Short of time? You could:
- give Activity **7** as homework.

1 Introduction *(10 minutes)*

Intermediate
Before they discuss, elicit the meanings of: *keep them at a distance, coming round, keep themselves to themselves* **and** *in and out of each other's houses all day*.

Advanced
You can ask them to suggest other words to describe these neighbours *e.g. for 2: disorganised, untidy.*

> **ANSWER KEY**
> **1** nosy **2** chaotic **3** intriguing **4** reserved **5** inconsiderate **6** helpful

2 Analysing the question *(5 minutes)*

It is important to analyse the question beforehand – candidates lose marks if they don't answer the question exactly. They should underline: <u>why is this so</u> and <u>what can be done to improve contact between neighbours?</u>.

> **ANSWER KEY**
> **a** false **b** only briefly **c** false **d** true – this answers the question: *why is this so?* **e** true – this answers the question: *what can be done to improve contact between neighbours?*

3 Brainstorming ideas *(10 minutes)*

Brainstorming is an essential part of preparing to write an answer. Many answers fall down because candidates run out of ideas.
- Tell your students to think of as many ideas as possible. Tell them not to discuss or evaluate ideas at this stage – just list them.

Intermediate
- To get them started, you can suggest: *people too busy* for causes and *community associations* for solutions.
- Make sure they list them in brief note form.

Advanced
- You may get the groups to do this against the clock – *e.g. by giving them 5 minutes and then seeing which group has the most ideas on their lists.*
- Get feedback from the whole class and put all their ideas on the board.

4 Studying a sample answer *(10 minutes)*

- When they have chosen the correct sentences, elicit the function of these sentences – *i.e. to tell the reader the purpose of the paragraph.*

> **ANSWER KEY**
> **1**b **2**c **3**a

Intermediate
Writing an introductory sentence of this type will help them:
- structure their answer.
- focus on the purpose of the paragraph they are writing.

- You can then elicit the structure of the sample answer by asking them what the purpose of each paragraph is:

Paragraph 1 introduces the problem, **Paragraph 2** explains the causes, **Paragraph 3** suggests solutions, **Paragraph 4** concludes saying how life will be better with these solutions.
- Ask them to highlight useful words and phrases in the sample answer.

Intermediate
To help them focus on highlighting, suggest:
- examples of comparisons *e.g. much more isolated lives.*
- linking words and phrases *e.g. firstly.*

> **ANSWER KEY**
> **them:** people, **they** (line 2): people, **this:** more mobile lifestyles, **the ones:** relationships, **there:** in the street, **them:** new neighbours, **them:** people

5 Using reference devices *(10 minutes)*

Using reference devices is a way of avoiding repetition of words and phrases. After deciding what each one here refers to, you can elicit:
- Which ones refer to people? (*they, them*)
- Which refers to a place? (*there*)
- Which refers to an idea expressed just before? (*this*)
- Which refers to some, but not all, of the things it refers to? (*the ones*)

> **ANSWER KEY**
> **1** this **2** those, the ones **3** The ones / Those **4** This / It

Intermediate
For extra practice, ask them to work in pairs and write 3 sentences with several words repeated in them. When they have finished, they should pass them to another pair to rewrite using reference devices.

6 Expressing causes *(10 minutes)*

Intermediate
Elicit the following structures by writing on the board and asking them to deduce them from the sample answer:
- .... + object + infinitive (*cause*)
- .... + object + infinitive without *to*. (*make*)
- .... + noun / gerund (*lead to*)

Advanced
After doing the exercise, they can write their own examples. Ask them to write down causes of disagreement between parents and teenagers.

> **ANSWER KEY**
> **1** makes **2** cause **3** leads **4** causes **5** lead

7 Writing task 2 *(10 minutes)*

You could combine preparation for this with Listening Section 2 – Coping with Stress on page 12.
- You can give the writing task for homework but it may be a good idea to do the first three steps in class with Intermediate students. Encourage your students to use the sample answer in Activity **4** as a model.

1 Introduction

Work in pairs and discuss these questions.
- What is happening in the two pictures?
- What sort of people are more suited to each way of working?
- Which way of working would you prefer and why?

2 Analysing the question

Read the following writing task and underline the key words and phrases.

> Computers and modems have made it possible for office workers to do much of their work from home instead of working in offices every day. Working from home should be encouraged as it is good for workers and employers.
>
> Do you agree or disagree?
> You should write at least 250 words.

3 ⏺ A brainstorming session

Listen to Rashid and Su-Mei brainstorming the composition. Complete the notes below. Write ONE OR TWO WORDS for each answer.

- Workers can work when they want i.e. more
  (1) ....
- Saves on (2) .... – reduces stress
- Can combine job with (3) ....
- Less likely to be (4) .... (saves employers money).
- Saves on (5) .... – this reduces costs
- Workers need (6) .... at home – supplied by employer
- Lose (7) .... of work
- Employers must (8) .... to do work – work more difficult to (9) ....
- Can hinder (10) .... work.

4 Introductory paragraphs

Work in small groups. Look at these first paragraphs written by IELTS students. Say what is good and what is bad about each paragraph and choose the most suitable one.

a My father works in a tall office block in downtown Boston all week and on weekends he often brings work home. When he does that, there's a really bad atmosphere at home as my mother has to keep quiet else he can't concentrate. So I guess it wouldn't be too good for their marriage if he always worked from home.

b Nowadays, new technologies have made it possible for many office workers to work from home rather than travelling to their offices every day. There are strong arguments in favour of employers giving their workers this opportunity, but on the other hand there are also strong arguments against.

c In recent years the vast expansion of information and communications technology has made teleworking much more practical. Although in many cases office workers could be made geographically independent by using modems, faxes and cell phones, few companies or employees take full advantage of this possibility.

d When computers first came into offices in the 1960s, there were many imaginative predictions of the way they would revolutionise our lives. However, few people predicted the arrival of the personal computer in the 1980s, which would sit on our desks and give each of us enormous computing power. Then the invention of the Internet in the 1990s gave us the possibility of connecting with computers in other parts of the world.

e Working from home is many people's ideal and there are strong arguments in favour of it.

 From *Instant IELTS* by Guy Brook-Hart © Cambridge University Press 2004 **PHOTOCOPIABLE**

5 Linking words

Read the sample answer. Which of Rashid's and Su-Mei's ideas have been used?
Choose a word or phrase from the boxes opposite for each space in the sample answer below. For Questions 1–6, choose from the first box. For Questions 7–12, choose from the second box.

In recent years the vast expansion of information and communications technology has made teleworking much more practical. Although in many cases office workers could be made geographically independent by using modems, faxes and cell phones, few companies or employees take full advantage of this possibility.

There are a number of strong arguments in favour of allowing workers to work from home. Firstly, costs for employers would be reduced (1) .... businesses would require less office space, which is often situated in the centre of large cities. (2) ...., workers' lives would be improved in a variety of ways. (3) ...., they would not need to travel to get to work, which would give them more free time.

(4) ...., they could combine their work with their family life, which is a major advantage if they are parents of young children or they have old people to look after.

(5) ...., travelling to a centralised workplace also has a number of points in its favour. (6) .... many employees would miss the social aspect of work (7) .... seeing colleagues and meeting customers.

(8) .... employers would need to be able to trust their workers to work at a high standard and finish their work on time, (9) .... supervising teleworkers is even more complicated than supervising workers in the same office.

(10) ...., working from home might inhibit teamwork and creative work and so perhaps is only really suitable for people doing routine office work.

(11) ...., I believe that (12) .... many workers welcome the opportunity to go out to work, others would find the chance to work from home very convenient. Where possible, I think workers should be offered the choice, but not forced to work from home unless they wish to.

Questions 1–6

Also   because   The first is that   For example
On the other hand   Secondly

Questions 7–12

A further point is that   Finally   In conclusion
since   such as   while

6 Giving examples

Arguments which are supported by examples are more convincing and you should include some in your answer. **Work in groups to think of a number of examples for each of these arguments and then complete the sentences.**

1   English is essential in a wide variety of jobs including...
2   Companies can find a number of ways of reducing costs such as...
3   A number of traditional jobs have been disappearing in recent years. For example,...
4   In the last twenty years we have seen a number of women doing traditional men's jobs like...

7 Writing task 2

Do the following writing task. You should spend about 40 minutes on this task. You should:
- analyse the question. (1–2 minutes)
- brainstorm as many ideas as you can. (2 minutes)
- make a plan for your answer. Decide how many paragraphs you will need and choose ideas from the list you have just brainstormed. In your plan, note down examples you want to use as well. (2 minutes)
- write your answer following your plan. (30 minutes)
- check your work carefully for mistakes. (4 minutes)

It is often difficult for young people to find a good job without previous work experience. Governments should encourage employers to choose young people when they need new workers.
Do you agree or disagree?
You should write at least 250 words.

"DON'T SUPPOSE YOU HAVE ANY JOBS GOING?"

RECEPTION

SOLICITORS

Estimated class time: 1 hour 5 minutes

🕐 **Short of time? You could:**
● ask your students to do Activity **7** for homework.

1 Introduction *(5 minutes)*

For example, people who value the social aspect of work may prefer the office, while people with family commitments may prefer working from home.

2 Analysing the question *(10 minutes)*

● It is important to analyse the question beforehand – candidates lose marks if they don't answer the question exactly. The question is framed in the form of a suggestion or proposal, so that they will have to argue for and against it.

> **ANSWER KEY**
> **Students should underline:** Working from home should be encouraged as it is good for workers and employers.

3 🔊 A brainstorming session *(10 minutes)*

For the complete recording script see page 128.
Before they look at the listening activity:
● Ask your students to brainstorm ideas for the writing task. Brainstorming consists of thinking of and noting down as many ideas as possible.

> **Intermediate**
> To get them started, refer your students back to the ideas in the introduction.
> They should list them in brief note form.

> **Advanced**
> You can get groups to do this against the clock – *e.g. by giving them 5 minutes and then seeing which group has the most ideas on their list.*

● Ask your students to work in pairs and try to predict the answers, the type of word, or type of information required.

> **Intermediate**
> Ask them to paraphrase *saves, reduces, combine, supply* and *hinder team work* (possibly using a dictionary) and then ask them to suggest things which could be *saved, reduced* etc. by working from home.

After listening, they can compare the ideas they heard with the ones they brainstormed earlier.

> **ANSWER KEY**
> **1** flexibility   **2** travelling / travel time   **3** family life   **4** off sick
> **5** office space   **6** office equipment   **7** social aspect   **8** trust workers
> **9** supervise   **10** team

4 Introductory paragraphs *(10 minutes)*

Getting the introductory paragraph right is important for creating the right impression on the reader, and also because it is much easier to make the rest of the answer flow logically from a good opening paragraph.
● Point out that they are looking at style and content, not for mistakes in the English.

> **ANSWER KEY**
> **Suggested comments:**
> **a** Avoid personal anecdotes – remember you should present a formal written argument. Avoid contractions and a colloquial style.
> **b** This merely repeats the ideas and (largely) the phrasing of the question. Waffle.
> **c** This one is fine as a general model. In the first sentence it states what situation has arisen while the second states why the question is worth discussing. The style is moderately formal and impersonal.
> **d** Irrelevant. You are asked to write a discursive essay, not a history of the computer.
> **e** Too short.

5 Linking words *(15 minutes)*

Linking words are very important in this type of writing task. Students will gain marks if they use them correctly.

> **Intermediate**
> **Before doing the activity, ask your students to classify the words in the boxes as words which introduce:**
> another point in the argument
> an example
> a reason
> a contrast or comparison
> the other side of the argument
> a conclusion.

> **Advanced**
> **When they have done the activity, you can ask your students to:**
> suggest other linking words and phrases which could be used in the spaces (not the ones given).
> underline or highlight other linking words *e.g. 'so' and relative pronouns, to make them aware of them.*
> underline or highlight useful vocabulary in the sample.

> **ANSWER KEY**
> **1** because   **2** Secondly   **3** For example   **4** Also   **5** On the other hand   **6** The first is that   **7** such as   **8** A further point is that
> **9** since   **10** Finally   **11** In conclusion   **12** while.

6 Giving examples *(5 minutes)*

> **Intermediate**
> **You may have to get them started by suggesting ideas e.g.:**
> ● travel agent
> ● using machines instead of people
> ● typists
> ● engineers or company directors.

> **Advanced**
> **This can be done in the form of a game where each group has to think of as many reasonable examples as possible for each sentence in 5 minutes.**

7 Writing task 2 *(10 minutes)*

You can give the writing task for homework, although with an Intermediate class, it may be a good idea to do the first three steps during the lesson.
Encourage your students to use the sample answer in Activity 5 as a model, and to use linkers and examples in their answers.

1 Introduction

Several students were asked their opinions about studying abroad and studying in their own country. Below are some of the things they said. Work in small groups. Discuss which ideas you agree with and which you disagree with.

a

'It's a long time to be away from my family and friends – I'm not sure my friends would remember me when I came back.'

b

'I want to feel that I'm a world citizen, and to do that it's necessary to travel and mix with students from other backgrounds.'

c

'I think it's better to study in my own country and to learn about my own culture. If I study at home, I'll be more ready to work in my country when I finish my course.'

d

'There's no doubt about it: I'll get a better job when I've done a course abroad. If I can, I'll find a job abroad. I don't want to come back and work in my home country.'

2 Analysing the question

Work in pairs.

- Look at the following writing task title and underline the key words and phrases.
- Then answer the question below.

> Nowadays many students have the opportunity to study for part or all of their courses in foreign countries. While studying abroad brings many benefits to individual students, it also has a number of disadvantages.
> Do you agree or disagree?
> You should write at least 250 words.

Which of these things should you include in your answer to this question? Write **YES**, **NO** or **MAYBE** by each.

1 What problems students may have studying abroad and what is good about it. ....

2 What countries gain and lose from people going abroad to study. ....

3 Whether governments should subsidise students' studies abroad. ....

4 Your personal experience of studying abroad, or the experience of people you know. ....

5 What is wrong with your own country's education system. ....

3 Brainstorming ideas

Work in small groups.

- Brainstorm ideas for the writing task title.
- Note down your ideas in two columns, **Advantages** and **Disadvantages**, as you talk.

4 Using linking phrases

Read the following sample answer.

- Complete the answer by filling the gaps with a word or phrase from the box below. (You can't use them all, and you can use some of them more than once.)

In recent years there has been a vast increase in the number of students choosing to study abroad. This is partly (1) .... people are more affluent and partly (2) .... the variety of grants and scholarships which are available for overseas students nowadays. (3) .... foreign study is not something which every student would choose, it is an attractive option for many people.
Studying overseas has a number of advantages.
(4) ...., it may give students access to knowledge and facilities (5) .... laboratories and libraries which are not available in their home country. (6) ...., by looking abroad students may find a wider range of courses than those offered in their country's universities, and (7) .... one which fits more closely to their particular requirements. (8) ...., studying abroad has a number of drawbacks. These may be divided into personal and professional.
(9) .... students have to leave their family and friends for a long period. (10) ...., studying abroad is almost always more expensive than studying at one's local university. (11) ...., students often have to study in a foreign language, which may limit their performance and mean they do not attain their true level.
(12) ...., however, the disadvantages of studying abroad are usually temporary in nature. Students who study abroad generally become proficient in the language quite soon and they are only away from their family and friends for a year or two. (13) ...., many of the benefits last students all their lives and make them highly desirable to prospective employers.

although	because	finally
firstly	in my opinion	such as
for example	moreover	secondly
furthermore	on the other hand	therefore
in contrast	due to	what is more

5 Categorising linking phrases

Look at the linking words and phrases in the box at the bottom of the previous page and copy each of them into your notebooks under one of these headings:

Listing your points	Contrasting points
Introducing your opinion	Introducing an example
Giving reasons	Expressing a consequence

6 Analysing the sample answer

Look at the sample answer and complete this plan for it.

> *Plan*
> *Paragraph 1:*   *Introduction including why more students study abroad*
> *Paragraph 2:*   *Advantages:*
> *access to knowledge and facilities*
> *(e.g. (1) ....)*
> *(2) .... – one which fits exact requirements*
> *Paragraph 3:*   *Disadvantages:*
> *Personal: – (3) ....*
> *(4) ....*
> *Professional: – study in foreign language – (5) ....*
> *Paragraph 4:*   *My opinion: disadvantages – temporary advantages – (6) ....*

7 Formal vocabulary

Find words and phrases in the sample answer which mean:

a   a big rise
b   people are richer
c   different
d   choice
e   do not exist
f   a bigger choice

g   needs
h   disadvantages
i   reach
j   good at
k   very attractive
l   possible

8 Writing task 2

Do the following writing task. You should spend about 40 minutes on this task. You should:

- analyse the question. (1–2 minutes)
- brainstorm as many ideas as you can. (2 minutes)
- make a plan for your answer. Decide how many paragraphs you will need and choose ideas from the list you have just brainstormed. In your plan, note down examples you want to use as well. (2 minutes)
- write your answer following your plan. (30 minutes)
- check your work carefully for mistakes. (4 minutes)

> In some countries it is common for students leaving school to do a gap year in which they travel, do voluntary work, or do a job before going on to higher education. Although this may benefit students in a number of ways, it also has a number of disadvantages.
> To what extent do you agree or disagree?
> You should write at least 250 words.

Estimated class time: 1 hour 15 minutes

⏱ **Short of time? You could:**
- give Activities **7** and **8** for homework.

1 Introduction *(10 minutes)*
Your students should work in groups of 3 or 4.

2 Analysing the question *(10 minutes)*
It is important to analyse the question beforehand – candidates lose marks if they don't answer the question exactly.

> **ANSWER KEY**
> **Students should underline:** many benefits to individual students and a number of disadvantages.
> **1** YES **2** NO – it's about advantages and disadvantages for individual students **3** NO **4** MAYBE – as examples **5** NO

3 Brainstorming ideas *(5 minutes)*
Many answers fall down because candidates run out of ideas. Tell your students to think of as many ideas as possible. Tell them not to discuss or evaluate ideas at this stage – just list them.

Intermediate
- To get them started, refer your students back to the ideas in the introduction.
- Make sure they list them in brief note form.

Advanced
- You may get the groups to do this against the clock.
- You can go a stage further and ask them to brainstorm vocabulary connected with their ideas.
- To get them started, for being away from family and friends elicit:
- *miss family and friends*
- *homesickness.*
- Point out that their answers will also be assessed for vocabulary.

4 Using linking phrases *(10 minutes)*
In the test candidates gain marks by using linking words.

Intermediate
- **You may have to orientate your students through the list of linking words first.**
- Ask them to categorise the words as roughly meaning *also*, *but*, *for example*, *because* and *others*.
- **NB In some cases answers are correct for grammatical reasons as well as semantic reasons. For further work on linking words you can use** *Advanced English Grammar In Use* **Units 96, 97 and 98.**

> **ANSWER KEY**
> **1** because **2** due to **3** Although **4** Firstly / For example
> **5** such as **6** Furthermore / Moreover / What is more / Secondly
> **7** therefore **8** On the other hand **9** Firstly **10** Furthermore / Moreover / What is more / Secondly **11** Finally / Furthermore / Moreover / What is more **12** In my opinion / On the other hand
> **13** Furthermore / What is more

5 Categorising linking phrases *(10 minutes)*

> **ANSWER KEY**
> **Listing your points:** firstly, furthermore, moreover, finally, secondly, what is more
> **Contrasting points:** although, in contrast, on the other hand
> **Introducing your opinion:** in my opinion
> **Introducing an example:** for example, such as
> **Giving reasons:** because, due to
> **Expressing a consequence:** therefore

Advanced
- **Ask them to work in groups and brainstorm other words and phrases for each category. e.g.:**
- **Listing your points:** *lastly, also*
- **Contrasting points:** *while, whereas, however, in spite of, despite*
- **Introducing your opinion:** *I think, I feel*
- **Introducing an example:** *for instance, like*
- **Expressing a consequence:** *in consequence, consequently, as a result, so*

6 Analysing the sample answer *(10 minutes)*
Candidates should express their opinion clearly in writing task 2. To do this, they should:
- make notes before writing.
- divide their ideas clearly into paragraphs.

Intermediate
- **To make the structure completely explicit, before they look at the activity ask them which paragraph:**
- expresses the writer's opinion
- gives reasons why more students study abroad
- gives advantages
- gives disadvantages
- gives reasons for the writer's opinion

> **ANSWER KEY**
> These should reflect these ideas – they needn't be grammatically accurate as these are rough notes:
> **1** laboratories & libraries **4** more expensive
> **2** wider range of courses **5** limits performance
> **3** away from family and friends **6** permanent

7 Formal vocabulary *(10 minutes)*
Answers are also assessed for range of vocabulary: a discursive essay is moderately formal.

> **ANSWER KEY**
> **a** a vast increase **b** people's increased affluence **c** variety of
> **d** option **e** are not available **f** a wider range **g** requirements
> **h** drawbacks **i** attain **j** proficient in **k** highly desirable **l** prospective

Intermediate
- When they are doing the test, they should concentrate on using vocabulary they are confident with and aim to write clearly and correctly.
- However, when writing for practice, or for homework, encourage them to use a dictionary and experiment with new words.

8 Writing task 2 *(10 minutes)*
You can give the writing task for homework but it is a good idea to do the first three steps with Intermediate students during class time.
Encourage your students to use the sample answer in Activity 4 as a model, and to use linking words and phrases and vocabulary from Activity 5 in their answers.

SPEAKING MODULE PART 1

Free time
Speaking Module Part 1

- What do you enjoy doing in your free time?
- How much time do you have each week for doing these things?
- Why do you like doing these activities?
- How did you start doing this activity at first?
- Is there some other hobby or sport you would like to try? Why?
- How has the way people spend their free time changed over the years?

Holidays
Speaking Module Part 1

- What do you do when you have a holiday?
- Where do you like to spend your holidays? Why?
- Can you describe a typical day in your holidays?
- Why are holidays important to you?
- If you could take a holiday anywhere in the world, where would you go? Why?

Your town
Speaking Module Part 1

- Can you describe your town or village to me?
- What jobs do people in your town do?
- What things are there to do in your town in your free time?
- What do you like about your town?
- How has your town changed over the last twenty years?

Shopping
Speaking Module Part 1

- How much time do you spend shopping every week?
- Do you enjoy going shopping? Why (not)?
- What is your favourite shop and why do you like it?
- What problems are there with shopping in your area?

Transport
Speaking Module Part 1

- How did you come here today?
- What is public transport like in your town?
- How do you think it could be improved?
- Do you think people should use public transport more? Why (not)?

Places to go in your free time
Speaking Module Part 1

- What do people do in your town in their free time?
- Where can they go out for entertainment, or to enjoy themselves?
- Which do you prefer: eating in restaurants or eating at home?
- Which are the best places to eat out?

Your neighbourhood
Speaking Module Part 1

- Can you describe the house where you live to me?
- What is there to do in the area where you live?
- What do you like about the area where you live?
- How do you think it could be improved?
- Do you think it is better to live in the centre of town or outside in the country? Why?

Reading
Speaking Module Part 1

- Do you enjoy reading? Why?
- What sort of things do you read?
- Tell me something about your favourite book.
- What are the advantages of reading instead of watching television or going to the cinema?

 From *Instant IELTS* by Guy Brook-Hart © Cambridge University Press 2004 **PHOTOCOPIABLE**

SPEAKING MODULE PARTS 1, 2 AND 3

You
Speaking Module Part 1

- Do you work or study?

Study
- What are you studying?
- Why did you choose that subject?
- What do you find most interesting about your course?
- What do you hope to do next?
- What are your ambitions for the future?
- What are the advantages of studying instead of working?

Work
- Can you describe your job to me?
- How long have you been doing it?
- Why did you choose to do that job?
- What things do you enjoy about your work? Why?
- And what things don't you like? Why not?
- What are your plans for the future?

Sports and games
Speaking Module Part 1

- What sports are most popular in your country?
- What sports and games did you most enjoy playing when you were a child?
- Do people take as much exercise as in the past?
- Why is exercise good for you?

Beautiful places
Speaking Module Part 2

Take one minute to prepare a talk on the following subject. Take notes if you like and remember to include reasons and examples. You should then speak for between one and two minutes.

> Describe a beautiful place to visit in your country.
> You should say:
>   where it is
>   how to get there
>   what there is to do when you are there
> and explain why you recommend this place.

Beautiful places
Speaking Module Part 3

Attitudes to tourism
- Why do you think people like to travel to different places in their free time?
- How do you see tourism changing in your country in the future?

Conserving the countryside
- Why is it important to protect the countryside?
- In what ways is the countryside in danger in your country?

Historic buildings and monuments
- Why are historic buildings and monuments important to a city?
- Is it better to keep old buildings, or build new modern ones?

Family
Speaking Module Part 2

Take one minute to prepare a talk on the following subject. Take notes if you like and remember to include reasons and examples. You should then speak for between one and two minutes.
Describe the person in your family who you most admire.

> You should say:
>   what their relationship is to you
>   what they have done in their life
>   what they do now
> and explain why you admire them so much.

Family
Speaking Module Part 3

Attitudes to family
- In what ways have families in your country changed in recent years?
- Should husbands and wives have different roles within the family?

Family or friends
- Which are more important to you: your family or your friends?
- What conflicts can arise between a person's family and a person's friends?

Family responsibilities
- What responsibilities do parents have towards their children?
- And what responsibilities do children have towards their parents?

Shopping
Speaking Module Part 2

Take one minute to prepare a talk on the following subject. Take notes if you like and remember to include reasons and examples. You should then speak for between one and two minutes.

> **Describe your favourite shop.**
> **You should say:**
> **where it is**
> **what things it sells**
> **what sort of people are its customers**
> **and explain why you like the shop so much.**

Shopping
Speaking Module Part 3

Things to buy
- What typical things can visitors to your country buy?
- What things do young people like to buy in your country?

Money
- Is it a good idea to save money? Why (not)?
- Do you think that people are happier if they have money? Why (not)?

Shopping
- What can shops do to make shopping more pleasant for their customers?
- Do you think that in the future people will do most of their shopping using the Internet? Why (not)?

Eating and food
Speaking Module Part 2

Take one minute to prepare a talk on the following subject. Take notes if you like and remember to include reasons and examples. You should then speak for between one and two minutes.

> **Describe a special occasion when you had a really enjoyable meal.**
> **You should say:**
> **what the occasion was**
> **who was at the meal**
> **what you ate**
> **and explain why the meal was so enjoyable.**

Eating and food
Speaking Module Part 3

Attitudes to food
- What do you think a healthy diet consists of?
- Which do people in your country prefer: traditional food or fast food such as hamburgers or pizzas?

Learning about food
- Do you think children should be taught about healthy diets and cooking at school? Why (not)?
- At what age do you think children should be taught to cook?

Food aid
- What can be done to prevent poor people in the world going hungry?
- Should rich countries help poor countries with more than just food?

Travelling
Speaking Module Part 2

Take one minute to prepare a talk on the following subject. Take notes if you like and remember to include reasons and examples. You should then speak for between one and two minutes.

> **Describe a memorable journey you have made.**
> **You should say:**
> **where you were going**
> **how you were travelling**
> **why you were making the journey**
> **and explain what made the journey so memorable.**

Travelling
Speaking Module Part 3

Travelling and learning
- What do people learn from travelling?
- Do you think the growth of international tourism is a good thing? Why (not)?

Tourism and culture
- How has tourism changed the way people in your country live?
- How should tourists behave when they visit your country?

Ways of travelling
- What do you think is the best way for a tourist to travel if they want to learn about your country?
- What are the advantages and disadvantages of travelling by plane?

From *Instant IELTS* by Guy Brook-Hart © Cambridge University Press 2004 **PHOTOCOPIABLE**

School
Speaking Module Part 2

Take one minute to prepare a talk on the following subject. Take notes if you like and remember to include reasons and examples. You should then speak for between one and two minutes.

> **Describe a school which you went to.**
> You should say:
> > when you went there
> > how many people studied there
> > how long you spent there
> **and explain what you liked and disliked about it.**

School
Speaking Module Part 3

Attitudes to education
- How has education changed in your country in the last ten years?
- Is a good education more important to a boy or a girl? Why?

The focus of education
- How well do you think schools prepare young people for working life?
- Do you think schools should teach subjects like art, music and dancing? Why (not)?

Education and technology
- How important is it for schools to have computers for their students?
- Is the Internet a valuable educational tool?

Adventure
Speaking Module Part 2

Take one minute to prepare a talk on the following subject. Take notes if you like and remember to include reasons and examples. You should then speak for between one and two minutes.

> **Describe an exciting experience in your life.**
> You should say:
> > when the experience took place
> > where the experience took place
> > what happened exactly
> **and explain why the experience was so exciting.**

Adventure
Speaking Module Part 3

Safety and danger
- In what ways is life becoming safer, and in what ways is it becoming more dangerous?
- Should people always avoid danger, or is it a good idea sometimes to take risks?

Taking risks
- What risks should people try to avoid?
- Do you think people take fewer risks as they grow older? Why (not)?

Adventure
- How important is it to have adventure in our lives?
- What do people learn about themselves from having adventures?

Newspapers
Speaking Module Part 2

Take one minute to prepare a talk on the following subject. Take notes if you like and remember to include reasons and examples. You should then speak for between one and two minutes.

> **Describe a newspaper or magazine you enjoy reading.**
> You should say:
> > what kind of newspaper or magazine it is, *e.g. fashion*
> > how often you buy it
> > what articles and information it contains
> **and explain why you enjoy reading it.**

Newspapers
Speaking Module Part 3

Attitudes to newspapers
- In what ways are newspapers better for learning about the news than listening to the radio or watching television?
- Do you think newspapers should be completely free to say whatever they want?

Tastes in reading
- What do people enjoy reading in your country?
- Do you think it is important for people to read a lot? Why (not)?

Public and private lives
- What sort of stories do newspapers and magazines publish about well-known or famous people in your country?
- Do you think the media should be allowed to publish stories about the private lives of public figures?

The materials provided here are not intended for use all in one lesson – you can use different parts of them in different lessons, perhaps for 15 or 20 minutes' practice at any one time.

The speaking test lasts between 11 and 14 minutes and consists of 3 parts. Students are assessed for ability to communicate effectively. This takes into account fluency and coherence, lexical resource, grammatical range and accuracy and pronunciation.

Speaking Module Part 1

You can tell your students that in Part 1 of the speaking module candidates have to answer a number of general questions about themselves and other familiar topics. This part of the test takes between 4 and 5 minutes.

Suggested classroom treatment

- You will have to cut up the question cards and the checklist.
- Ask your students to work in pairs.
- Give them a complete set of cards which they place face-down in front of them and the checklist.
- Students take it in turns to play the role of interviewer and candidate.
- The interviewer should take one of the question cards and use them to ask the candidate questions. The candidate should not see the questions.
- Tell the candidate to avoid giving short answers. Tell them to give reasons for their answers and examples when possible.
- When they have answered the questions on a card, they should discuss the questions on the checklist* together.
- They can then change roles and repeat the procedure using another question card.

Intermediate

When they have done the checklist, they can brainstorm vocabulary which would have been useful in answering the questions, either with you or using a dictionary, and then repeat the exercise using the same question card to give 'improved' answers.

Speaking Module Parts 2 and 3

You can tell your students that:

- in Part 2 candidates are given a task card with prompts on it. They are given a minute to prepare and make notes. They then have to speak for 1 or 2 minutes. Finally, the interviewer asks 1 or 2 'rounding off' questions.
- in Part 3 the interviewer asks a number of questions which are linked to the subject on the card and discusses these questions with the candidate. The discussion lasts 4 or 5 minutes.

Suggested classroom treatment

- You will have to cut out the question cards and separate Part 2 from Part 3. Also cut out the checklist below.
- Ask your students to work in pairs as candidate and interviewer. Give the candidate a prompt card for Part 2, and the interviewer the corresponding questions for Part 3.
- Candidates should take 1 minute to prepare their talks.
- Meanwhile interviewers should study their questions and think of 2 or 3 more they can ask on the same subjects.

Intermediate

You can ask candidates to work in pairs and prepare their talks for Part 2. In this case, give them 4 or 5 minutes. Meanwhile interviewers can also work in pairs and prepare their questions.

- Students should then do Parts 2 and 3 in pairs. You can remind candidates before they start that they should give reasons and examples – this is a way for them to give longer answers and demonstrate how much English they know.
- When they have finished, ask them to work down the checklist* together.
- You can then ask them to change roles and either work with the same cards or use different ones.

*The best answer for all the questions on the checklist is 'YES'. You can explain that they will not be assessed for all the points on the checklist, but that some of the things on it will help to make a good impression on the interviewer.

Checklist

Dealing with the questions	YES	NO
1 Did the candidate understand and answer the questions?	☐	☐
2 Did the candidate ask you to repeat questions he / she didn't understand?	☐	☐
3 Did the candidate give quite long answers to the questions?	☐	☐
4 When appropriate, did the candidate give reasons for his / her answers?	☐	☐
5 Did the candidate support his / her answers with examples?	☐	☐
6 Did the candidate express his / her opinions and ideas clearly?	☐	☐
Body language and voice		
7 Did the candidate look positive, confident and friendly?	☐	☐
8 Did the candidate look at you directly when speaking?	☐	☐
9 Did the candidate speak clearly, so you could hear him / her?	☐	☐
Dealing with problems		
10 When the candidate made a mistake, did he / she ever try to correct it?	☐	☐
11 When the candidate couldn't think of the correct word, did he / she find other ways of expressing the idea in English?	☐	☐
12 Did the candidate answer completely in English?	☐	☐

Listening Section 1 A House to Rent p.5

Track 2

Woman: Hi. Bellingham Real-Estate Agents. Could you hold, please.
Man: OK.
Woman: Sorry about that. What can I do for you?
Man: Yeah. I'm looking for some tenants for my house and I was hoping you could advertise it for me.
Woman: Sure. No problem. Is it here in Vancouver?
Man: No, it's just outside in Richmond.
Woman: Very nice. It's a house, you say?
Man: Yes. It's a family house, it's er two-storey, quite modern. **1**
Woman: Right. And you're wanting to rent out the whole place, that right?
Man: No, no, just two rooms are for rent – that's two bedrooms plus the use of the rest of the house – it would really suit a couple of students.
Woman: OK. Can you just tell me the address, please?
Man: Yeah sure, it's 3281 Number One Road, Richmond. **2**
Woman: OK, that's quite a ways out. And how much were you thinking of for these rooms?
Man: I thought $700 per room would be a pretty fair price. **3**
Woman: Is that per month?
Man: Sure.
Woman: OK. You'd get at least a thousand if you were in Vancouver.
Man: Yeah, I know.
Woman: Hum. Any other costs?
Man: Er! just the cleaner who comes in once a week. **4**
Woman: Cleaner, OK. And how much would your tenant have to pay her?
Man: Him, actually, it's a guy and… er… that would be another $30 a month.
Woman: OK, and it's nice? I mean it's got a view and things?
Man: Sure, it looks out over the ocean. No garden, but there's lots **5** to look at from the lounge.
Woman: OK, and your name is?
Man: Peter Truboise. **6**
Woman: Truboise – is that B–O–Y–S?
Man: No, it's T–R–U–B–O–I–S–E.
Woman: Truboise. Nice name. And your address?
Man: It's the same one as I just gave you.
Woman: Fine, as above. Got a phone number you can give me?
Man: Sure. I'm calling you from it. It's 60474106. **7**
Woman: And a cell?
Man: Yup. That's 903 2773987.

Track 3

Woman: Good. Now let's get down to the serious stuff. What have you got in the kitchen? A fridge, of course.
Man: Yes, a fridge, and there's a dishwasher. **8**
Woman: Got facilities for washing clothes?
Man: Yeah. A washing machine in the basement, and a dryer too.
Woman: OK. Gas or electric stove?
Man: Electric, and there's a microwave as well. **8**
Woman: Fine. Now what about the house? Anything worth mentioning?
Man: Sure – there's a room for playing ping pong and pool. **9**
Woman: Great and how's it heated?
Man: It's got central heating but no fireplace. **9**
Woman: That's too bad. I like an open fire in winter. Air conditioned?
Man: No.
Woman: No conditioning. I suppose you've got a TV?
Man: Sure.
Woman: Cable?
Man: Er afraid not. I've never gotten around to putting it in.
Woman: Fine. What sort of tenant are you looking for – students, you said?
Man: That's right. Although it's quite a way from the university, though – I guess they'd need a car.
Woman: That's true. Still, there's a shopping mall just a block **10** away – I'm looking at a map right now.
Man: Yup, just a small one – no movie theaters or anything like that. We're right by the beach though and that's something.

Woman: Sure. Especially in this weather. I wish I was there myself! Any other entertainment in the area?
Man: There's a cocktail lounge on the corner and a couple of hamburger joints. You'd have to go downtown for a movie though. Oh, and Boyd Park is only a couple of hundred yards **10** away.
Woman: OK Mr Truboise, I'll post this up for you and I hope you have some luck.
Man: Thanks, bye.
Woman: Bye, and take care.
Man: Sure, thanks.

Listening Section 1 At the Doctor's p.8

Track 4

Doctor: Good morning.
Martin: Morning.
Doctor: Come in. Sit down. Now, you're a new patient, aren't you?
Martin: Yes, that's right.
Doctor: OK, so I'd better get some basic details down first. Right, we'll start with your name.
Martin: Martin Hansen.
Doctor: Do you spell that S–O–N or S–E–N?
Martin: H–A–N–S–E–N.
Doctor: OK. And you are a first-year student?
Martin: Yes, I am.
Doctor: Studying?
Martin: Medicine, actually. **1**
Doctor: Ah! Good choice. I hope you enjoy it.
Martin: Thanks.
Doctor: And your address?
Martin: Yes, it's 13 Chatham Street. **2**
Doctor: That's C–H–A–T–H–A–M, isn't it?
Martin: That's right.
Doctor: And your phone number?
Martin: 01734 24655. **3**
Doctor: 01734 26455.
Martin: No, you got the 6 and the 4 the wrong way round. It's 24655.
Doctor: Huh! Sorry, right. And when were you born?
Martin: On the 15th of June 1986.
Doctor: Here in New Zealand?
Martin: Yes.
Doctor: Fine. Now, let's get some of your medical background. Have you ever had any serious illnesses or accidents?
Martin: A broken leg I got playing football when I was 17. I was **4** in the school team.
Doctor: What position did you play in?
Martin: I was the goalkeeper.
Doctor: A lot of standing around then!
Martin: Yes, when we were winning.
Doctor: Right. Anything else?
Martin: No, apart from that, nothing.
Doctor: And, have you had any operations of any kind?
Martin: No, the only time I've been to hospital was when I broke **5** my leg.
Doctor: Fine. Any allergies?
Martin: Yes, to dust and cats. **6**
Doctor: What form does that take? How do you react?
Martin: They both make me sneeze a bit. Nothing else.
Doctor: So you're not allergic to antibiotics like penicillin as far as you know?
Martin: I don't think so.

Track 5

Doctor: Good. So what's your problem?
Martin: Well, recently I've been getting this pain here, just behind **7** my eyes and in my forehead.
Doctor: I see. Have you felt sick or dizzy at all, or vomited?
Martin: No, not at all, though the pain is pretty intense sometimes.
Doctor: And how's your health generally? Have you had any colds or flu recently?
Martin: I had a cold a couple of weeks ago, but that's gone. It was only a sniffle really.

Doctor: Good. Are you studying a lot? Are you getting enough sleep?

Martin: Yes, I'm studying quite a lot – I've got some exams coming up in December, but I'm making sure to sleep plenty.

Doctor: What time do you go to bed?

Martin: Usually around 11. I sleep <u>about 8-and-a-half hours</u>, and   **8** I'm up about 7.30 so I have time to go jogging for half an hour before going in to the university at 9.

Doctor: Very healthy. And has this pain kept you awake or stopped you jogging?

Martin: Yes, it makes getting to sleep harder. <u>It's much worse at</u>   **9** <u>the end of the day</u>. I hardly notice it in the morning.

Doctor: What about food? Are you eating properly?

Martin: I think so. My girlfriend cooks my meals.

Doctor: Right. And do you wear glasses?

Martin: No.

Doctor: Aha. When did you last visit an optician?

Martin: I don't remember. When I was a child, I suppose.

Doctor: OK. <u>Well I think first you should get that done again</u>, just to make sure it's not the cause. In the meantime, <u>take an aspirin</u> <u>or two when you're in pain</u>, and come and see me again in a   **10** week. Ask the receptionist to give you an appointment with the optician. He's here on Tuesday and Thursday mornings …

Listening Section 2 Coping with Stress p.12

Track 6

Disc jockey: And now, after that old favourite from 'The Corrs' entitled 'I never loved you anyway', we have Dr Claire Greenhill to talk to us today about stress in the workplace. Is it getting worse Dr Greenhill?

Dr Greenhill: I'm not sure whether it's getting worse or just that more people are talking about it. Certainly lots more people are complaining about it. I've just completed a study of 5,000 workers from 20 different countries. And I've taken a multi-cultural approach to the subject.

Disc jockey: And what have you found?

Dr Greenhill: That broadly speaking the causes of stress are similar the world over. For example, Ramon from Mexico City says that society measures people by individual success. But, he says, increasingly work is organised in teams. This means there's a conflict between personal goals and the need to cooperate with one's colleagues. He finds this an acute source of stress, actually.

Then there's Kikuko, from Osaka, Japan, who says she's under a lot of stress because the company she's worked for for 30 years is in difficulties. She says it's because her bosses made a number of bad decisions, but really <u>what worries her most is that she</u>   **1** <u>might lose her job</u>. You know, she's in her 50s and at that age it's not easy to find another one. She says that she also feels overworked and well that's getting her stressed out too.

Well, then there's <u>Boris, from Odessa in the Ukraine. He puts</u>   **2** <u>overwork at the top of his list of stressors</u>. Then there are other factors. Both he and his wife have full-time jobs so that when they get home they don't get to relax much either. I guess that's a problem most of us can relate to!

Disc jockey: We always hear about <u>computers, e-mail and cell</u>   **2** <u>phones</u> as things which get people tearing their hair out. Is this true?

Dr Greenhill: Mmm. In many cases, yes, but not as much as you might think – <u>only 15% of respondents give this as the main</u>   **3** <u>cause – Etienne from Quebec, Canada, is one</u> – though he also mentions change and the feeling of being a victim of circumstances beyond his control. Other people talk about the amount of work which comes with continual change as being more stressing than new technologies themselves. People feel they lack stability in their working life.

But we must remember that in many places it's really lack of new technology that puts people under most pressure. Take <u>Nagwa from Sohag in Egypt, for example. She says that for her</u>   **4** <u>the main source of stress was working in noisy, hot, unventilated</u> <u>conditions</u> day in day out and with no end in sight. So it seems, we can't win either way!

Track 7

Disc jockey: So, what can we as individuals do to make things easier for ourselves?

Dr Greenhill: Well, I've talked to a number of specialists about this – doctors and psychologists – and here are a few suggestions for reducing stress without you having to change your job! First, vary your diet: fish, pasta, vegetables, fruit and so on. Try not to live off sandwiches and fast food – a <u>balanced diet</u> in other   **5** words. Also, we tend to drink too much coffee. Caffeine, the drug in coffee, gets us more nervous. So, if you want to feel less stressed, <u>drink less coffee</u>. It's tough at first but you'll notice the   **6** difference within just a few days. Finally, <u>take regular exercise</u>.   **7** It's a great way of relaxing and of course it makes you more healthy too!

For particular causes of stress there are various things you can do. If your problem is that you think you've got too much work on your plate, what you probably need to do is <u>manage time</u>   **8** <u>better</u>. You have to learn to deal with the things which are really vital. Don't waste time on trivialities. There are courses to help you with this. If you are worried about unemployment, <u>make</u>   **9** <u>plans</u> so that if it happens you are ready for it. Do things like set money aside and update your CV so it's attractive to new employers. As for new technologies, <u>do training courses</u> so   **10** that you feel at home with them and so that you don't feel frightened of them. So in the end the best way to deal with stress is for you to take control of your life and not allow yourself to be a victim of circumstances.

Disc jockey: Thank you, Dr Claire Greenhill on fighting stress, and, just when you thought you could relax, here's Dolly Parton working 9 to 5…

Listening Section 2 Mentoring p.14

Track 8

Pat Baker: Hi! It's good to see you all here today and what a pity the weather is so bad for your first day at university! It could at least have stayed sunny today! Now, my name is Pat Baker, I work for student services and I'm going to tell you all about our mentoring scheme for new students. We've had it in place for a few years now and people starting at university for the first time in general find it a very positive experience at these meetings. What happens is this: each of you, if you want to that is, will be assigned a mentor – that is, <u>someone who's been studying here</u>   **1** <u>for a year or two</u> and who can show you the ropes, in other words, show you how things work, give you advice if you need it and just generally be a friendly contact for you in the university. Of course you'll have your tutors and lecturers who will also help you with academic problems, but this is someone more your own age who has been through the same experience quite recently.

What the mentor does is have a group of usually two or three students and <u>he or she organises meetings preferably about</u>   **2** <u>once every two weeks</u> – we generally find that more than that's just too often – where you chat about your problems, university life or just about things in general and your mentor will give you the benefit of his or her experience.

If you're joining this scheme, you'll be meeting your mentor today just after lunch. If you haven't signed up by the way, it's not too late. Come and see me after the talk. Don't be frightened about this first meeting: it's going to be quite short so you won't have time to tell your mentor all your difficulties – you'll just get to know each other a little bit and, <u>most</u> <u>importantly, fix a time and a place for your next meeting</u>,   **3** which you can have when you're feeling more relaxed and not so overwhelmed by the newness of it all!

Track 9

Pat Baker: Mentors, as I've said, have been through the same experience as you quite recently, so they can understand your problems. They'll be able to tell you about <u>academic systems</u>,   **4** which are so different at university from what you were used to at school. Also, because at university you are much more independent and you have to spend so much time studying on your own, they can suggest <u>techniques for studying</u> which will help you to keep up-to-date with your work. **5**

This university is an enormous place, so another thing which they'll be able to help with is <u>university facilities</u> – you know, **6** anything from sports halls to libraries to medical services and they can probably help you get involved in all sorts of <u>social</u> **7** <u>activities</u> too – parties, clubs, sports, whatever.

So, as you can see, this is a pretty useful scheme, but it does rely on people keeping in touch. The telephone's pretty useful if you have one, but students are busy people and often out doing things, so e-mail is probably better. Your mentor will be able to show you how to get an <u>e-mail account</u> … they don't cost **8** anything to students. They're free. For people who have never been <u>away from home</u> before, a mentor is a useful contact and **9** support – somewhere between a friend and a parent. And no doubt as the year progresses and you start getting nervous around exam time, your mentor will be ready with useful tips on the best way to <u>pass your exams</u> – after all, they did the same **10** ones either last year or the year before and they passed them!

Listening Section 3
Bridging the Digital Divide p.17

Track 10

Tutor: So, Sanjay, I asked you to find out about how the villagers of Veerampattinam are managing to bridge the digital divide. How did you get on?

Sanjay: Oh, I found it very interesting. Veerampattinam is a small village on the east coast of India, near Pondicherry – that's, south of Chennai. Now this village, in the year 2000, had no telephone connection and no electricity supply. It was just the sort of place which we'd expect to be completely left behind as the technological revolution rushed ahead. But, that year they had an Internet connection installed in the village and now each day <u>a local volunteer</u> in the village checks for information which **1** is useful to the villagers.

Female student: Really? But how was that possible if there was no telephone or electricity?

Sanjay: Well, quite simple really: they installed a <u>solar panel</u> to **2** provide the power, and, instead of an old-fashioned telephone line, the Internet connection was provided by a <u>wireless</u> **3** <u>transmission system</u> – all very hi-tech!

Tutor: And then what does the volunteer do with the information – print it out in a newspaper?

Sanjay: No, that would be far too slow and expensive. He just picks up a microphone and broadcasts the information to the whole village using a <u>public address system</u>. You know, simple **4** ideas are often the best and villagers can hear what they want to know while they're having tea in the local café, or doing their shopping. They don't even have to go to a meeting!

Track 11

Female student: So what sort of information do these villagers get from the Internet?

Sanjay: Well, I'll give you a few examples. Veerampattinam is on the coast, and quite a lot of the villagers are fishermen. From the Web <u>they can find out what weather conditions will be like the</u> **5** <u>next day</u>, and if they know about the weather they know whether it'll be safe to go fishing. This Internet connection can actually save lives.

Tutor: Now that really is remarkable.

Sanjay: Another useful application is that they can find out <u>how</u> **6** <u>much crops are selling for in the markets</u> of Pondicherry and Chennai. You see a lot of the villagers earn a living from farming, so you can imagine how useful that is. Also, by looking on the Internet <u>people can find out about jobs which are on</u> **7** <u>offer</u>, and then go and do them. This in turn brings more money into the area.

Tutor: But, wasn't the system very expensive to install? How did they manage it?

Sanjay: The system was the idea of M.S. Swaminathan – you may have heard of him.

Female student: Wasn't he the man behind the Green Revolution?

Sanjay: Yes! <u>He did his PhD in plant genetics</u> at Cambridge in the 1950s. Actually he was a major force behind the agricultural revolution. The agricultural revolution largely solved India's food problems. And his foundation designed and paid for this installation. When you think about it, it's a much cheaper solution than installing electricity and telephone lines to the village, though those will come with time, I expect.

Tutor: Do the villagers have the know-how to use something as sophisticated as the Internet?

Sanjay: Well, the technology is sophisticated, but the Internet itself is very user-friendly. That's why it's such a powerful tool. And it's very important that the people who handle the information are not technicians from outside who have their own interests and priorities, and certainly not civil servants who might tell the villagers what they think they should know. No, <u>it has to be the</u> **9** <u>local people who know what information they need and can</u> <u>look after their own interests</u>. I'll give you an example: you remember I told you one of the pieces of information which villagers want is how much crops are selling for in the markets? Well, if they get this information then they're in a much better position to negotiate with <u>the intermediaries who come to the</u> **10** <u>village</u> to buy their produce and may tell all sorts of stories to get prices down.

Tutor: That's true. So once again it proves the old saying that 'information is power'. Thank you very much Sanjay. That was very good. Well done.

Sanjay: My pleasure.

Listening Section 3
Changes in Intelligence p.20

Track 12

Farouk: Hi, Martin. Hi, Maria. How are you getting on with your project? You've got to give the seminar on Friday, haven't you?

Maria: Hi, Farouk. We're getting on fine. It's just so interesting! Do you want to hear about it?

Farouk: Well, I've got ten minutes before my next lecture, so why not? Let's hear it!

Maria: Great. And it'll help us to sort out who said what, won't it Martin?

Martin: That's right. You know, what we've been looking at is research done by a number of psychologists from different parts of the world on intelligence quotients – how they've been rising over the last 50 years.

Farouk: Really?

Maria: Yes! Some psychologists have measured increases in intelligence of up to 25 points in one generation.

Farouk: Amazing. What's causing us all to get cleverer?

Martin: There's a political scientist from New Zealand called <u>James</u> **1** <u>Flynn</u>. Well, he's a pioneer in this field, and he's found that people perform the visuo-spatial tasks in intelligence tests much better than they did 50 years ago. <u>Partly he puts this down to</u> **1** <u>people playing with their PCs and watching TV</u> – things like that.

Farouk: <u>What about diet?</u> Does that have anything to do with it? **2**

Maria: Perhaps. <u>Robert Howard, a Sydney psychologist, thinks that</u> <u>it does</u>. Just as eating better has made children taller, their average intelligence has also risen. <u>He also says that parents are</u> **3** <u>having fewer children, so they're able to pay more attention to</u> <u>them when they're small. It's fairly clear that stimulation in</u> <u>childhood has a positive effect on kids' intelligence.</u>

Farouk: IQ tests have verbal and numerical elements too. Have these also been improving?

Martin: Yes, but only moderately. It's the visuo–spatial element which has made the big difference and <u>Flynn also suggests that</u> **4** <u>modern activities like driving may play a part in this.</u>

Maria: There's a British researcher, <u>John Rust, who has made the</u> **5**

general point that modern life is much more complicated than it was fifty years ago. Our intelligence has had to develop in order to cope with it all.

Martin: Remember also that far more children have the   **6** opportunity to go to school nowadays. Howard thinks that must be a leading factor in improved IQ test performance.

Farouk: Well, yes, that would seem fairly obvious.

Maria: To come back to John Rust: he suggests that as science and **7** knowledge develop, ideas become more complex. Well, the people who produce these ideas, the Einsteins and Hawkings are obviously highly intelligent people, but, he says, ordinary people's intelligence has also had to develop to cope with these new theories.

Track 13

Farouk: Are there any limits to intelligence or will the human race just continue to get cleverer and cleverer?

Martin: Er, actually, research in some Western industrialised   **8** countries such as Australia and some European countries suggests that intelligence rose quite steeply for 2 or 3 decades and then levelled off a few years ago. Some pessimists think that quite soon we may see it beginning to dip – in some countries students seem to be less motivated than before. In that sense there may well be a limit to intelligence.

Maria: On the other hand, this rise in intelligence started to   **9** happen some years later in East Asian countries – the so-called Asian tigers – and it still hasn't levelled off.

Farouk: Is higher intelligence what has caused exam results to improve here in Britain, do you think?

Maria: Well, that's rather a political question, so it depends who you ask, but you must remember that 30 years ago only about 5% of school-leavers here went on to university. But there's been a vast expansion of the university system, and nowadays about 30% of young people get a higher education. So I guess exams **10** must have been getting easier for all those people to get in.

Listening Section 4
Emblematic Buildings p.23

Track 14

Lecturer: Right, today we're going to consider emblematic buildings, that is, buildings which are closely associated with the city where they're situated and which almost represent the city to the outside world. You know, if you think of Athens, you think of the Acropolis and the Parthenon, or for Sydney you think of its Opera House.

Recently, a lot of other cities round the world have been following the example of Sydney and putting up emblematic buildings – Bilbao for example, in Northern Spain, opened its own Guggenheim Museum in 1999. This houses an important collection of modern art and attracts a million visitors to the city **1** every year. In other cities, modern additions to existing buildings have proved a tremendous attraction, as is the case of the glass **2** pyramid in front of the Louvre in Paris – a museum which gets about 5 million visits a year. This is only surpassed by Paris's other emblematic building, the Eiffel Tower, with 6 million.

Projects of this type can make a big difference to a city. Let's take the example of Valencia, a city in Eastern Spain. Relatively few people used to visit Valencia some years ago – in 1992, it received only 75,000 tourists. However, its city authorities embarked on an extremely ambitious project to create a City of Arts and Sciences and, when it opened in 2001, its futuristic **3** Science Museum received no less than 4 million visitors in the first year.

The effect of these buildings is tremendous, and even cities in relatively poor countries are doing the same thing – just look at the new library in Alexandria in Egypt as an example.   **4**

Track 15

Lecturer: These emblematic buildings bring many more visitors to their cities, but that's only one of a number of benefits that

arise. In Valencia, the City of Arts and Sciences breathed new life **5** into a depressed industrial area of the town, and this has now become a prime residential zone as well as a tourist attraction. The effort and vision which goes into completing a project like this also has the effect of enhancing the city's image. Previously, **6** if people thought about Valencia at all, it was seen as a provincial backwater whereas now it sticks in people's minds. Valencia's progressive and energetic. The City of Arts and Sciences has put Valencia on the international map and that brings in plenty of new investment from outside as people   **7** realise what excellent business opportunities the city offers.

Nowadays, the competition amongst cities to attract attention from tourists, politicians and business people is fierce, and in Valencia they realised that it's not sufficient to have just one emblematic building which will serve for a single short visit. For this reason they've built an entire complex of buildings.

Looking at the next slide, which shows a plan of the City of Arts and Sciences, you'll see what I mean. You park your car in a building which amazingly has a garden with palm trees and **8** sculpture on its roof. You go down some steps and in front of you, you're faced with the colossal Science Museum with its huge white arches. This, and the combined planetarium and large screen film theater nearby are surrounded by artificial **9** lakes, and from a distance they appear to be floating on water.

The effect is magical as the whole complex is built in shining white concrete which reflects in the water. Further along, beyond the planetarium is the new opera house and theater **10** complex, which, from a distance looks like a vast ship. In the opposite direction, they've built the equally breathtaking oceanographic park, which is the largest in Europe and features, amongst other things, an underwater restaurant …

Listening Section 4 Changes at Work p.27

Track 16

Dr Pendleton: Hello. This afternoon I'm going to begin by outlining some of the main changes that have occurred in the labour market and in working practices over the last 20 years. One of the most significant changes has been the vast move, especially in industrialised countries, from manufacturing to service industries. Although this has freed many people from heavy and repetitive work in factories, many people find their work in service industries equally boring and just as badly paid.

Another important change has been that most people no longer expect to spend most of their working lives with the same company or organisation. As a result people set themselves objectives which they work towards, and they use the various jobs they do and the different companies they work for as steps towards these objectives. For individual workers I think this has **1** helped them become more independent and given them more control over their lives.

In most companies the management team has become less hierarchical. This is often called downsizing or delayering. In other words, there are fewer managers and fewer levels of management. As a result, there are not so many opportunities **2** for promotion and people often feel frustrated because they find themselves at the same level for many years without the chance to rise in the company.

Competition from new products and from different parts of the world means that nowadays companies have to adapt very fast to changing markets and this requires them to be very flexible. Increasingly this means they don't employ workers directly, but employ other small specialist companies or individuals to do the job when they need them. This means they don't have the expense of employing workers when they don't need them. I believe that for workers who are subcontracted there are **3** various gains: they're often better paid for the work they do, they work in smaller, more human organisations and they're able to organise their working lives in ways which suit them, instead of having to fit into the routines of a large company.

Of course, the biggest areas of change have come with the technological revolution. Workers now have the chance to go job hunting on the World Wide Web, so they have more **4** opportunities to find better or more suitable jobs. Statistics show that generally people work much harder than in **5** the past with much longer hours. New technologies are largely responsible for this, especially mobile phones and beepers or pagers. These things force employees to stay in contact with their offices even in their free time and at weekends. I think this is a pity as people need to be able to relax and have time for themselves.

Another effect of technological change is that jobs evolve very rapidly, and workers have to be continually going on training courses in order to remain employable. As a university teacher, I can hardly complain about this, but it can place an enormous strain on workers if they're obliged to retrain for jobs well into their late 50s when they're getting close to retirement, so I'm **6** not sure if it's a good thing or a bad thing.

Track 17

Dr Pendleton: New technology and global competition have, between them, meant that the life cycle of products isn't nearly **7** as long as it used to be. This has had a profound effect on companies and on the way we work. In order to cope with sudden changes in the market, companies need much greater **8** flexibility from their staff. As a result large numbers of tenured **9** or permanent jobs have disappeared. Apart from university lecturers like myself, few people can expect nowadays to have a job for life, and temporary short-term employment has become the norm for many people. However, we have to be positive. One wonderful change which has come out of the technological revolution is the opportunity for office workers to telecommute, that is, for them to work from home, with their **10** computer and their modem. This enables them to organise their working lives around their families and cut out the long journeys to and from work which are the bane of most office workers' lives.

Academic Reading Passage 2
Increased Life Expectancy p.41

Track 18

Lecturer: One of the most profound changes which has taken place in the last 100 years is the increase in life expectancy. For example, here in Canada in 1920 the average lifespan for men and women was just 59 years old. Forty years later, in 1960, **1** people could expect to live to the age of 71, and by 1990, this had risen to 78 – in other words, an increase of almost 20 years **2** over a period of just 70 years.
As we all know, life expectancy has not risen so fast in all parts of the world. In Africa as a whole life expectancy is still just 51. In other words, it has still not reached the level of Canada more than eighty years ago, and in Asia it stood at 65 years old in **3** 1998. This, of course, does not take into account variations in individual countries – for example, in China the average life span **4** is now 70, while in Japan, perhaps the country in the world with **5** the greatest longevity, people live an average of 80 years. Even in Hong Kong, which is now a part of China, people live to the **6** age of 79. In Australia, another Commonwealth country, life **7** expectancy is now 80 – that is 77 for men and 83 for women, which brings me to another point …

General Training Reading Passage 2
Distance Learning p.60

Track 19

Jeremy: So, how are we going to summarise the advantages of distance learning?
Fiona: Well, I think the most obvious one is that you can do a distance course from almost anywhere in the world – as long as you have a postal service or a telephone connection – and in

that sense you're completely independent of the place where **1** you're studying.
Jeremy: Yes, and along with that the advantage is that you can study whenever it suits you at any time of the day or night, which means studying doesn't interfere with other commitments **2** like your job or your family life.
Fiona: Exactly. So distance courses are possible at any age, not just **3** when you're young and free of responsibilities.
Jeremy: Another thing we should add is that the materials which are used for teaching are extremely closely controlled in terms of **4** quality, unlike face-to-face learning where things are left much more to the individual teachers concerned.
Fiona: Right. Can you think of anything else?
Jeremy: Um, not right now. Look, we haven't got too much time. Let's get on to the advantages of F2F.
Fiona: F2F?
Jeremy: Face-to-face.
Fiona: Ah. OK. Well, obviously being in contact with teachers and other students means that there's a free flow of information – **5** you're not just dependent on what comes through the post or over the phone line.
Jeremy: That sounds good: 'free flow of information'.
Fiona: And studying with other people helps you to have more **6** ideas.
Jeremy: That's right. I've just had one: it helps you to keep up **7** your interest in the subject and your motivation to carry on studying. I should think if you're on your own on a distance course it's very easy to lose interest and motivation without anyone else around who's interested in the same thing. All day alone in a room on your own studying. Think of it!
Fiona: Yes, distance learning requires a lot of self-discipline from students as you're not so closely supervised as when doing a **8** face-to-face course.
Jeremy: Good point. And when you have a question or you want some comments on your work you may have to wait for someone to answer your e-mail rather than getting the answer in real time like we do. **9**
Fiona: Real time! You've got all the jargon, haven't you?
Jeremy: I'm studying it! It means immediately – your questions are answered immediately. Now, any more points because I have to get down to the theatre club in five minutes?
Fiona: Well, just that point: face-to-face studying gives you the opportunity to take part in the university's wider educational **10** culture – theatre, photographic clubs, student unions and so on.
Jeremy: Great. I think that's a good set of notes. Probably enough for our tutorial tomorrow. I must rush. See you, Fiona!
Fiona: See you tomorrow, Jeremy.

Academic Writing Task 1
Describing a Process p.86

Track 20

University lecturer: Good morning. Now I guess most of you are new to graduate studies and particularly research at post-graduate level, so I thought today I'd start by outlining a typical research process because I know you're all going to be pretty much involved in some kind of research quite soon. Now, if I can just get the data projector to work! Yes, that's it, um, you can see the chart here which shows the process.
First of all, you have to have some idea of what you want to research before you start – this I've called 'Sources of research ideas'. In some cases this will come from research you've done before and you've realised that there are still some questions to be answered, so further research is necessary.

Another source will be your personal experience – you've been **1** working somewhere on something and you've noticed a problem or something which you feel deserves investigation. Or quite possibly your only motive for carrying out research will be **2** curiosity. There's something bugging you and you want to know the answer. Well why not? If you didn't suffer from incurable curiosity, you wouldn't have got so far with your university studies.

From there – your research idea – you have to state the research

BOSTON PUBLIC LIBRARY

3 9999 05222 993 5

WEST ROXBURY

question. What is it you want to find out? What's the focus of your research going to be? For most university teachers teaching of course is a pleasure, but their overriding passion is for research, and this is how human knowledge advances. Once you've formulated your question <u>you have to design your</u> **3** <u>research methodology</u> – in other words, how you're going to carry out your research and find your answers. Also, you have to clarify who your readers are going to be. If no one is going to read your research, it'll all be in vain – it won't advance human knowledge at all, so at least make sure you're researching something which will interest other people as well!

Going on from there, <u>you should identify your sources of</u> **4** <u>information – where will you get the data</u>, the facts which will form the basis of your research, and what methods will you use for obtaining these facts? You see you can't just rush into research headlong. You have to prepare yourself pretty carefully before you start and discuss what you're going to do at length with your supervisors.

When you've done all this, then <u>you can then proceed with</u> **5** <u>data collection</u>. This can be very enjoyable, but you must remember to be objective, and not just collect data which supports your ideas. Keep an open mind about the results of your research. If you think you know the answer before you start, you're not going to be a very good researcher! When you think you've got enough data, you can go on to analyse it – this should include discussing it with other students and with your supervisor. Finally, you can write your report, which will include your findings and conclusions, <u>together with</u> **6** <u>any recommendations</u> and implications of what you've found out. All in all it's a complex process with many pitfalls, but if you do it well, it can be a source of immense personal satisfaction.

General Training Writing Task 2
Working from Home p.112

Track 21

Rashid: Well, let's brainstorm arguments in favour first. What do you think?

Su-Mei: Fine. Um, I think an obvious argument is that workers can do their work when it suits them – they don't have to fit it into fixed working hours, you know.

Rashid: In other words it gives them <u>greater flexibility</u>. **1**

Su-Mei: That's right.

Rashid: Good. I'll note that down. What else?

Su-Mei: Well, obviously they don't have all that <u>travelling time</u> **2** which causes so much stress to most commuters.

Rashid: Sure. Travelling in the rush hour can be really uncomfortable, especially when the weather is bad. And how about family life? <u>Working from home allows you to do your job</u> **3** <u>and have a family life</u> – being with your husband or wife and children more.

Su-Mei: I'm not sure if that's an argument for or against – some people go to work to have a break from their families!

Rashid: Ha! Well, it helps workers when their children are sick. They can look after them and carry on with their work.

Su-Mei: Not just when their children are sick. When they're sick as well, they're more likely to be able to continue working.

Rashid: OK, so I'll write down <u>'less likely to be off sick'.</u> **4**

Su-Mei: Right. And another point: working from home means companies can reduce their costs because <u>they don't need so</u> **5** <u>much office space</u>, which is very expensive.

Rashid: That's true. But on the other hand workers need to have some <u>office equipment</u> at home. You know, um, a computer, a **6** fax and so on – which obviously the employer must supply.

Su-Mei: Right. That could be an argument against then.

Rashid: Possibly. Can you think of any others?

Su-Mei: Sure. One of the things I most enjoy about work is meeting my colleagues and occasionally the customers. I'd miss the <u>social aspect</u> of my job. **7**

Rashid: Yes. You could get very lonely if you always worked from home.

Su-Mei: And I don't think it suits everyone, you know. Not

everyone has the self–discipline to work from home.

Rashid: That's true. <u>Bosses have to trust workers to complete their</u> **8** <u>work and to work responsibly</u>. If you can't trust workers then you can't let them work from home. It becomes <u>hard to</u> **9** <u>supervise</u> whether they're doing the work properly or not.

Su-Mei: Yes, bosses can become like teachers checking children's homework to see if they've done it!

Rashid: Anything else?

Su-Mei: Well, not all jobs are suitable for working from home. Nowadays lots of people work in teams, and <u>teams have to see</u> **10** <u>each other</u>.

Rashid: The face-to-face thing, which is essential in many jobs.

Su-Mei: That's right.

Rashid: Hey. It's good working with you – I think we've got some really good notes for this writing task, don't you?

Su-Mei: Sure. It's fun. We've probably got too many ideas for a 250-word answer, though. I guess the next thing is to write a plan and decide which ideas to include and which to leave out.

Rashid: And we must decide what our opinion about all this is – you remember what the teacher said: 'If you don't give your opinion, you haven't answered the question'. Shall we do that together then – work out our opinion, I mean?

Su-Mei: Sure. Great.

From *Instant IELTS* by Guy Brook–Hart © Cambridge University Press 2004 **PHOTOCOPIABLE**